DONALD TRUMP, TIGER WOODS, BERNIE MADOFF, AND DICK CHENEY: THE ANATOMY OF EVIL

John Doe, Ph.D.

DONALD TRUMP, TIGER WOODS, BERNIE MADOFF, AND DICK CHENEY; THE ANATOMY OF EVIL

THE ANOMIC PERSONALITY OF OUR TIME

JOHN DOE, Ph.D.

DONALD TRUMP, TIGER WOODS, BERNIE MADOFF, AND DICK CHENEY: THE ANATOMY OF EVIL
THE ANOMIC PERSONALITY OF OUR TIME

iUniverse books may be ordered through booksellers or by contacting:

iUniverse
1663 Liberty Drive
Bloomington, IN 47403
www.iuniverse.com
1-800-Authors (1-800-288-4677)

ISBN: 978-1-5320-6848-5 (sc)
ISBN: 978-1-5320-6888-1 (e)

Library of Congress Control Number: 2019901770

Print information available on the last page.

iUniverse rev. date: 02/26/2019

Contents

CHAPTER ONE

DONALD TRUMP

Introduction: Leading up to the Election: The primaries, Hillary vs Donald, Putin, Comey and Giuliani? A rank order of threat

I never intended to add Donald Trump to the "anomic" triumvirate of Tiger Woods, Bernie Madoff and Dick Cheney. This book has been five years in the making, and Trump was not even a candidate for the presidency when I started writing. I never watched his game show, *The Apprentice,* though it ran for fourteen seasons since 2004. I read that when the losing contestant was chosen by Trump and others on the show, Donald would give his signal judgement, "You're Fired!" This could almost be seen as a dark harbinger of things to come—a dystopia in the making.

A central concept in the book is "anomie," a term used by Emile Durkheim, the French sociologist. (Durkheim, E. Le Suicide) [Durkheim, E. *Le Suicide*. Paris: Alcan, 1897.] He used it to describe *a state of society* marked by excessive deregulation. Emotional states *in the individual* like boredom, "tantalization" and perpetual dissatisfaction give us further insight into the "derangement" or "insatiable will" that Durkheim described as typical in the victims of a society in a state of anomie. Thus societal and personal deregulation are linked, and emotional states, particularly tantalization (dissatisfaction with any level of achievement), are rampant.

The anomic personality is a set of behaviors and attitudes (excessive striving, limitless goals, narcissism, grandiosity, lack of empathy, etc.). It is based on a personality type known as the Aggressive Narcissist. Traits especially prevalent in the Anomic Personality are: 1. Relentless pursuit of goals. 2. Limitless goals. 3. Treats people as objects. 4. Cunning, smooth talker. 5. Usually charismatic. 6. Sexual addiction. 7. Strong drive for power.

Tiger Woods is an example of sexual anomie; a deregulation of <u>sexual</u> activity. Bernie Madoff had <u>money </u>as his primary goal, and became deregulated in his search for <u>wealth</u>. Dick Cheney sought unregulated <u>power</u>, and virtually ran the country as Vice President. <u>Donald Trump is deregulated in all three areas; sex, money and power.</u> He is a "winner," not a "loser," in the zero sum game of survival in our former democracy, now morphed into a kleptocracy. The anomic personality thrives in a societal condition of excessive decontrol (anomie), that breeds rampant inequality and makes for extreme striving for sex, money and power at the expense of others.

When Trump became president it struck me that he was the epitome of the anomic personality, a concept which I have constructed. It was only fitting that he be first in line to introduce this new personality type, which could be considered at best a "culturally patterned defect" (a term introduced by Erich Fromm). This describes a behavior that is so prevalent in a society that it is not generally seen as offensive, and in fact has become part of the culturally normative (acceptable or even encouraged) behavior.

Trump's striving for unlimited sex, money and power, and his voluminous tweets and revealing books made him ideal as an avatar of the anomic outlier. His popularity among his white male less-educated base, and his extreme unpopularity among the large majority of the nation made a powerful argument for putting him up front, before Tiger, Bernie and Dick. This brief summary of the central concepts in the book had to be placed up front. They will be expanded in the chapters following Chapter One.

Another reason to put Trump up front is that at this writing, the Mueller investigation may be on the verge of making public its findings about the "Russian Connection." Charges of money laundering, tax evasion, and obstruction of justice may be brought against Trump and members of his administration. If Trump decides to get rid of Mueller by firing any Department of Justice head or FBI member who does not pledge "loyalty" to him (as in the case of Preet Bharara, Sally Yates, and James Comey, *seriatim*) it will cause a "constitutional crisis" and may be grounds for charges of "obstruction of justice." Congress may then act to impeach the President, or invoke other laws that allow for replacement of a president seen as unfit for the position. In 2018 U.S. Deputy Attorney General Rod Rosenstein has been severely criticized by Trump, and may be his next victim. Jeff Sessions was No. 1 in the Department of Justice, but recused himself from the Russian Investigation, much to Trump's anger. Next in line after Rosenstein came Rachel Brand, Associate Attorney General. Perhaps fearing a dismissal ("firing?"), she took a job with Walmart, obviously at much higher pay, and wisely away from the turmoil in the White House.

If Rosenstein is fired, and Brand has left, it leaves Associate Attorney General Noel Francisco in line to succeed Rosenstein. Francisco is also Trump's choice. He clerked for Justice Scalia, one of the most conservative judges in recent years, and is known to be quite conservative himself. Trump may then have a "loyal" Attorney General who will do his bidding and fire Mueller. That would probably be the end of the Russian investigation, and Trump could go free of all the possible charges that might have been made against him. Putting this story up front can alert readers to the seriousness of our national crisis. Our democracy and our warming planet are at risk. Trump's tweeted grade-school-level wise-cracks about "Little Rocket Man" (Kim Jong-Un) could lay the groundwork for a nuclear war with North Korea.

On 11/7/2018 Trump fiored Jeff Sessions, and appointed Matthew Whitaker to serve as interim Attorney General. Whitaker is a Trump loyalist, and his appointment is brelieved to be a move to take down the Mueller investigation.

Trump's vicious attacks on his fellow-aspirants during the G.O.P. primaries, and his similar attacks on Hillary Clinton ("crooked Hillary" and "lock her up") showed a propensity for demeaning others, often with a sly sense of humor. When he won the election, apparently with the help of Putin, Julian Assange, and various hackers who got into Hillary's e-mails, it was clear that the election was "rigged," a term Trump often used during the campaign to accuse the Democrats. Last, but not least, it appeared that there was a conspiracy to use an announcement by FBI Director James Comey *two days before the election,* that the earlier (July) finding (that no criminal charges were warranted against Democrat Hillary Clinton for using her private email server for government work) had been confirmed. The excuse was that a new batch of emails had been found on a laptop belonging to disgraced former Congressman Anthony Weiner and his wife, Huma Abedin, chief aide to Hillary. The announcement of the investigation of this new set of e-mails (some between Abedin and Hillary) was made on October 28th, *ten days before the election*. The excuse for the eight-day delay before announcing that Hillary was not incriminated by the Abedin/Hillary emails was due to the volume of the documents. Of course, there was no reason to make either the October 28th or the Sunday November 6th announcements. The Anthony Weiner investigation was completely separate from the investigation of Hillary's emails. The chance to further denigrate Hillary through an unrelated investigation must have seemed very tempting, and, in the light of recent discoveries, was just what was needed by Trump, Rudy Giuliani, and Erik Prince to change voters' minds at the last minute against Hillary.

There was suspicion all along that the Comey comments and their timing might have been coerced. And this has been laid out in great detail in a current article. "Information presently public and available confirms that Eric Prince, Rudy Giuliani, and Donald Trump conspired to intimidate FBI Director James Comey into interfering in, and thus directly affecting, the 2016 presidential election. This conspiracy was made possible with the assistance of officers in the New York City Police Department and agents within the New York City field office of the Federal Bureau of Investigation."
(Abramson, S. 2017) ["The Domestic Conspiracy That Gave Trump The Election Is In Plain Sight." Seth Abramson, The Huffington Post, 1/17/2017] p.163

A few details show the incredible cunning and manipulation involved, in what is believed to be the blackmail of Comey, forcing him to make both the October and November announcements. On October 25th and 26th on Fox News, Rudy Giuliani (former mayor of New York City) said that "in a few days there would be a 'surprise' in October that would turn the tide against Hillary Clinton." (op. cit.) This surprise, of course, was the announcement of the finding of the Hillary/Abedin emails on the Weiner laptop. It was a premature announcement, for which Giuliani was to pay dearly. On November 29th he announced that he would not be a candidate for any position in Trump's cabinet. In fact, he had been the leading candidate for Secretary of State, until he said the "surprise" was coming. A loose mouth might have brought down Trump's presidency. Now he's designated as Trump's lawyer for the Russian investigation, and perhaps to handle any "flip" by Trump's former personal lawyer, Michael Cohen, due to the reluctance of most defense lawyers to deal with Trump's tantrums and volatility.

With what did this trio blackmail Comey? Here is where Eric Prince steps in.

Eric Prince was "the founder of Blackwater private security, one of Trump's biggest donors, a conspiracy theorist who'd previously accused Huma Abedin of being a terrorist in the employ of the Muslim Brotherhood."{sic} (Abramson, ibid.) Prince said he had sources in the NYPD (N.Y.C. Police Department), and he gave the leaked information to Breitbart News (notorious for its racist, anti-Semitic, alt-right journalism, and its former Executive Editor, Steve Bannon.) Trump chose Bannon to be his chief strategist and senior counselor. Bannon had obviously written or heavily edited Trump's inaugural address due to style and substance, His views have had great, or even the greatest, weight with Trump, until they fell out. For this reason, a slight digression here may be prognostic of the next four years. Steve touts "enlightened capitalism." The onus is on the individual, driven by faith and conscience. The state must not force people to behave in ways it arbitrarily defines as correct. This is the assessment of a "close friend" of Steve's. In my view, the right wing concept of "freedom" is freedom from any regulation *of their choice*. Bannon is Irish Catholic, and supports the church doctrine on abortion. But even as I write, thousands of women, of Catholic and all faiths the world over, are marching to protest Trump's inauguration. They don't want the state to force them to give birth to a Down Syndrome baby, or a baby conceived during a rape, or a child they are not prepared to have for whatever reason. They don't want Roe vs. Wade overturned. Bannon, as Trump's counselor, was strongly for the overturn of the Roe vs. Wade decision. Luckily, he was "fired" by Trump.

Justice Scalia's replacement is the fatal blow. Neil Gorsuch, a very conservative judge, was confirmed to the Supreme Court on April 7th, 2017. This will mean a conservative majority for decades, and up till 2018 is probably the greatest damage Trump has done to our democracy.

To return to the conspiracy, Prince gave an interview to Breitbart News, which was undoubtedly meant for Comey's eyes at the FBI. In it Prince enumerated the slanderous and totally false information about the Clintons that would be revealed publicly if Comey didn't pursue the Weiner/Hillary/Abedin email investigation, announce the new findings, and go public with the indictments. Examples of the slander that Prince wrote were: "[NYPD] found a lot of other really damning information from Weiner's computer, including money laundering, including the fact that Hillary went to this sex island with convicted pedophile Jeffrey Epstein. Bill Clinton went there more than twenty times. Hillary Clinton went there at least six times." "There is all kinds of criminal culpability through all the emails they've seen of that 650,000, including money laundering, underage sex, pay for play..."

To start a chapter about Trump without first briefly describing his childhood, family background, his later education, career and marriages, might seem odd, if it were not necessary first to let the reader become aware of the illegitimacy of his election. Aside from the Prince/Giuliani/Trump conspiracy, the hacking of the DNC (Democratic National Committee) server and John Podesta's computer was accomplished through hackers in the service of Vladimir Putin. Trump's praise of Putin seemed unusual, since Russia has been "the enemy" in the U.S. since shortly after World War II, invading and annexing Crimea, and railing against NATO, Europe's protection against further Russian annexation. In light of revelations that Trump rewarded Putin with monitoring of exiled Russian oligarchs, this quid pro quo (hacking of Democrats, especially Hillary, in exchange for monitoring Russian exiles) bordered on treason.

The enormity of the skullduggery and the immediate threats to our democracy and to Planet Earth (rank-ordered later) outweigh the usual biographical details that I will give for Tiger, Bernie M., and Dick Cheney. Those details will be woven in with Trumps personality and character in later sections.

Trump's promises and plans:

Because Trump is often vague about the details of his plans and because he has changed his mind, his wives, and his subordinates many times, it was a bit foolhardy to predict so soon after his inauguration in November 2016 what course he would follow with respect to any issue. Two sources can help us make a brief review of his stated goals and promises;

"How Hard (or Easy) It Will Be for Trump to Fulfill His 100-Day Plan." Buchanan, L. et al., *The NY Times,* 11/21/2016.) and ("Donald Trump's Top 10 Campaign Promises." Qiu, L., Politifact, 7/15/2016.)Trump's promises range from the usual GOP wish list, "cut taxes," to the unusual "Build a wall and make Mexico pay for it." The Buchanan list follows, with some explanatory material from the Qiu list.

The following promises don't need Congress for approval:

Suspend immigration from terror-prone regions: He would temporarily ban Muslims from entering the U.S. "Trump banned citizens of seven Muslim-majority countries from entering the US for at least the next 90 days. The executive order bars all people hailing from Iraq, Syria, Iran, Libya, Somalia, Sudan, and Yemen – or at least 134 million people, based on 2013 World Bank census data – from entering the United States." A revised order (3/6/2017) dropped Iraq from the ban. (Diamond, J. 2017) ["Trump banned citizens of seven Muslim-majority countries from entering the US for at least the next 90 days. "Jeremy Diamond. *CNN Politics,* 1/27/2017.]

Eleven people were stopped from entering the U.S. at J.F.K airport. Two of them hired lawyers to sue the government. Interestingly, countries like Saudi Arabia and Egypt are not on the executive order list. Could those be countries that might offer opportunities for building a Trump Hotel? The other seven countries are a sop to the base, who attribute job loss to Muslim immigrants, and are repeatedly told that Muslims are terrorists.

After Trump's executive order, there was a protest at JFK International Airport by over a thousand people, and protests at major airports in the U.S. At JFK, lawyers for the A.C.L.U. (American Civil Liberties Union) wrote a brief asking for a stay of the executive order. Brooklyn federal judge Ann M. Donnelly issued a nationwide stay against Trump's "Muslim Ban" on 1/28/2017. Those being held who had valid visas could remain in the U.S. Between 100 and 200 people were being held at the airports. This was a major defeat for Trump. It remains to be seen how he will retaliate.

End foreign trade abuses: In early 2018 Trump suddenly announced that there would be a 25% tariff on steel and a 10% tariff on aluminum. His sudden announcement blindsided his staff, who would normally take several months of discussion and planning before such a drastic move. Our allies were aghast, and our stock market took a big dip. Impulsivity like this is a byproduct of his extreme grandiosity. He has claimed that he can "do it alone," and boasts that he has a very high I.Q.

Withdraw from the Transpacific Partnership. Renegotiate NAFTA:

(This might need Congressional approval.) In view of strained relations with China over Trump's telephone conversation with the President of Taiwan (a breach of 40 years of diplomatic protocol considering Taiwan part of "one China"), his plan to use tariffs to control trade with China (specifically their cheap exports) bodes ill for future relations.

Label China as a currency manipulator:

Choose Supreme Court nominee: I have already discussed the very conservative long-term effects of any Trump appointment to the SCOTUS.

Limit federal regulations: As of 1/23/2017 a massive deregulation program is in the works.

Roll back environmental regulations: The environmental section of the governmental website has been dropped. Government data on ocean and air temperature, air and water pollution, and related environmental subjects are in danger of being erased. Scientific groups involved in these data collections are scrambling to save these records before they are destroyed. Setting back science in favor of oil and coal profits may go down in history as Trump's worst offense.

Rescind Obama's actions on guns:

Approve the Keystone XL pipeline: After months of demonstrations during which protesters were injured, and a veto by Obama, the new administration will approve any and all legislation that benefits the oil, coal, and energy industries, no matter how it impinges on our citizens. Eminent Domain will rule the land.

Tighten lobbying restrictions: If this is carried out, it will be a welcome and surprising increase in regulation.

Freeze federal hiring: This has already started. Cabinet appointments are way behind schedule compared to other transition periods, and thousands of lesser positions are awaiting.

*Overturn protections for certain undocumented immigrants:*_The Dreamers are the children of undocumented immigrants. Born and raised in the U.S., they are at risk through no fault of their own. Trump targeted them for deportation, but was blocked by a Federal Court judge in January, 2018. Presumably, the Dreamers (DACA) and all illegal immigrants are at risk because attacking them, ostensibly for taking away jobs from the "base," is a common ploy that is being used in many countries around the world.

Cancel payments to U.N. climate programs: This is in keeping with the attack on the environment and environmental regulations. Cuts to the United Nations climate program would help U.S. oil and coal industries, at the expense of eventual climate control worldwide.

*Propose term limits on Congress:*_I am not sure how this will impact the passage of legislation helpful to the 99%, as opposed to vested interests (the 1% or even 10 %?)

The Following Promises Might need Congressional Approval:

Deport undocumented (criminal?) immigrants:

Impose tariffs on companies moving overseas: A good move. (Trump has imported workers rather than U.S. citizen-workers, for example, at his Mar a Lago Hotel and Golf Club. Outsourcing is one of the factors impacting U.S. workers, particularly those below college level education. Trump's "base" needs restrictions on outsourcing, or tax credits for those companies that hire U.S. labor.

Stop funding "sanctuary cities:" A sanctuary city is one that protects undocumented immigrants against prosecution for violating immigration laws of the country to which they have immigrated. This is in keeping with Trump's diatribes against immigrants. "When Mexico sends its people, they're not sending their best," he said. "They're sending people that have lots of problems...they're bringing drugs, they're bringing crime. They're rapists. And some, I assume, are good people." (Miller, T., 2015) [Donald Trump defends calling Mexican Immigrants 'rapists.' "Miller, T. CBS News, 7/2/2015]

The Following Promises Need Congressional Approval:

Repeal Obamacare and Replace it with a market-based alternative: With Republican control of both the House and Senate, repeal is likely. (Yes, on 5/4/2017, the House narrowly passed a bill to repeal and replace Obamacare, The Affordable Care Act. The bill has to pass the Senate, and even if it passes the Senate, it has to go through several stages to become law.)

"Obamacare caused the percentage of Americans *without insurance* to fall sharply, to the lowest level ever. Repeal would send the numbers *right back up* — 18 million newly uninsured in just the first year, eventually rising to more than 30 million, according to Congressional Budget Office estimates. And no, Republicans who have spent seven years failing to come up with a real replacement won't develop one in the next few weeks, or ever." (Krugman, P., 2017) [Krugman, P. "Things Will Only Get Worse." The *N. Y. Times, opinion pages,* 1/23/2017.] What will the "base" do when their health insurance stops?

Build a Wall and make Mexico pay for it: Mexico has said it will *not* pay for it. It might be 1200 miles long, from Brownsville to El Paso, Texas, and 30 feet high, and cost billions. This is a "pie in the sky" promise to his base, especially those in the Southwest, who fear a growing Hispanic political power in their states. Hispanics comprise 12.5% of the U.S. population, and non-Hispanic Blacks make up a similar 12.1%. When Trump dog-whistled "Make America great (White) again," he should have mentioned that only 62% of the nation are non-Hispanic Whites. That's 62% White versus a 24.6% Hispanic-Black minority. What's to worry, guys, except that a majority of them are poor and undereducated, due to the GOP's cuts in education (via Betsy De Vos), cuts in food stamps, and its economic policy (some examples being low minimum wage, union busting).

End Common Core: Again, part of the onslaught against public education.

Pass a Security bill:

Cut taxes: This is a Republican mantra. Under Trump's plan, the top 0.1 % would receive greater tax relief than the bottom 60%. The deficit would grow by $10 trillion over the next decade. Such a large deficit would threaten the continuation of Social Security Trump has also promised to continue SocialSecurity. Modus operandi; promise everything, deliver little or nothing.

Pass an infrastructure bill: Since the new administration plans to make low-interest, long-term loans to investors to build *toll* roads, the infrastructure program will be a gift to the 1%. Toll roads, rather than highways, will be a long-term source of income for the wealthy. Of course, owners will have to pay for repairs. Schools and public housing can also be privatized in this way, making contractors or investors the owners of public property.

Pass an ethics bill: On 1/23/2017 the House voted to gut an independent ethics watchdog committee. Democrats raised a hue and cry. Of course, gutting ethics was a very bad choice for the opening action of the 115th Congress. Trump thus protected his promise to "drain the swamp" of special interests. He also showed how he can control Congress with his tweeting.

Restrict lobbying by former members of Congress: The five year ban is longer than the current two year ban for senators, and one year ban for House members.

Pass a child care bill: Trump proposed a six weeks' mandated maternity leave. "Because all his methods of paying for childcare involve rewriting the tax code, they effectively only reward the wealthy, those who make enough to need a tax break. Under his plan, parents will be able to deduct the cost of childcare from their tax bill, up to a certain amount."(Luscombe, B., 2016) ["Donald Trump's Childcare Policy Is Perfect—For Ivanka Trump's Friends." Belinda Luscombe, *Time* Sep 14, 2016.]

Pass a law enforcement bill: "In a proposed federal budget prepared by the president elect's transition team, the Department of Justice and related agencies come in for almost $1.3 billion in cuts in the first fiscal year alone. This represents less than 1 percent of the department's $29 billion annual budget, but the targets are telling. The Office of Community Oriented Policing Services and Violence Against Women grants would be eliminated altogether, as would the autonomous Legal Services Corporation. Funding would be reduced for the department's Civil Rights and Environment and Natural Resources divisions. The programs and departments slated for the chopping block mirror closely (but not precisely) those in the *Blueprint for Balance,* a proposed federal budget that the conservative Heritage Foundation published last year. (The Marshall Project, 2017) [Trump Budget Draft Targets Cops, Crime Victims." The Marshall Project. 1/19/2017]

That the Civil Rights Division would face cuts, (or worse) is hardly surprising, since civil rights seem to be anathema to this new administration.

A rank ordering of catastrophe and threats

By examining the list of Trump's promises and plans, one can easily guess at the extensive damage they will do to the 99%.The separations of families by deportation of immigrants, the cuts in education, the loss of legal services, the threat to Social Security due to a huge deficit following massive tax cuts, raises in health care premiums due to privatization and loss of child care support payments, are a few examples. But there are even greater threats to our country and to the entire world that follow logically from statements made or past behavior of the new president or members of his cabinet. Depending on our personality, our social class and income, our age and perhaps our gender, we are bound to have differing views on what threatens us the most. My ranking of threats has been heavily affected by what I read, what I hear from family and friends, and my advanced age. Contrary to the politician's short-term view, I think in terms of my younger wife, my children, my grandchildren and the future generations. While the nuclear threat is still with us, global warming seems like a time-bomb, ready to go off if we do not take drastic steps to stop or mitigate it. Other short and long-term threats, national or international, are also of concern:

1. Global Warming: (See 6 below.)
2. Nuclear War: arming and attack by rogue states (Isis), or North Korea, or less likely by Russia or China. Threats by Trump to "nuke" ISIS suggest that the U.S. might initiate a "first strike."

Vice President Joseph Biden asked how we could trust this man with the code for the "nuclear football" which could set off a worldwide nuclear Armageddon.

3. Middle East Wars possibly escalating to World War III: Sunnis versus Shiites vs Kurds, Israelis vs Palestinians. Opposing armed groups are fighting in Libya, Syria and Yemen.

4. Over-population: Massive Migration, and Food Shortages: These are all possible even without Global Warming or Nuclear War. They are happening right now.

5. SCOTUS: With the election of Trump, a conservative appointment to the Supreme Court will lead to perhaps 30 years of conservative decisions because of a 5-4 conservative majority. *(Neil Gorsuch, a conservative, was confirmed as Supreme Court Justice on April 7th, 2017.)*

6. The continuing post-election Republican majority in the House of Representatives and the Senate means that progress on Global Warming will be stopped in its tracks. While Obama was in office, the recent meeting between the United States and China looked as if it might set an example for other nations to follow. Tensions between China and the U.S. have heightened, after Trump decided to accept a phone call from Taiwan's president. *(On June 1st, 2017 Trump withdrew from the Paris Accord.} The Democrats' mid-term majority win may mitigate some of these threats.*

7. An Angry Awakening: Given that nearly half the U.S. voting population has shown itself partial to a regressive platform of: racial, religious and ethnic discrimination and misogyny, elimination of the current or Democrat-proposed social safety net (including Social Security and Obama Care, public school support, free college education for families under $125,000, minimum wages of $15, and LGBT recognition, for example) a resurgence of anger and violence may follow months after the election. The threat is that a large portion of the disaffected, especially high-school-and-lower-educated White males have voted against their best interests. When they find out that their Social Security checks are cut or gone, and their medical care has been privatized to take care of insurance company profits, Hell will have no matching fury. They

are already blinded by anger and by the twisting of truth by skilled G.O.P. wordsmiths. Their sudden leap in suicide, alcoholism and addiction rates, in contrast to those of other demographic subgroups, is cause for alarm. "Anger in" as shown in these rates can suddenly turn to "anger out," in U.S homegrown militias and racist organizations. A recent comment struck me dumbfounded; that the Trump campaign is full of the famous "dog-whistle" statements and slogans. Remember that actual dog-whistles are beyond the range of the human ear, but German Shepherds can hear them. Similarly, statements like "Make America Great Again" a major Trump slogan, actually fall on his followers' ears as "Make America White again." "Lock her up," a chant at some Trump campaign gatherings, was part of his attack on Hillary, claiming that she is a criminal because she disregarded State Department cybersecurity guidelines by using a private email account and server. How clever of Trump's campaign managers to take part of the well-known children's song, "London Bridge Is Falling Down," and apply it to Hillary. "Take a key and lock her up, my fair lady." "Lock her up" has become an ominous chant at Trump rallies, *even two years after his election.* "Crooked Hillary" was another effective slogan, based on an unproven allegation, despite years of the Whitewater investigation.

8. Inequality: I have devoted many pages to a discussion of how a recent worldwide leap of inequality of all kinds, but especially inequality of income and wealth, may lead to the destruction of our capitalism as we now know it—a system only partially leavened by the creation of a safety network of social supports. The anomic personality thrives in a societal condition of excessive decontrol, (anomie) that breeds rampant inequality and makes for extreme striving for sex, money and power at the expense of others.

9. Child-rearing: Survey after survey show that the large proportion of parents who are punitive, cold, or labile in relation to their children threatens to continue to produce children who are antisocial, depressed, or anxious. Some of these children become leaders who are narcissists, Machiavellians, or even psychopaths. Many fail to care for other human beings due to their early treatment

by their parents. The anger engendered, especially by antisocial and narcissistic parents, prepares young men and women for war, where they can legally "act out" their anger, instead of going into depression or crime. Education of parents and teachers in child rearing, (see much later discussion) is of some hope in avoiding wars that we as a nation initiate.

How will Donald deal with the two worst threats?

Global Warming: Hillary would probably have followed in the footsteps of Obama, who recently (2016) in Hangzou, China, submitted his plans to reduce carbon emissions, along with President Xi Jinping, to the UN Secretary General, Ban Ki Moon. Donald, on the other hand, doesn't believe in global warming. 'I don't believe in climate change,' he told CNN in September 2015 after a long history of calling it both a 'hoax' and a Chinese invention to undermine US. Business interests! In May 2016 he vowed to "renegotiate…at a minimum' the Paris agreement, one of the Obama administration's landmark achievements." (Timm, Jane C, 2016) [Timm, Jane C. "A Full List of Donald Trump's Rapidly Changing Policy Positions" *Politics*, 8/30/2016] On July 1, 2017, Trump announced that the U.S. will withdraw from the Paris Climate Accord.

Nuclear proliferation: "So, North Korea has nukes. Japan has a problem with that. I mean, they have a big problem with that. Maybe they would in fact be better off if they defend themselves from North Korea,'" (Trump said this on Fox News in April.) Host Chris Wallace followed up, asking, 'With nukes?' 'Including with nukes, yes, including with nukes,' Trump said."

Trump surrounds himself with like-minded people, and presumably, they will be some of the decision-makers. Steve Bannon, who was elevated by Trump to lead the NSA (National Security Agency), was perhaps the most extreme in his worldview. He was fired after it seemed that Bannon, not Trump, was running the show as depicted in the book Devil's Bargain, by Joshua Green. (Green, J. 2017) [Green, J., *Devil's Bargain*, New York, Penguin Press, 2017] Lt. General H.R. McMaster replaced Bannon as head of the NSA on 4/5/2017. This agency has historically been headed by someone with technical expertise in the military or in espionage and cyber defense, not by an editor of a newspaper, Breitbart News. Trump himself is uninformed and impulsive, a bad combination in the nuclear age. Bannon should have known that if you work for an Aggressive Narcissist, a Machiavellian, a person exhibiting Psychopathy and Sadism; (see Trump's Personality Traits and The Dark Tetrad) your chances of staying long on the payroll are the same as the chances of a snowball in Hell.

Trump's cabinet picks:

There is such a plethora of information on the background, careers, political activities, and special idiosyncrasies of Donald's cabinet that it might take volumes to describe and evaluate. I will give short shrift to all but the most egregious choices—that is, those individuals who will do real damage to our country if they wield their power in the same direction and at the same victims as before their current appointments. Most of them are vetted and confirmed, some still in consideration, or need Congressional approval. With few exceptions they seem to exhibit an alt-right approach to their domain. They could be like the criminal jury selected to try Jabez Stone in "*The Devil and Daniel Webster*," by Stephen Vincent Benét. For example, Webster chose people like the pirate Bluebeard, John Hathorne, the executor of the Salem Witch trials, and Walter Butler and Samuel Girty, two Loyalists—loyal to King George III, thus traitors.

A quote from a *Public Citizen* post-election letter says it all. "The candidate who ran against Washington D.C. corruption and insider deal-making has now turned to a rogue's gallery of corporate insiders—lobbyists, corporate lawyers, staff from corporate-backed think tanks and corporate executives themselves—to run his transition team. A former pharmaceutical industry executive is in charge of health care. The head of a climate change denying group is overseeing environmental policy. A former chief economist at Bear Stearns is in charge of economic policy." The fox is guarding the henhouse.

John Kelly: Homeland Security: Kelly's last job was as leader of the U.S. Southern Command in 2013. I2008 he was commander of I Marine Expeditionary Force. He had extensive experience in Western Iraq during the U.S. Occupation. He warned about vulnerabilities on the border with Mexico. In charge of prisoners at Guantanamo who were on a hunger strike, he labeled their force feeding as "long-term non-religious fasting." Human rights campaigners are suspicious of his Guantanamo behavior, because of the prejudice against Muslims and deportations which climaxed recently (1/29/17) in huge protests at major airports over detained Muslims. He shows high intelligence, and is sophisticated in his view of war. He wrote "...it was mostly about unfulfilled promises and the heavy-handed military approach taken by some that caused events to spiral out of control" (in Iraq). He shares the conservative viewpoint, preferring an American "melting pot" with common values as opposed to: "an unruly gaggle of 'hyphenated' or 'multi-cultural' individuals." He has plusses and minuses, but is competent to do the job, unlike many other appointees. [https://www/the guardian.com/us-news/2016/dec/07/john-kelly-homeland-security-trump-cabinet] His views on the Civil War are antediluvian (before the Biblical flood). Former generals are not likely to be of a liberal persuasion. A General Joe Stillwell comes along once in a century.

Tom Price, Secretary of Health and Human Services: "The evidence that the coming betrayal (of the white working class) is obvious in the choice of an array of pro-corporate, anti-labor figures for key positions. In particular....was the selection of Tom Price, and ardent opponent of Obamacare and advocate of Medicare privatization, as Secretary of Health and Human Services. This choice probably means that the Affordable Care Act is doomed, and Trump's most enthusiastic supporters will be among the biggest losers." (Krugman, P., 2016) ["Yes, the white working class is about to be betrayed. [Seduced and Betrayed by Donald Trump." Krugman, P., *The N.Y. Times. Opinion pages,* 12/3/2016] Price is a six term congressman from Georgia and an orthopedic surgeon. Medicare and Medicaid insure more than 100 million people. The appointment may also signal a wish to cut research funds for the National Institutes of Health.

Price's investments, discovered as part of a *TIME* review of Congressional and lobbying records, raise new questions about Trump's Cabinet, which ethics watchdogs say has not taken care to avoid appearances of conflicts of interest.

According to a *TIME* review of Congressional financial disclosures, Price held between at least $60,000 and $250,000 in stocks in health care-related companies as of the end of 2016. Because of his conflict of interest, he is a very bad choice.

Steven Mnuchin Treasury Secretary>: He is a former Goldman Sachs executive. Did Trump's base think he would appoint so many billionaires and inhabitants of Wall Street to represent them?

Mnuchin's time at the head of OneWest Bank, and whether it treated homeowners facing foreclosure fairly, was the central issue during his testimony. He has no government experience.

James N. Mattis, Defense Secretary: Mattis, known as "Mad Dog Mattis," led a Marine division to Baghdad during the 2003 invasion, and led the U.S. Central Command from 2010-2013. He is now retired from the service. He would presumably lead the fight against ISIS, giving advice as a leading military member of the National Security Council (NSA). This body sets major policy and readies it for the President's signature. In a much decried move, Trump at one time elevated Steve Bannon to the NSA as a regular Principals Committee member, while Mattis as Defense Secretary, and the newly appointed Director of National Intelligence, Daniel Coats, were demoted. These positions will not be regular members of the Principal's Committee. They will attend at the request of the Principals. The promotion of Bannon to the Principals Committee was feared to create a politicization of the NSA. (Bannon was fired by Trump, 8/18/2017.)

John McCain has best expressed this fear. John McCain harshly criticized the elevation of White House strategist Steve Bannon to President Donald Trump's National Security Council, calling the move "radical" because it minimizes the role of the chairman of the Joint Chiefs of Staff. (Bannon was replaced, see *supra*.)

Mattis is one of the few people with the intelligence and force of personality who could stand up to Bannon. He believes that Trump's conciliatory statements toward Russia are ill informed. He is an independent thinker. When Trump asked Mattis what he thought of waterboarding, Mattis said "I've never found it to be useful." Trump denies that it changed his position on waterboarding. Mattis has made some outrageous statements, and earned the nickname "Mad Dog Mattis." For example, he said to Iraqi military leaders shortly after the Iraq War's beginning, "I come in peace. I didn't bring artillery. But I'm pleading with you, with tears in my eyes. If you fuck with me, I'll kill you all."

The struggle for dominance in the National Security Council continued apace. Navy Admiral Michael Mullen, formerly Defense Secretary and Chairman of the Joint Chiefs of Staff under both G.W. Bush and Obama, threw his weight behind Mattis, and against Bannon. "Every president has the right and the responsibility to shape the Security Council as he sees fit. But partisan politics has no place at that table. And neither does Mr. Bannon." ["I was on the National Security Council. Bannon doesn't belong there." Michael G. Mullen, *The New York Times, Opinion Pages,* 2/6/2017.]

Scott Pruitt, Environmental Protection Agency Administrator: "Pruitt is controversial with Democrats because he has spent much of his energy as attorney general fighting the agency he is now leading. He repeatedly sued the EPA during the Obama administration, challenging the agency's legal authority to regulate toxic mercury pollution, smog, carbon emissions from power plants and the quality of wetlands and other waters. He has proudly described himself as 'a leading advocate against the EPA's activist agenda.' (Brady et al. 2017) ["Democrats boycott controversial EPA nominee Scott Pruitt's committee confirmation vote." [Brady D. et al. *CNN Politics.com,* 2/1/2017]

Elaine L. Chao, Transportation Secretary: She has an MBA from Harvard, and was Secretary of Labor under George W. Bush. Twelve miners died and three rescue workers died in mine disasters in 2006-7. Chao had cut more than 100 coal mine safety inspections previous to the disasters. Despite her later efforts, mine deaths shot up to 49 during her watch. She is the wife of Senator Mitch McConnell, no doubt some help in getting her appointment. In addition, she is from Taiwan, (population 23.4 million) favored by Trump over China with its 1.357 billion. Compare this to the U.S. 316.5 million. Her job will be to increase and repair America's infrastructure. Someone with an engineering degree or with experience in construction might have been a better choice. She was almost unanimously approved for the position.

Betsy DeVos, Education Secretary: Mrs. DeVos has devoted many years of her life to creating Charter schools in Detroit, Michigan. She has funded much of the work with her own wealth. She has managed to increase the proportion of Charter Schools in Detroit to 80%, leaving only 20% untouched. I wrote about the use of school vouchers and exorbitant teacher salaries to privatize the public schools in New York City in later sections called "Education and Inequality." and 'Educational Inequality and Mental Health." Suffice it to say that Republicans have continually tried to destroy the public school system, and shut down the Education Department. How does Trump's base reconcile this with their own wishes to see their children well-educated? They have fallen for the head feint that Charter Schools produce better-achieving students. They don't. By cherry-picking students and teachers the Charter School advocates try to convince us that they are better than public schools.

DeVos is an extreme example of the fox guarding the henhouse. Her background links her to some of the most ultraconservative figures in the country. Of course, birds of a feather flock together, just as Democrats and Liberals are more likely to be linked. Your associates reinforce your political convictions. In criminological theory, this is known as "differential association."

DeVos is married to Dick DeVos, the former CEO of multi-level marketing company Amway, and is the daughter-in-law of billionaire and Amway co-founder Richard DeVos. Her brother, Erik Prince, a former U.S. Navy SEAL officer, is the founder of Blackwater USA, later renamed Academi.

"In 1997, employees of Blackwater killed17 Iraqi civilians. Four guards were convicted of murder or manslaughter. Prince was recently (2016) under investigation for trying to provide private military services to Libya." (Blake, A., 2016) [Blake, A. "Former Blackwater chief under investigation for deals with China, Libya: report." *The Washington Times*, 3/24/2016.]

Eric Prince has sat in on meetings with Trump that were devoted to choosing candidates for the cabinet and other positions. In addition, Prince had connections to the NYPD and the FBI NYC field office. It was there that he supposedly got the scandalous (but fictitious) information about the Clintons and a "sex island" that he then turned over to Breitbart News. The threat to release this lurid misinformation supposedly forced Comey to announce more news about Hillary two days before the election. Prince and his sister, Betsy DeVos, have been involved in what seems to be a campaign of anti-Muslim, pro-Christian activities, and their influence on Trump should not be underestimated. If Trump ever needed a private army, I am sure Eric Prince could provide one. Prince's record throws a dark shadow on the appointment of his sister. He accused Huma Abedin, Hillary Clinton's aide, of being a "Muslim terrorist." He was at a secret meeting in the Seychelles Islands with a Russian banker, a close associate of Putin, ostensibly to talk business. George Nader, a Middle East specialist, with ties to the United Arab Emirates, was at the Seychelles meeting. He refuted Prince's version of the meeting. He has cooperated with Special Counsel Mueller's investigation. Representative Adam Schiff, (Dem., CA) said that the island meeting was an attempt to set up a "back-channel" communication between Trump's soon-to-be-official administration and the Kremlin, thus bypassing the FBI and the CIA and all U.S. intelligence agencies.

President Donald Trump's choice of billionaire Betsy DeVos to be education secretary was confirmed by the U.S. Senate on Tuesday, 2/7/2016, but only after Vice President Mike Pence was called in to break a tie that threatened to defeat her. The tie-breaking vote, which Senate officials said was unprecedented to confirm a Cabinet nominee, followed an all-night debate on DeVos as Senate Democrats tried to pressure at least one more Republican to oppose her and defeat the nomination. Ultimately, only two Republican Senators, Susan Collins of Maine and Lisa Murkowski of Alaska, joined the 46 Democrats and two independents in opposition to DeVos. That left 50 Republicans supporting her in the 100-member chamber. Critics have called her unprepared to lead the Department of Education after a rocky Senate confirmation hearing.

Under the U.S. Constitution, the vice president also serves as president of the Senate, with the power to cast votes only when there are ties on nominations or legislation. (Ernst, J., 2017) ["U.S. Vice President Mike Pence (R) swears in Education Secretary Betsy DeVos joined by her husband Dick DeVos at the Eisenhower Executive Office Building at the White House in Washington, U.S." Jonathan Ernst, Reuters, 2017.] Historically, Cabinet nominees with weak support in the Senate ask the president to withdraw their nomination, which DeVos did not do.

DeVos is married to the heir and former chief executive of Amway, which sells household and personal care items. She is also the daughter of the founders of Prince Corp, a Michigan car parts supplier, and sister of Erik Prince, the founder of the security company formerly known as Blackwater USA, now called Academi.

As Monday night's debate wound down, Schumer said of DeVos: "She disdains public education where 90 percent of our students are." Senate Majority Leader Mitch McConnell, urging her confirmation, said it was time to "end the unprecedented delay by Democrats" on the Cabinet nominations by Trump, who took office on January 20th.

DeVos has been an advocate of charter schools, which operate independently of school districts and frequently are run by corporations. Democrats are concerned she will promote charter schools in a way that would undercut public schools, which have long been the anchor of the U.S. education system.

Teachers unions, a major constituency for the Democratic Party, roundly opposed DeVos, a philanthropist and investor, to lead the department, which sets education policy for younger children and universities and also administers a college financial aid program of $1 trillion.

The Consumer Federation of America urged DeVos to confront the problem of millions of Americans in default on student loans. "The new secretary needs to put borrowers and taxpayers first, rather than focusing on helping the student loan and for-profit college industries pump up their profits," it said.

Jeff Sessions, Attorney General: Following the cliffhanger vote on DeVos, the Senate promptly limited debate on Trump's choice of Senator Jeff Sessions of Alabama to be Attorney General. Sessions is for strict immigration enforcement. Like most Republicans, he is tough on crime and favors reduced spending. On 2/7/2017, Elizabeth Warren, Senior Senator from Massachusetts and consumer advocate, asked to read into the record a letter from Coretta Scott King

"I'm reading a letter from Coretta Scott King to the Judiciary Committee from 1986 that was admitted into the record. I'm simply reading what she wrote about what the nomination of Jeff Sessions to be a federal court judge meant, and what it would mean in history for her." King had written that Sessions used "the awesome power of his office to chill the free exercise of the vote by black citizens" — and that was the line Senate Majority Leader Mitch McConnell would later cite in his objection.

"I call the senator to order under the provisions of Rule 19," McConnell said after interrupting Warren's speech, in which he said she had "impugned the motives and conduct of our colleague from Alabama."

"The Senate has silenced Elizabeth Warren. And by doing so, majority Republicans just handed the liberal firebrand a megaphone –further elevating President Donald Trump's fiercest and most prominent critic in the Senate and turning her into a Democratic hero." (Bradner, 2017) ["Silencing Elizabeth Warren backfires on Senate GOP." Eric Bradner. *CNN politics, 2/8/2017]*

Sessions was approved, as have even the worst of Trump's nominees to date. He will be pushing for more "law and order," and his negative civil rights record clearly goes back to before 1986.

Trump, Personality Traits and Personality Type:

It is difficult to describe the personality of most people whom you do not know personally or who are inaccessible for various reasons. In the case of Donald Trump, his life is like an "open book." Not only has he written many books, mostly about himself, but many others have written about him. In addition, he has given numerous speeches, and several hundred of his tweets are online which give unusual insights about his feelings and ideation. Understanding this man is the first step in trying to Make America Sane Again. We must get inside the head of this prime example of The Anomic Personality as a negative model for future leaders of our country.

Personality traits are characteristic behaviors and feelings that are consistent and long lasting. Unlike traits, which are stable characteristics, states are temporary behaviors or feelings that depend on a person's situation and motives at a particular time.

We must look at Trump's behavior over as much time as possible, to determine if what we see now during his presidency has been stable.

Is his behavior merely the result of the stress of his current position? I think it will be clear that he has shown behavior over most of his life that is consistent with his current behavior, and he is not in a temporary "state."

I will discuss Tiger Woods in Chapter Three, a narcissist, Bernie Madoff in Chapter Five a Machiavellian/Psychopath and Dick Cheney, another Machiavellian, in Chapter Six. Donald Trump seems to show clear signs of "preclinical" Aggressive Narcissism, Machiavellianism, Psychopathy and Sadism. We can think of him as really Dark, since he partakes of *all four* of the dark symptom clusters. (Due to his obvious prejudice against Blacks and most people with dark or non-white skin, I don't think he would appreciate the Dark designation). The Tetrad is composed of symptom clusters, slightly overlapping in content, which are more likely to appear in "anomic" individuals. They are part of a "Dark Triad," to which a group of research psychologists recently added Sadism, creating a "Dark Tetrad."

I ponder whether Bernie M., having been arrested and convicted of his massive Ponzi scheme, could be considered a psychopath, not just a preclinical psychopath. The American Psychiatric Association had emphasized the reliable criterion of arrest or conviction over the unreliable self-reports (if any) of psychopaths in making a diagnosis. However, it is clear that Bernie had enough self-control to avoid arrest for many years. He was also functioning very well in a complex (though criminal) undertaking, which may make him a Machiavellian/with secondary Psychpathy Even in prison, he has cornered the prison market in cocoa for making hot chocolate! When researchers look at the relationships between the four types, as tested by various instruments, there are moderate correlations between all four members of the Dark Tetrad. While there is some overlap, each dimension is statistically distinct. If the responses to questionnaires are representative of actual behavior of the respondents, then the subtypes do in fact exist in real life. Moreover, experimental and observational studies seem to support the independence and validity of the four Dark Tetrad members.

The Dark Triad/Tetrad is based on research conducted by Paulhus and Williams (Paulhus, D.L. & Williams, K.M.) [Paulhus, D.L. and Williams, K.M., "The Dark Triad of Personality." *Journal of Research in Personality*, 36,556-563, 2002.] and many other peer-reviewed journal articles. There are many related articles by various authors. In the interest of brevity, and because of their creation of questionnaire instruments tapping these dimensions, I have focused on Paulhus and his co-workers.

In 2013, Paulhus and his colleagues introduced a companion dimension to the Triad, which they called Sadism. They now had a Dark Tetrad.

"Past research on socially aversive personalities has focused on subclinical psychopathy, subclinical narcissism, and Machiavellianism— the 'Dark Triad' of personality. In the research reported here, we evaluated whether an everyday form of sadism should be added to that list. Acts of apparent cruelty were captured using two laboratory procedures, and we showed that such behavior could be predicted with two measures of sadistic personality. Study 1 featured a bug-killing paradigm. As expected, sadists volunteered to kill bugs at greater rates than did non-sadists. Study 2 examined willingness to harm an innocent victim. When aggression was easy, sadism and Dark Triad measures predicted unprovoked aggression. However, only sadists were willing to work for the opportunity to hurt an innocent person. In both studies, sadism emerged as an independent predictor of behavior reflecting an appetite for cruelty. Together, these findings support the construct validity of everyday sadism and its incorporation into a new 'Dark Tetrad' of personality." (Buckels, E.E. et al., 2013) [Buckels, E.E., Jones, D.N & Paulhus, D.L. "Behavioral Confirmation of Everyday Sadism." *Psychological Science,* 24(11), 2201-2209. 9/10/2013]

A major issue for me is whether the responses to questionnaires or to suggested bug-crushing tell us only about people who are not currently in treatment (the" subclinical") but also about those who are or have been arrested, convicted, or in treatment for psychological or psychiatric disorders (the "clinical" portion of the population.) I think Paulhus is being overly cautious when he says "The term *dark personalities* refers to a set of socially aversive traits in the subclinical range. Not extreme enough to invite clinical or forensic attention, they can get along (even flourish) in everyday work settings, scholastic settings, and the broader community." (Paulhus, D.L., 2014) [Paulhus, D.L. (2014) Toward a taxonomy of dark personalities. *Current Directions in Psychological Science, 23,* 421-426.]

Because of my experience in psychiatric epidemiology and that of many others who have done studies that compared psychiatric interviews given to random community samples with questionnaires covering psychiatric symptomatology and role functioning given to those same samples, I feel that the measures Paulhus has constructed tell us just as much about the "clinical" as they do about the "subclinical." In our random sample of a large city (anon. anon.) some 24% of the (anon.) respondents were judged to show some impairment in functioning as judged by psychiatrists rating their responses. A similar score (symptom score) based on the responses alone (an instrument that would parallel Paulhus' Dark Triad scales) showed similar results. *In short, there was much overlap between the treated and untreated in functioning and symptomatology.*

Because of these findings, I think the Dark Triad and Tetrad can shed some light on Donald Trump's personality and behavioral traits. He is, after all, still nominally in the subclinical range, "functioning" out there in the community, calling foreign leaders by phone, tweeting, fighting with the press, and charging the taxpayers for his visits to the Mar a Lago hotel.

Let's take the "gist" of the traits suggested by the Short Dark Triad questionnaire items and those in the Everyday Sadism list, and see if they match some of Trump's behavior or pronouncements For example, "I enjoy mocking losers to their face." (Sadism) In November, 2015, at a rally, Trump did an unflattering impression of Serge Kovaleski, who has a congenital joint condition. In response to a wave of criticism, Trump tweeted "Meryl Streep, one of the most over-rated actresses in Hollywood, doesn't know me but attacked last night at the Golden Globes. She is a Hillary flunky who lost big. For the 100th time, I never 'mocked' a disabled reporter (would never do that) but simply showed him 'groveling' when he totally changed a 16 year old story that he had written in order to make me look bad. Just more very dishonest media!" The sadism item and Trump's behavior coincide, suggesting that he exhibits sadistic behavior. He used the incident to strike back at Meryl Streep, exhibiting psychopathy. Although overall Donald is a Machiavellian, in this incident he seems more like a (subclinical) psychopath. The Psychopathy scale items "Payback needs to be quick and nasty" and "People who mess with me always regret it." support this interpretation. Remember, there are low intercorrelations between the four scales, which suggests that the traits tend to be scattered across the Tetrad, and any individual can have some traits in all four dimensions. (Note that sadism tends to be more independent from the Triad, while the Triad members are more overlapping or correlated.)

Let's start by reviewing the content of some of the items in the Narcissism scale, and add any that are in our previous discussion of narcissism and the Anomic Personality Trait List. An example of a trait that is covered in our previous discussion of narcissism, but not in the narcissism scale, is the <u>constant demand for love and praise</u> that stands out in Trump's relations. In the midst of a 77 minute rant there was what I would label as a significant "tell" or giveaway. "I watch CNN it's so much anger and hatred and just the hatred….. The tone is such hatred. I'm really not a bad person, by the way." In the midst of an unprecedented rant, there is a cry for recognition and even love that is different from the grandiose bragging we usually hear. It's heard in an unguarded moment. If we are ever able to vet candidates for high office in some intelligent way, we must be aware of the danger of electing an extremely needy person who must prove him-or-her-self to be "good." And as a nation we are seeing the creation of more anomic personalities, who will do whatever it takes to prove they are "good." No matter how hard they strive, they will not be satisfied. There is never enough sex, money or power to convince them of their worth.

Let's start with the traits of the narcissist. following the list of traits in "Aggressive Narcissism, Hare's Factor 1:

AGGRESSIVE NARCISSISM

Glibness: Fluent speech or writing, but insincere or deceitful. Trump continually fails to answer questions by reporters directly, often changing the subject or attacking the reporter or questioner on a personal basis. (See "cunning," below.) **Superficial charm:** He acts "presidential" and pleasant in the company of Obama or those he wishes to coopt for his cabinet, but is disdainful and aggressive toward those of lower status.

Pathological lying: He has lied consistently during the campaign and since he assumed office. He not only called Hillary "crooked" without evidence, but seems to have been involved in the conspiracy to smear the Clintons with details of a "sex island" and sex with juveniles along with Eric Prince and Rudy Giuliani. In his 77 minute rant at the White House (2/16/2017) Trump said that his Electoral College victory was the largest since Ronald Reagan's. But he actually won fewer Electoral College votes than three of the four presidents since Reagan: Barack Obama, Bill Clinton and George Bush.

When a reporter pointed that out, Mr. Trump brushed it off. "I was given that information," he said. Here again lying is denied with a *glib* response. Lying by Donald and his associates has become so obvious that his spokeswoman, Kellyanne Conway, counselor to the president, said the White House press secretary, Sean Spicer, gave "alternative facts" when he blatantly lied describing the inauguration crowd as "the largest ever" during his first appearance before the press this weekend. This is glibness and cunning in defense of glibness and cunning. It is reminiscent of "creating our own reality," attributed to Karl Rove during G.W. Bush's reign.

Grandiose sense of self-worth:

"I'm intelligent. Some people would say I'm very, very, very intelligent." (*Fortune*, April 3, 2000) [N.B.: Trump quotations with reference are from (Kruse, M., 2015) ["The 199 Most Donald Trump Things Donald Trump Has Ever Said." Kruse, M. *Politico*, 8/14/2015]

"Part of the beauty of me is that I am very rich." *(ABC's "Good Morning America," March 17, 2011)* "Show me someone without an ego, and I'll show you a loser." (Facebook, Dec. 9, 2013)

"... of course, it's very hard for them to attack me on looks, because I'm so good looking." (*NBC's* "Meet the Press," Aug. 9, 2015)

"Sorry losers and haters, but my I.Q. is one of the highest — and you all know it!" (Twitter, May 8, 2013)

Donald's fear of being a loser, or his fear of failure, is evident. The grandiosity is a cover for this fear. He is at work 24/7 to keep up his successful self-image, and the flow of kudos and admiration and power that it brings.

Cunning/manipulative: During his 77 minute "rant" he called on Jake Turx, an ultra-Orthodox Jewish reporter from Ami Magazine. "Are you a friendly reporter?" he asked. "I haven't seen anybody in my community accuse either yourself or anyone on your staff of being anti-Semitic," Mr. Turx said. But, citing bomb threats against Jewish centers, he said, "What we haven't really heard being addressed is an uptick in anti-Semitism and how the government is planning to take care of it." Mr. Trump bristled, taking it as a suggestion that he *was* anti-Semitic even though the reporter specifically said the opposite. "I am the least anti-Semitic person that you've ever seen in your entire life," Trump said.

Mr. Turx protested that he was not suggesting otherwise. "Quiet, quiet, quiet," Mr. Trump said. "See? He lied. He was going to get up and ask a very straight, simple question." Instead, Mr. Trump said, the question was "repulsive" and "very insulting." Well, Turx did *not* say he would ask a very straight simple question. Trump turned Turx' inoffensive question into an attack, and shut him up, which was both cunning and manipulative.

Lack of remorse or guilt: An Obama "program called Deferred Action for Childhood Arrivals (DACA).....has provided work permits to more than 750,000 immigrants who came to the country illegally as children. Trump had promised during his campaign to 'immediately terminate' the program, calling it an unconstitutional 'executive amnesty,' but he has wavered since then. Last week, he said he would 'show great heart' in determining the fate of that program." (Nakamura, D., 2017) [Nakamura, D. "Trump administration seeks to prevent 'panic' over new immigration enforcement policies." The Washington Post, 2/21/2017.]

Due to Trump's ban on Muslim immigrants from seven middle-eastern countries, millions of families will be broken up. In 2015, a normal year, 333,000 immigrants were deported under Obama. The new guidelines (announced 2/21/2017) by Homeland Security Secretary, John F. Kelly, will expose not thousands, but millions to deportation. Where is the "heart" in this directive? Remember, Trumps grandparents and his wife, Melania, were immigrants. "I'm all right Jack!"(This expression originally depicted a sailor climbing up the rescue ship's ladder to safety and saying "I'm all right, Jack, let the others in the lifeboat drown."

Emotionally shallow: "You know, it really doesn't matter what they write as long as you've got a young and beautiful piece of ass." (*Esquire*, 1991)

Callous/Lack of Empathy: (+ Sadism) The President has never apologized to the numerous people he has publicly disparaged and bad-mouthed. These include Megyn Kelly, ("There was blood coming out of her whatever," {note fear of contagion}, The Khans (father and mother of a slain U.S. Muslim soldier,) Meryl Streep, ("Hillary flunky who lost big. "One of the most overrated actresses in Hollywood.") John Lewis, Bill de Blasio, Angela Merkel, Maureen Dowd, Alicia Machado, Arianna Huffington, ("She is unattractive both inside and out. I fully understand why her former husband left her for a man—he made a good decision.") Lindsey Graham ("no honor"), Carly Fiorina, ("Look at that face! Would anyone vote for that? Can you imagine that, the face of our next president?") John McCain ("He's not a war hero. He was a war hero because he was captured. I like people who weren't captured.") Elizabeth Warren, ("Pocahontas," "Phony Native America Heritage.") Tony Schwartz (his former biographer), "A hostile basket case who feels jilted."

For a full list of the "307 People, Places and Things Donald Trump has Insulted." see Quealy, K. & Lee, JC. *The New York Times*, 2/7/2017. I already mentioned that he has been involved in several thousand lawsuits over his whole career, so many of them are related to business, not show or-monkey-business (otherwise known as the campaign for the presidency.) His tweets do not fall on deaf ears. He currently (2017) has 1,415,216 tweet followers.

The fact that some of his tweets are clearly sadistic, and that his reference to blood coming out of a woman's vagina suggestsa fear of contagion, illustrates the principle that *any single instance of behavior can partake of multiple traits.* The origins of Trump's misogyny may never be uncovered, but his poor relationships with women, his "pussy-grabbing" that inspired so many thousands of pussy hats in protest, his fear of vaginal blood suggest poor early attachment. This may also be suggested by a further incident, which did not receive much publicity.

In 2011 Elizabeth Beck, an opposing lawyer, was deposing Trump, and asked for a break to pump breast milk for her infant daughter. She said Trump responded; "He got up, his face got red, he shook his finger at me and he screamed, 'You're disgusting, you're disgusting,' and he ran out of there." Disgust tends to center around food, and the facial expression accompanying disgust centers around the mouth and wrinkled nose. To avoid "pisspot determinism," which I have so severely criticized in later discussion, let me say that during adolescence Donald's father must have been a major influence (in addition to breast feeding). There was enough anger in Trump to get him kicked out of school at age13, and sent to a military academy where he could get more discipline.

The breast-milk incident also illustrates the Mach trait of treating people (women) as objects. A penchant for handwashing is found in Donald's quotes. The theme of disgust and contamination pops up again and again. "Know what? After shaking five thousand hands, I think I'll go wash mine." [*New Yorker*, May 19, 1997.]

Failing to accept responsibility for his own actions:

"I inherited a mess at home and abroad." ["I inherited a mess" BBC News. 2/16/2017]

"Bill Owens, the father of Chief Petty Officer William "Ryan" Owens, the the Navy SEAL who died in the (Yemen) operation, demanded an investigation into his son's death over the weekend. Owens further revealed he *couldn't bear to meet Trump at the airport as* Ryan's casket was carried off the military plane last month. Asked about the matter during an interview with Fox News' "Fox 'n Friends," Trump repeatedly said "they" were responsible for the outcome of the mission, in reference to the military. 'This was a mission that was started before I got here. This was something they wanted to do,'" he said. 'They came to me, they explained what they wanted to do — the generals — who are very respected, my generals are the most respected that we've had in many decades, I believe. And they lost Ryan.' (Bobie, I., 2017) [Bobic, I. "Donald Trump Blames Seal's Death on Military. "They Lost Ryan." *The Huffington Post, Politics,* 2/28/2017.] Former presidents took full responsibility for government failings; Barack Obama (the Benghazi attack), George W. Bush (the Katrina Hurricane and the Iraq Invasion), and Ronald Reagan (the Iran-Contra Scandal). President Truman had a sign on his desk, saying "The Buck Stops Here." Trump was "passing the buck." (Around 1850-1900, poker players changed the dealer with every hand to avoid cheating. A buckhorn knife was used as a marker in front of the dealer. When finished, he would "pass the buck" to the next dealer.).

In addition to this list of quotes suggesting Trump's sharing of the Aggressive Narcissist traits in Hare's Factor I, there are similar narcissist traits tapped by the Dark Triad narcissism factor and scale. The gist of these traits are: loving the center of attention, considering oneself special, being "above average," loving compliments, and deserving and demanding respect. All of these have been covered by quotes in the discussion of the Hare trait list. Note that since Factor I contains the word "aggressive" (Narcissism), it contains some traits that could very well be considered to be Machiavellian, such as "cunning/manipulative." Given the sharing of traits across the Narcissist-Machiavellian-Psychopath continuum, the striving for purity of traits within those categories was not our goal, and indeed may be impossible due to the reality of overlap.

MACHIAVELLIAMISM:

The main traits of the Mach are being secretive, manipulation of others (perhaps more so than with aggressive narcissists) using people as objects, exploitation of others, anger at criticism, my ends justify my means, sexual dominance (males), kiss-up-kick-down hierarchical behavior and worldview. Additional Mach traits suggested by the Short Dark Triad Mach scale items are: careful timing of retaliation in excess of the injury you sustained, storing damaging information on others for future use against them.

Secretive: "It's always good to do things nice and complicated so that nobody can figure it out." (*New Yorker*, May 19, 1997) [Similar to "cunning, manipulative" in aggressive narcissism.]

Uses people as objects:

"I have black guys counting my money. ... I hate it. The only guys I want counting my money are short guys that wear yarmulkes all day." (*USA Today*, May 20, 1991.) (Also hierarchical view.)

"She's not giving me 100 percent. She's giving me 84 percent, and 16 percent is going towards taking care of children." (*TIME*, May 23, 2011).

"When a man leaves a woman, especially when it was perceived that he has left for a piece of ass—a good one! — there are 50 percent of the population who will love the woman who was left." (*Vanity Fair*, September)

Women: "You have to treat 'em like shit." (*New York* magazine, Nov. 9, 1992) (Also falls in Sadism dimension.)

My ends justify my means:

"It's very possible that I could be the first presidential candidate to run and make money on it." (*Fortune*, April 3, 2000) Trump has charged the taxpayers for his stays at Mar a Lago, and has discussed building hotels in various foreign countries, setting up conflicts of interest.

When you need zone changes, you're political. ... You know, I'll support the Democrats, the Republicans, whatever the hell I have to support." *(BuzzFeed*, Feb. 13, 2014).

"I'll do nearly anything within legal bounds to win." (*The Art of the Deal*.)

Hierarchical view of the world, kiss up, kick down:

"I think if this country gets any kinder or gentler, it's literally going to cease to exist." (*Playboy*, March 1990) Machiavelli said "....it is much safer to be feared than loved." This is a basic tenet of the Mach.

"It's been said that I believe in the power of positive thinking. In fact, I believe in the power of negative thinking." (*The Art of the Deal*, 1987)

Anger at Criticism: "I really value my reputation and I don't hesitate to sue." (*Village Voice*, Jan. 15, 1979) Extreme litigiousness over business and interpersonally. Retaliation is often excessive.

Excessive retaliation: "Anybody who hits me, we're gonna hit them ten times harder," [On "Hannity" tonight, Donald Trump warned his fellow GOP candidates about using attack ads against him. Fox News, 11/3/15.]

Obama made fun of Trump at the White House annual correspondent's dinner, which is usually a roast of the press and political figures. Obama said "I know he's taken some flak lately, but no one is prouder to put this birth certificate matter to rest than 'The Donald,' "And that's because he can finally get back to focusing on the issues that matter, like: Did we fake the moon landing?" This was one of a series of jibes. Trump had to chuckle at some of them, but he showed his Mach membership by continuing to proclaim the "birther" story until September 16th, 2016. This was *five years* after Obama had released his original long-form birth certificate showing he was born in Honolulu, in the U.S. State of Hawaii.

The traits of **retaliation** and perhaps an **obsessive** component are evident. (Perone, T., 2011) [Perone, T. "Obama Mocks Trump at White House." The N.Y. Post, 5/1/2011.]

"Let me tell you something about the rich. They have a very low threshold for pain." (*New York* magazine, Feb. 11, 1985)

Misogyny:

"There's nothing I love more than women, but they're really a lot different than portrayed. They are far worse than men, far more aggressive." (*The Art of the Comeback*, 1997) Projection of own aggression onto others, especially women.

PSYCHOPATHY

It is important to remember that we are looking for signs of *subclinical* psychopathy in the President. This is because he is not in treatment, and to our knowledge has never been in treatment. We can extract the gist or essence of these traits from the content of the Psychopathy scale in the Dark Tetrad and from the general literature on the subject. Let's take each scale item in turn. *Psychopathy scale items are shown in curly brackets or "braces."* {}

{I like to get revenge on authorities"}

The episode attacking Obama's citizenship for well over five years, even after release of proof that he was born in the state of Hawaii seems to exemplify this revenge trait.

His numerous lawsuits also attest to his penchant for revenge. He has been involved as plaintiff or defendant in 4,095 lawsuits in three decades. The great majority of these lawsuits stem from his business, such as tax matters, and personal injury to employees. He has also sued individuals for defamation, such as Miss Pennsylvania, Bill Maher and author Tim O'Brien, but has never successfully concluded any of these cases to date.

{"I avoid dangerous situations."}

Trump shows some caution, so he does not qualify for *clinical* psychopathy on this trait. He wisely backed down (after five years) on his "birther" attack. He shows only minimal caution appointing people who seem volatile or loose cannons. A flagrant example is Michael Flynn, whom Trump appointed National Security Adviser. Flynn Regularly broke rules in his whole military career. General McChrystal, his former boss, tried to get him to "tone it down." He was a poor choice, and was soon fired after he lied to V.P. Pence about whether he discussed U.S. sanctions against Russia with the Russian Ambassador. U.S. intelligence officials said that there actually had been discussion at that pre-election meeting about lifting the sanctions in case Trump won the election.

Trump has declared several bankruptcies. This shows that he is indeed a risk taker, and doesn't always avoid dangerous situations. His relationship to Putin, though still clouded in mystery at this time, must have involved major risks. After all, Putin spent 17 years as a mid-level agent in the Soviet KGB foreign intelligence service. Would you put your trust in a Soviet spy?

{"Payback needs to be quick and nasty,"} and {"People who mess with me always regret it."}

"For many years I've said that if someone screws you, screw them back. When somebody hurts you, just go after them as viciously and as violently as you can." (*How to Get Rich,* 2004)

"But when somebody tries to sucker punch me, when they're after my ass, I push back a hell of a lot harder than I was pushed in the first place. If somebody tries to push me around, he's going to pay a price. Those people don't come back for seconds. I don't like being pushed around or taken advantage of. (*Playboy,* March 1990)

{"It's true that I can be mean to others."}

"I can be a killer and a nice guy. You have to be everything. You have to be strong. You have to be sweet. You have to be ruthless. And I don't think any of it can be learned. Either you have it or you don't. And that is why most kids can get straight A's in school but fail in life." (Playboy, March 1990).

{"People often say I'm out of control."} There seem to be no Trump quotes that would agree with that statement. Being narcissistic, he would be unlikely to make *public* statements about being out of control. However, a subclinical psychopath might answer yes to such a question in an interview. Of course, thousands, maybe millions of people say and think that "the Donald" *is* out of control.

The Russian connection, the cabinet changes and conflicts, the botched calls to foreign leaders such as Australia and Taiwan, the precipitous ban on Muslims, and the numerous rants and tweets, might all be considered as signs of being out of control.

Given his quotes and his known behavior, there is little doubt that Trump shows signs of *subclinical* psychopathy, in addition to the other three dimensions of the Dark Tetrad. Moreover, he is in constant danger of arrest or impeachment, should any further revelations about the Russian connection come to light, or should any of his "pussy-grab" encounters devolve into a lawsuit with a complainant who refused to be bought off. Stormy Daniels, a minor porn star and prostitute, was paid hush money of $130,000 by Trump's lawyer, Michael Cohen, out of his own pocket. Stormy claims that she and Trump had a year-long affair, and Trump wanted to shut her up with "hush money" before the 2016 election. On March 12th, 2018, Stormy, whose real name is Stephanie Clifford, offered to return the money in exchange for dissolving the "hush agreement." She would then be able to publish any correspondence, videotapes or photographs without fear of retribution. This ploy has two effects. It puts Trump squarely in the relationship, which he has denied. Second, it threatens him with full disclosure of the details of the affair. Stormy could get many times the hush money for the publication of her story. Would it be possible that this one consensual affair would bring down the President, while the complaints of nineteen women about his sexual assaults have had no apparent effect on his standing with his base, or the GOP senators and representatives?

The establishment GOP would gladly sacrifice him, once he has done their dirty work of cutting Obamacare and Social Security. I think there are few who would like to be in his shoes, despite his wealth and beautiful wives.

SADISTIC TENDENCIES

Again, we turn first to another member of the Dark Tetrad for scale items that have been found to tap Sadism.(Paulhus, supra, 2015.) ["Sadistic Tendencies," Paulhus & Jones, *supra*, 2015.] There were seven items tapping "Vicarious Sadism." For example, "In car-racing, it's the accidents I enjoy most." Such activities as watching and liking "gory slasher films," "cage fighting" "horror movies," and "realistic blood spurts in video games," are not likely to be mentioned on tweets, or trumpeted as part of a public relations program.

Instead, we have selected some of the seven "Direct Sadism" items, along with some relevant Trump quotes, to illustrate this family of traits. Immediately recognizable as relevant is the item "I would never purposely humiliate someone." This is scored in reverse, as a *"disagree."* {"I would never purposely humiliate someone."}

"Rosie O'Donnell's disgusting. I mean, both inside and out. You take a look at her, she's a slob." ("Entertainment Tonight," Dec. 21, 2006) This was in retaliation for her calling him a 'snake-oil salesman." When you humiliate on television, it is *mass* humiliation watched by millions.

When discussing callousness as a trait of narcissism, I mentioned only a few of the numerous people he has insulted and humiliated. The humiliation lies in the ability of the sadist to find the weak points in the target's armor. Megyn Kelly was attacked for having a menstrual cycle! There is an almost universal taboo concerning menstrual blood, and Trump called on the taboo to denigrate Kelly. Some of the other previously mentioned people he humiliated were Meryl Streep, Angela Merkel, Arianna Huffington, John McCain, and Elizabeth Warren. Should there be any doubt of the consistency of this trait, one can always reference the "307 People, Places and Things Donald Trump has Insulted." (*supra.*)

{"I enjoy mocking losers to their face."}

"Karl Rove is a total loser." (Twitter, Feb. 7, 2013)

One of these "losers" was Serge Kovaleski, a disabled reporter, whose poorly controlled arm and hand movements Trump mimicked live, on TV.

"I do love provoking people." (*BuzzFeed*, Feb. 13, 2014)

{"I can dominate others, using fear."}

Trump has dominated many people through his numerous lawsuits. Fear of losing a trial has always been a deterrent for people who have less money than the complainant. Losing a case can wipe out the savings of the defendant. In the suit against *Gawker,* a New York City-based blog, the wrestler "Hulk" Hogan won $115 million for invasion of privacy and $25 million in punitive damages. Gawker posted a 9 second video clip of Hogan *in flagrante delicto* with the wife of his best friend. Gawker filed for bankruptcy (2016) and the company is up for sale.

This enormous judgement is of great concern to legal experts, who see it as a threat to freedom of the press and freedom of speech (part of the First Amendment). Even more ominous is the connection between the Gawker trial and Trump. Peter Thiel, co-founder of PayPal, helped Hogan win his case with a gift of $10 million. Thiel was "outed" by Gawker, and this was in effect "payback" for that revelation.

"Thiel is Chairman of Palantir, a spyware company. Palantir "has been found responsible for surveillance conducted by American agencies, according to a new report from *The Intercept*..... Palantir helped support the National Security Agency's controversial spy program XKeyscore, enabling the use of surveillance programming and the gathering of phone conversations of Americans, according to documents released by whistleblower Edward Snowden. The private company — co-founded by Thiel, who serves as chairman — previously denied its connection to another spy program called PRISM, which compiles individuals' internet histories. While Palantir remains mum as to their list of clientele on Capitol Hill, many assume that the administration of President Trump — a close friend of Thiel's —is already or will soon be a primary customer. The ability to obtain and exploit informational data by a man with severe temperament issues and a habit of impulsive action is certainly concerning." [Haley, B. "What Happens When Peter Thiel's Spyware Becomes Trump's Toy?" *Advocate* 2/23/2017]

There are other items in the Direct Sadism set which might apply to Trump, but he would never give a positive response to them during an interview. For example, "I enjoy making people suffer" is something he might agree with but he would never post it on his twitter feed. The ban on immigrants from six Middle Eastern countries is now making, or eventually will make, millions of people suffer. Children are being separated from their parents. Muslims who have lived in the U.S. for years are subject to deportation. With one stroke of the pen, Trump has made so many people suffer, but there is no proof that he enjoys that act. It may be just part of his suspicious worldview that it is a necessary ban, and he does not take any pleasure in the suffering it causes. However, he clearly enjoys the payback that obviously makes the target suffer when he calls his enemies losers, fat, ugly, or slobs.

Depression is linked to anger. When there is "anger in," directed at the self, you get depression. When there is 'anger out," the underlying depression may be controlled or reduced. Trump seems to have controlled his depression during a series of bankruptcies by being a "mean (sadistic) piece of shit." This is not a very positive self-image, but it is far better in his eyes than being a "loser," the worst epithet in his large vocabulary of mockery and aspersion.

"Hey, look, I had a cold spell from 1990 to '91. I was beat up in business and in my personal life. But you learn that you're either the toughest, meanest piece of shit in the world or you just crawl into a corner, put your finger in your mouth, and say, 'I want to go home.' You never know until you're under pressure how you're gonna react. Guys that I thought were tough were *nothin'*." (*New York* magazine, Aug. 15, 1994) Possibly a negative self-image; "a piece of shit." The lack of empathy for guys not tough enough is striking, and in keeping with the Machiavellian, his predominant social character.

ANOMIC PERSONALITY

When reviewing hundreds of Trump quotes, I never expected to find evidence of some of his deepest motivation. Because of his need for admiration and self-promotion he has produced more quotes and tweets than most other humans. The average anomic personality does not reveal in writing the emotional states and special behavior that is evident in unlimited striving. This revelation of Donald's intense struggle to be successful, epitomized by the tantalizing feeling of never gaining enough money, power and possessions to achieve satisfaction, is shown in these few quotes.

"I'm a guy who lies awake at night and thinks and plots." (*New York* magazine, Nov. 9, 1992) This sounds like an obsessive-compulsive routine. Much of the tweeting against his enemies is done in the wee small hours.

"..... the same assets that excite me in the chase, often, once they are acquired, leave me bored. For me, you see, the important thing is the getting, not the having." (*Surviving at the Top*, 1990)

"I truly believe that someone successful is never really happy, because dissatisfaction is what drives him." (*Playboy*, March 1990) "*The*

Art of the Deal, 1987). These two quotes are the essence of anomie (a deregulated state of *society*) as it manifests itself in the (deregulated anomic) *individual.* There is no limit to ambition, and no satisfaction at any level of achievement. Durkheim, as I said before, called this emotional condition in the individual a "derangement" and "an insatiable will." Others used terms like "drive" or 'instinct," which suggest biology (survival?) as the source, rather than society. No doubt, both are involved.

Emotional states like boredom and dissatisfaction give us further insight into the "derangement" or "insatiable will" that Durkheim described as typical in the victims of societal anomie.

The lack of satisfaction with any level of achievement results in what appears to be a compulsive striving that pervades all aspects of living, including sleeping and eating.

"I rarely stop for lunch." (*The Art of the Deal,* 1987)

"I don't sleep more than four hours a night." (Playboy, March 1990)

This lack of satisfaction at any level of achievement I call "tantalizing," after the mythical Greek King Tantalus, who could not reach the receding grapes above his head nor drink the receding water at his feet.

The traits of the anomic personality cut across the Dark Triad. They are: Overachiever, Pursues goals relentlessly, Goals are limitless, grandiose, Cunning, especially in use of language to manipulate, Pathological lying, Often charismatic, and Leadership, if any, tends toward coercion, dominance, and manipulation. Clearly, its main elements are Aggressive Narcissism, while coercive leadership falls in the Machiavellian dimension. The anomics are predominantly subclinical, for they are often functioning at a high level. As I have said before, they are the striving American, mostly male, and constitute a culturally patterned defect ("being fit in an unfit fitness"). Because they are surrounded by other anomics, they do not suffer any ostracism for their often nasty behavior.

Donald's view of the word is Manichaean. That means he sees everything in terms of "black and white" a dualism. There is no in-between, no shading. There is only love and hate, or good and evil. People are divided into winners and losers, and if you are a loser, you are worthless. Much has been said about our "zero-sum," or "winner-take-all" culture. There are the stars in movies and sports, the Kardashians famous for being famous, and the rest of us, whom Trump views as slobs, dogs, and losers.

"I don't like to lose." (*New York Times*, Aug. 7, 1983)

Perhaps the most revealing quote has to do with one of Trump's favorite songs, "Is that All There Is?"

> "Is that all there is, is that all there is
> If that's all there is my friends, then let's keep dancing
> Let's break out the booze and have a ball
> If that's all there is."

"During his final interview with Mr. D'Antonio, as their relationship had warmed and deepened, Mr. Trump turned philosophical. He recalled a favorite song, performed by Peggy Lee, 'Is That All There Is?' — a poignant ballad about unfulfilled dreams and dissatisfaction with life."

'It's a great song because I've had these tremendous successes and then I'm off to the next one. Because it's like, 'Is that all there is? That's a great song actually, that's a very interesting song, especially sung by her, because she had such a troubled life.'" Of course, it is *Donald* who has had such a troubled life, with little satisfaction as he meets his umpteenth goal. President of the United States? Is that all there is? (Barbaro, M., 2016) [Barbaro, M. "What Drives Donald Trump? Fear of Losing Status, Tapes Show." *The New York Times,* 10/25/2016.]

ANTI-INTRACEPTION:

This trait involves a dislike of subjectivity and imagination. It was found to be characteristic of the "authoritarian personality." "The authoritarian personality is a state of mind or attitude characterized by belief in absolute obedience or submission to one's own authority, as well as the administration of that belief through the oppression of one's subordinates. (Adorno, T.W. et al. 1950) [Adorno, T.W. et al. *The Authoritarian Personality.* Harper, 1950.] Trump fits this description pretty well, for he demands submission to his authority and he oppresses his subordinates. He throws them "under the bus" when he pleases, as with Michael Flynn, former National Security Adviser; Sally Yates, acting Attorney General (an Obama appointee) Corey Lewandoski, his campaign manager,. and in March 2018 Rex Tillerson, his Secretary of State, among many others. The traits of the authoritarian personality fit best to one member of the Dark Tetrad; namely Machiavellianism. Though the authoritarian F-scale was created to tap Fascism and race prejudice at the time of World War II, the racist, hierarchical attitude, Manichaean world-view (dualistic black-and white), and anti-intraceptive traits it elicited are still relevant to our parsing of Trump. These anti-intraceptive quotes were hard to find, but are very telling.

"Who knows what's in the deepest part of my mind?" (*BuzzFeed*). If Donald looks inside himself, he is afraid he will see "the toughest meanest shit" that he says he had to become in order to get through hard financial times.

"I don't like to analyze myself," Trump said in the tapes, "because I might not like what I see." He might see that "toughest meanest shit?"(Kludt, T, 2016) [Kludt, T. "Biographer: 'Interviews Showed Trump to be 'Calmer, More Sincere' "CNN *10/26/2016]* The tapes were of an interview of Trump by Michael D'Antonio.

The trouble with being strongly anti-intraceptive is that you are subject to the disparity between your unconscious self-image (piece of shit) and your conscious one, grandiose. There is a struggle, suggested by these two quotes, to keep the unconscious "bad" self from popping up and telling you that you are *not* so great, lovable, intelligent, etc. So part of the motivation for unbridled striving, aside from a cultural imperative (the anomie of our extreme winner-take-all capitalism) is the struggle, or "cognitive/unconscious dissonance", between the conscious self-image (good) and frequent *glimpses* of the unconscious bad self-image. The latter can come up in unguarded moments, when looking in the mirror, in dreams of guilt or accusation, or when experiencing a hurtful rejection by someone you love or admire.

In a prevous book I posit two groups with opposite social characters, the GOPS and the DEMS (rather thinly disguised labels). As the division between the two parties and their "bases" has radically deepened since the Obama presidency and the first year of the Trump presidency, the gap between these (Manichaean!) dichotomies has widened: "authoritarian versus permissive, selfish vs. caring, bellicose vs. peaceful, averse vs. empathic, imperceptive vs. perceptive, extroverted vs. introverted, anti-intraceptive vs. intraceptive, external locus of control vs. internal locus of control, rigid vs. flexible, close-minded vs. open-minded, sincere vs. authentic, self-reliant vs. acceptance of dependency, belief in absolute truths vs. relativistic truths, faith vs. science, particularism vs. universalism, homogeneity vs. multiculturalism, cynicism and irony disliked vs. cynicism and irony accepted as criticism of the establishment, instrumental values vs. intrinsic values, pragmatism vs. idealism, and intolerance vs. tolerance of ambiguity. Almost without exception, Trump exhibits the first, more conservative, member of each pair of traits. There are possibly a few exceptions. He is very cynical and uses some irony in his tweets. He has a negative view of the current establishment, whether Republican or Democrat, and would like to replace it with his own establishment, which would be very radical. The influence of Steve Bannon and Stephen Miller pushed him even further than his original radical positions. Also if he has any source of control, it is not like his base, who are mostly religious (at least in their identity) and look to God or some higher authority for their source of control. He sees himself as completely in control of his fate and the sole author of his decisions He plots and plans in the wee small hours to achieve that control. He would agree with the poet William Henley that "I am the master of my fate, I am the captain of my soul." He is not deeply religious, although he may give God credit in his speeches to his base, who are primarily religious.

There is neither time nor space to go into all of these traits at length, supporting them with quotes or behavior when possible. Many of them are so clearly "Trumpish" as to need no explanation. What is important is that the first member of each dichotomy falls into, or is linked to, one of the Dark Tetrads; Narcissism, Machiavellianism, Psychopathy and Sadism, almost without exception. This leaves me with a dark view of our national future, since these traits and values are part and parcel of the current Republican Party, and can only become more extreme under the guidance of Trump and his authoritarian cabinet.

I have not gone into the details of Trump's childhood and career because the focus has to be on the current political crisis, and what his character predicts for the near future. However, a few quotes suggest that his father's character and their relationship had a large role in forming his current behavior and worldview.

"We had a relationship that was almost businesslike." (*The Art of the Deal*, 1987)

"He was a strong, strict father, a no-nonsense kind of guy, but he didn't hit me." (*Playboy*, March 1990)

He taught me to keep my guard up. The world is a pretty vicious place." (*Esquire*, January 2004)

Well, despite being "strict and no nonsense," Fred Trump was very generous in supporting Donald. His first loan (1975) was one million, 14 million around 1985, and 3.5 million in 1990. But such huge loans probably came along with a father's high expectations of future success. After all, his son was a big investment. Donald Trump says he got 'only a small loan' from his father! (Fortune Staff, 2016) ["Donald Trump Says He Got 'Only a Small Loan' From His Father." Fortune Staff, *Fortune*, 9/26/2016.]

Trump, Personality Traits and Personality Type: Summary

Trump exhibits traits found in all four of the Dark Tetrad dimensions; Narcissism, Machiavellianism, Psychopathy and Sadism. Because of his (marginal) functioning at this time, and the fact that he is not in treatment or incarceration forces us to consider him, by definition, as preclinical in all these areas. Because of the added stress in a new role as President, he is at high risk of a failure in his defenses. His grandiosity may be punctured by the future disclosure of his connections to Putin and Russia by the CIA and FBI. His former dependency on Bannon and Miller, both extremists, puts him in a precarious position. The pressure of the alt-GOP, (my label), sponsored by the Koch brothers, to get rid of Obamacare immediately without considering the gigantic backlash it will cause, may lose him the support of much of his base. They will suddenly realize that they have no medical insurance. Trump's overweening need for approval would be starved by the loss of many of his supporters. He might compensate by becoming even more Machiavellian or sadistic. This would involve more regressive laws, further bans, stepped-up law and order, and more explicit race and religious discrimination. Presumably, before this went too far, Congress would step in and current V.P. Pence would become President.

I have already discussed the threats posed by Trump's presidency. Near term there are the threats of "eliminating ISIL," nuclear attack by North Korea, and the loss of our friendly nations, due in part to Trump's new tariffs on steel (25% and aluminum (10%). At home, we may face mass rioting due to loss of medical care, Social Security, food stamps, and myriad government services formerly available. Long term, global warming, nuclear war with Russia or Iran, famine and mass migration are threats. Not all threats will stop with Donald's departure. He has delayed the attack on global warming and cut many government programs that usually protect the environment. That has happened within the month of his inauguration, and worse is yet to come.

I previously wrote that I looked on the bright side, and did not go along with Berman, the author of *Dark Ages America, (supra)*. After the first months of Trumpism, I am veering more toward Berman's dark view. With a leader, cabinet and advisors who on first impression all seem to share many of the traits in the Dark Tetrad, I am rapidly joining Chicken Little, who said "The sky is falling" when an acorn fell on her head. She tells all the other animals, and they join forces to tell the King the news. In the more popular version, Foxy Loxey invites them to his lair, and eats them all.

If you told me the sky was falling when Trump first announced his candidacy in June of 2016, you could rightly have called me a paranoid liberal. Since then, a gigantic acorn *has* actually fallen on our heads, and there are even those on the right, such as Senators John McCain, Lindsey Graham, and Jeb Bush, former Governor of Florida, who are highly critical of Trump. In a few years, the sky will not fall, but it will be obscured by the pollutants that Trump et al. have returned to the air above us in order to save the coal industry. Yet he mocked the coal miners, whose jobs have been decimated by the invention of fracking and the surfeit of U.S. oil.

"I like the challenge and tell the story of the coal miner's son. The coal miner gets black-lung disease, his son gets it, then his son. If I had been the son of a coal miner, I would have left the damn mines. But most people don't have the imagination— or whatever—to leave their mine. They don't have 'it.'" (*Playboy*, March 1990) What they don't have is not "it,", but a father who supports them with about 24 million dollars in "loans." It's not lack of imagination that kept generations of miners in the mines with coal workers' pneumoconiosis. It's lack of money, education, and opportunity.

And it's his astounding lack of empathy and surfeit of grandiosity that allow Donald to say he has "it" and the miners don't.

The people who have been "left behind, and cling to their guns and religion" (via Obama) are the same people who drink, fight, pray, suffer, and "spend their way to the poorhouse" in *Hillbilly Elegy*, another look into the politically forgotten Scots-Irish (this time in Kentucky). But the author, J.D. Vance, says the poverty of the hillbillies is due to their "culture." He was a hillbilly who worked his way through Yale Law School (Trump said poverty and disease are due to "lack of imagination" or lack of "it"). (Vance, J.D., 2016) [Vance, J.D. *Hillbilly Elegy*, HarperCollins, New York, 2016.}This best-selling book got rave reviews in the New York Times and many other leading newspapers. But a review by Sarah Jones (Jones, S., 2016) [Jones, S. "J.D. Vance, "The False Prophet of Blue America." *The New Republic* 11/17/2016] tells a different story.

"*Elegy* is little more than a list of myths about welfare queens repackaged as a primer on the white working class. Vance's central argument is that hillbillies themselves are to blame for their troubles. 'Our religion has changed,' he laments, 'to a version 'heavy on emotional rhetoric and light on the kind of social support' that he needed as a child. He also faults 'a peculiar crisis of masculinity.' This brave new world, in sore need of that old time religion and manly men, is apparently to blame for everything from his mother's drug addiction to the region's economic crisis."

There follows a diatribe by Vance that could have come from the pen of those who want to distance themselves from the poor, and will cut any funding that sounds like a safety net. In fact, it could be a quote from almost any of Trump's current cabinet members (especially Betsy DeVos).

"We spend our way to the poorhouse. We buy giant TVs and iPads. Our children wear nice clothes thanks to high-interest credit cards and payday loans. We purchase homes we don't need, refinance them for more spending money, and declare bankruptcy, often leaving them full of garbage in our wake. Thrift is inimical to our being." (Vance, *ibid.*) This does sound like a GOP rant about "Welfare Queens," and is almost as dark as Trump's depiction of Mexicans as rapists.

"When Mexico sends its people, they're not sending their best. They're bringing drugs. They're bringing crime. They're rapists. And some, I assume, are good people." (Presidential announcement speech, June 16, 2015.)

How could so many reviewers and book buyers be so easily deceived by these old lies? Perhaps because they are so well packaged. Moreover, Maw ("Mamaw" in the *Hillbilly Elegy*) and Paw have always been amusing stereotypes in movies and television. In "Western" movies, Maw is handy with a gun, and Paw is kindly, but not when drunk or crossed. In the extremely popular Ma and Pa Kettle series in the 1940s, Ma (Marjorie Main) was raucous and resilient, caring for her fifteen children, while Pa (Percy Kilbride) was somewhat retarded and lazy. Somehow, stereotyping Appalachians seemed, and perhaps still seems, more politically correct than denigrating African-Americans or Hispanics.

In short, we must always be aware of explanations of poverty that are based on race, biology, low I.Q. and a "culture of poverty." That particular "culture" is a state, not a trait, induced by *malign*, not "benign" neglect. (Daniel Patrick Moynihan, serving as urban affairs adviser to Richard Nixon, said "...the issue of race could benefit from a period of benign neglect.") That continued neglect, extended to poor Whites as well as to African-Americans, Hispanics, and other minorities by Republicans, and by Democrats to a lesser extent, may have helped to bring us to the "Dawn of the Dark Ages," a fitting oxymoron. (I am thinking of patenting this phrase, for use if Trump is around for a full four year term.) What can we do to avoid repeat occurrences of Trumpism? First of all, we know that the Dark Tetrad consists of four dimensions, each of which is distributed from dark to light, as it were. Trump's statements, speeches, tweets and behavior seem to closely mirror these dimensions. Not all Americans are subclinical Psychopaths or Sadists by any means, though a good portion are Narcissists. In business and politics, the Machs abound. How can we move some people from the Dark Tetrad into more sympathetic, empathic, and caring behavior and attitudes? I have discussed the possible role of teaching child-rearing to expectant mothers and to high-schoolers of both sexes, so that they are less cold, punitive, and labile with their children. The importance of high-quality medical care, prenatally and during the full life-span cannot be exaggerated. Good physical health and mental health are inextricable, shown by almost every study that has been done. Body and mind are one. Jobs for parents, promised by Trump, can lift them out of poverty. He has only given lip-service to job-creation. He announced that Intel Corporation had agreed to add 3000 jobs, but soon afterward they cut 12,000 jobs! Two months before inauguration, Trump and Price visited the Carrier plant in Indiana for photo ops, after they closed a deal to "save 1000 jobs from moving to Mexico." United Technologies, the parent company of Carrier, was promised seven million in tax breaks. You can't bribe every corporation in America to keep their jobs at home. This gift sets a bad precedent. Moreover, 1000 Carrier jobs will *still* go to Mexico, and 11,000 will stay in Indiana. Who said there is no free lunch? (Lawler, D., 2016) [Lawler, D. "Donald Trump Touts Jobs–) *The Telegraph* (U.K.) Washington, 12/1/2016.]

Good housing is essential for protecting both children and their parents from the elements, (extreme temperatures, rain, snow, wind) and from pollution, insect and rodent infestation. The cuts already being made by the Environmental Protection Agecy; air quality, and water purity, are harbingers of worse cuts to come. As spelled out in detail before, Trump's cabinet is largely made up of people who have openly tried to demolish the very services they are supposed to supervise. Children can't study if they have lead poisoning from peeling old paint, breathe in perchloroethylene from dry cleaners, or live on streets where cars are pouring out carbon monoxide day and night.

Well, after this litany of government and corporate war against the poor and minorities, or at this point even against the 99% poor and middle class, what can we do to avoid another veritable Dark Age? How can we avoid having "snake-oil salesmen" sell the "Brooklyn Bridge" to unsuspecting "marks" If we can understand why almost half the voting population can fall for this "consummate con game," perhaps we can avoid a repetition of this radical rip-off. With the election of Trump, we are entering the explosive phase of a shift from a democracy to a kleptocracy run by a billionaire president and his millionaire/billionaire cabinet.

Attachment: a major reason why people vote against their own interests.

(a new theory of the origins of excessive attachment to undeserving leaders and the Kardashians.)

I am suggesting that *the overwhelming need for attachment has made "the base" vulnerable to a "bait and switch" con of gigantic proportions.* The bait is a promise of jobs, of making "America Great (White) Again," (a dog-whistle promise of White supremacy), and a promise of ethnic cleansing (now Muslims, later who knows?). These promises have been promoted by various memes that are capable of arousing strong emotions when repeated or shouted. "Crooked Hillary" and "Lock Her Up" were still being shouted at what appear to be Trump campaign rallies for the mid-term 2018 or the 2020 election. This has an obvious function for the base, that of blowing off steam. The anger at being passed by, combined with the fear of changing mores and changing technology such as automation, is directed at protesters, minorities, immigrants, and "elites" who have "made it."

How did leaders in history get their "base' to bond with them? Some, like Gandhi, gained traction through fasting. He was a sophisticated lawyer, but his starving body and ragged garments made him one with his people. Attachment is facilitated by some similarities between the leader and follower, such as starvation. Hitler was a failed artist, a war veteran, and a "victim" of the Versailles Treaty. These qualities appealed to the *Kleinbeampte*, the small officials, such as conductors, customs officials and police, who became the backbone of the S.S. They too had failed to rise in the system. The nobility and industrialists stood by, thinking that they would maintain their power. Killing the Jews and Gypsies provided the targets for the people's anger. The promise of the Third Reich was greatness and power that would last a thousand years. It lasted only 12 years (1933-1945). Slogans ("*Deutschland über alles*" and music (*Die Wacht Am Rhein*, and the popular song, *Lili Marlene that was* even sung by the Allied forces, made for strong bonds.

Not surprisingly, Hitler's rise coincided with the worldwide Great Depression of 1929, when the New York stock market crashed. Loans to the Weimar Republic by U.S. financiers were halted, and many German banks failed. By 1933, 26 per cent of the workforce was unemployed. Children were dying of starvation. With each year, the NSDAP Nazi Party grew stronger. Much of Hitler's base was desperate.

The parallel to the U.S. (and worldwide) Great Recession is hardly an accident. The recession (really a depression) between 2007 and 2009 was due to the housing bubble and U.S. banks selling subprime mortgages to investors. Unemployment was at 4.7%, but rose to 10% by 2009. The "base" (especially unemployed White males) was exposed to many losses;

of identity, self-esteem, social supports and control over life events. This was a recipe for intense longing for authority, a resurgence of religion, and a homogeneous community life that preceded the rise of Hitler, and that also preceded the coming of Trump. The authority has been handed over to a president and a cabinet who have very little authority or expertise in the positions they occupy. Religion has been pushed front and center by speeches and by legislation. Roe vs Wade may be in danger of being overturned once Trump's conservative new appointment to the Supreme Court, Neil Gorsuch, is installed. At the very least, abortion may be ruled illegal in the U.S. by a 5-4 vote. Betsy DeVos' real goal is to destroy the public school system and build up the parochial ("charter") schools. Her appointment as Secretary of Education is more evidence of the goals of Trump, Bannon and Miller (though their goals do not completely overlap). The return to a homogeneous community life (One People, One Empire, One Leader, or "*Ein Volk, Ein Reich, Ein Fuhrer*") contributed in part to the Holocaust. Killing the "others" in your society, such as Jews and Gypsies, is a very efficient way to obtain homogeneity. Similarly, Trump's travel ban on Muslims from six countries and his plan to drive out undocumented immigrants has great appeal to his White, high-school-or-less-educated base. Immigrants are seen as taking jobs away from White Americans. Trump's proposed wall along the Mexican border has the same appeal. Isolate, or persecute the "other." Create homogeneity. It is a little late to "make America Great (White) again." Non-Hispanic Whites comprised only 61% of the U.S. population in 2016, compared to 76% in 1990. They were the only group to experience more deaths than births. You see in the speeches and writings of some of our current leaders and cabinet members the condemnation of "multiculturalism," and the praise for the old "melting pot" approach, that wants quick assimilation of immigrants, and "no more hyphenated Americans." (John Kelly.)

I think we have laid the groundwork for showing how attachment is possible to a leader who exhibits a lot of the ideation, values, and behavior found in the Dark Tetrad scales. *Why did the people in Trump's base vote for him when, with few exceptions, he has not acted in their own best interest?* I have written a book asking this same question, but looking at *past* presidential elections. George W. Bush didn't act in the interest of the poor, working class, or middle class, but he got a lot of their votes. Possible reasons were social class differences in personality, and value systems. Poor education could also account for being misled or not understanding the issues involved. Being exposed to a barrage of euphemisms, twisted language, and camouflaged legislation could be factors. Depression and anxiety interfere with the ability to focus attention on politics and complex issues. Rapid social change in values and technology create anger that is directed away from politicians by propaganda and slogans. The anger is redirected purposely at minorities, immigrants and vaguely defined "elites." ("pointy-headed intellectuals," "Wall Street"). The energy that could go into action in their own interest goes into shouting "Lock her up."

To explain why people don't vote in their own best interests, and why Trump's base clearly didn't vote in their own best interest, I am setting up a chain of hypotheses.

1. Attachment to a parent, usually the mother, is a universal human need, and is found in the animal kingdom as well, particularly among mammals.

2. That it is necessary for survival of the infant.

3. That in proto-humans during the long period of infancy and adolescence, there were minimal requirements for proper development (for example, nourishment, walking, language, brain development) that demanded strong and continued attachment and bonding between mother and child.

4. *The average life span of the Cro-Magnons, the first modern humans, was only 20 years.* During that short time they had to transmit whatever technology and skills they had to their children. That demanded they teach how to build fires for warmth and cooking, make clothing from animal skins, and fashion stone tools, bows and arrows, spears, and fish hooks. Transmitting these skills required attachment between teacher/ parent and student/child.

5. There was a pressing need for very strong child-parent attachment during prehistoric times, due to predators. Huge cave bears were hunted by the Neanderthals, and were finally extinguished by the Cro-Magnon hunters. Children could not be left alone. The bears and the early humans fought for the shelter of the caves.

6. Given poor shelter, (caves), predators, and the presence of vermin, reptiles, insects and arachnids in the forests, children without strong

attachment were sure to die at a much greater rate than those with strong attachment. *Thus 21ˢᵗ century man has inherited a very strong attachment need in his DNA, through the process of natural selection.* Our predators are now mostly human, except in some African countries, the Amazon forest, and the Polar Regions.

7. In the U.S. we now have wide variation in the degree, length and quality of parent-child bonding. By and large, however, it is fair to say that Americans bond with and attach to their parents for a very long period compared with some other cultures. Our "adolescence" extends well into the mid-twenties, and as jobs become scarce during various depressions or recessions, older children are even coming back to live with their parents when they are in their twenties or thirties. (This was hardly possible in a Cro-Magnon family, since parents died on average at around 20.) Housing shortages and high rentals contribute to this trend. Some nations look upon us as child-coddlers. As discussed before, the recent growth of narcissism among our youth has been documented in many studies, and we have the label for it, "the me generation." The ubiquitous "selfie" has been around ever since there was still water. Narcissus, in Greek mythology, fell in love with his own reflection in a lake. How many selfies does it take to satisfy a narcissist? As many as their iPhone can hold, until it needs recharging.

8. Prolongation of adolescence doesn't necessarily mean prolongation of parent-child attachment. There may be a bimodal relationship between attachment and social class. Poor and working class parents on one end of the income/education distribution tend to encourage their children to work outside the home early because of the need for money. Upper-class parents are known for sending their children to prep, military and "finishing" schools, away from home. The middle class has a reputation for keeping children close to the apron strings, through college, and later. A humorous example is found in *Barefoot Boy With Cheek*, a novel by Max Schulman. A boy goes away to college, but his actual "Jewish mother" (a stereotype) keeps visiting him there with the excuse that she is knitting him a woolen sweater. (Many of Schulman's books were made into popular movies.)

While the length and intensity of *child-parent attachment* may vary with changes in the economy, values, and forms of government, I think *the greatest change making for general attachment to figures other than parents has come about due to the increase in the human life span.* Remember that the Cro-Magnons lived to 20. What happens to the propensity to bond that's in the DNA? (It is in animal DNA also, but they don't have much longer life spans than in prehistoric times, except for pets, who don't vote for president and don't swoon over movie stars.) Now, after our 20 year bonding to our parents, we still have another 60 more years plus in which to bond to other figures. It seems to me that the prevalence of attachment to figures outside the childhood home is simply due to the fact that the majority of young adults move outside the home to get jobs, to get higher education or job training, and to marry.

Now they attach to "significant others" they meet in adult life. That may mean their teacher, girlfriend or boyfriend, wife or husband, boss, pastor, or their general practitioner/internist (before they lose their Obamacare due to the Trump agenda). *But in our fractionated culture, people are more likely to attach to figures with whom they have no immediate contact, except through the media.* Thus the bonding with total strangers, such as Kim Kardashian and Paris Hilton, Leonardo DiCaprio and Scarlett Johanssen, or Tiger Woods and Venus Williams. It makes no difference whether your attachment-target is famous for skills and accomplishments, or if they lack both of these qualities, as in Kim and Paris.

Mother-child attachment we call "love." Girlfriend-boyfriend bonding we call "love." Husband-wife attachment we call "love." Volumes have been written by psychoanalysts about "object choice," and the factors that determine it, especially early childhood experience and parental character. Marriage counselors have also written about the pitfalls of poor choices of mates. Here I propose that we take a look at the randomness found in choice of marital partners. For example, people with the same first letter of their family name or surname tended to get married at a greater rate than those whose last names began with different letters. This had been caused by the alphabetic seating of high school students in the last century, but has changed due to the relaxation of seating assignments.

The construction of reality is the problem here. It was probably Karl Rove who said "We create our own reality." Well, he was no philosopher, but he unwittingly raises this very important question. What is reality, and how much of what we see, hear and touch is not what it seems. "Skim milk masquerades as cream." "Truthiness" reigns. Kellyanne Conway, Trump's counselor and mouthpiece, invented "alternative facts," a prizewinning oxymoron.

Way back in 1822 Stendhal (Marie Henri Beyle) published *De L'Amour*, in which he described love as an illusion; the construction of the lover. "Friendship has its illusions, no less than love." The poet Thomas Moore, wrote "Romantic love is an illusion. Most of us discover this truth at the end of a love affair or else when the sweet emotions of love lead us into marriage and then turn down their flames. (Moore, T., brainyquote.com) [Thomas Moore, https://www.brainyquote.com/quotes/quotes/t/thomasmoor138407.html]

The construction of the leader is like that of the lover—partly an illusion.

John F. Kennedy had plenty of charisma. He was handsome, well spoken, rich, and had a beautiful wife, Jackie. She coined the term "Camelot" for his presidency after his assassination. This referred to the castle and court of legendary King Arthur. Our country, at least the Democrats, couldn't get enough of him. I saw people weeping everywhere as the news of his death came in. I was with two psychiatrist friends sitting in the adolescent ward of a mental hospital when the news came in. They immediately locked down the ward, because there were many suicidal girls there. As clinicians, they knew the power of attachment, and loss. Did the fact that Kennedy had a fling with Marilyn Monroe and other stars make a difference in the romantic halo that surrounded John and Jackie? Not a bit. *We* make the image of the person or leader we love, and it often has little to do with reality.

10. I'd like to propose that there is a large element of randomness in the attachments we have given as examples. People bond with others they have never met, and will never meet. So it is with attachment to movie stars, chosen for their physical beauty and sometimes for their acting ability. The characteristics of one blonde starlet or one handsome leading man don't differ by very much. Famous athletes tend to be somewhat similar. Politicians with some exceptions are almost caricatures of the narcissistic smooth talker. The party labels are deceiving, for promises are made and broken by Democrats and Republicans, though perhaps at different rates. Many people found it difficult to vote for Trump, because of his character, and for Hillary, because she was "crooked." The Trump base of angry,

often unemployed White males heard the promises of "making America Great Again" suggesting White Christian homogeneity. They listened to his promises of jobs. They heard he would cut or gut Obamacare and eventually Social Security. How could they believe that a border wall would get rid of all the non-Whites or minorities who comprise about 40% the nation? How could they reconcile voting for "the Donald" when they knew that they were dependent, or might easily *become* dependent, on Medicaid, Medicare, and Social Security?

The usual answer, expertly spelled out by Paul Krugman, is that the base doesn't consider Social Security, Medicare, or other benefits they receive to be government programs. I find that hard to believe, since every threat to cut these programs is accompanied by a tirade against "Big Government." Or "government spending."

"Given this reality (that Social Security, Medicare and Medicaid are crucial to the Trump base of white working-class voters, (*my paraphrase*) why are so many people opposed to "big government"? Many have a distorted view of the numbers. For example, people have a vastly exaggerated view of how much we spend on foreign aid. Many also fail to connect their personal experience with public policy. Large numbers of Social Security and Medicare recipients believe that they make no use of any government social programs.....Many, perhaps most voters don't see how such (drastic spending) cuts would affect their lives.(Krugman, P., 2017) [Krugman, P. "Conservative Fantasies Run Into Reality" *The New York Times*, 3/19/2017, Op-Ed.]

Another explanation is that the White working class is stupid. As defined, the Trump base has high-school or less education, but a majority are definitely not stupid. The reason they didn't "*see*," pre-election, how Trump's well-publicized cuts would impinge on their lives is, in my view, that they were *blinded* by bonding to a charismatic TV personality. What drove them to form this self-defeating bond?

The answer is that anxiety and depression and the latent fears of the base create a blind bonding to the leader to whom they attach. The specific issues like health care and financial security take a back seat, while love for the leader and hatred for the "enemy" (the media, minorities, Muslims) prevail.

Justin Frank quoted before in relation to his diagnosis of Trump as psychotic (which seems to me going overboard, since he is still functioning, though poorly, in a job more complex than almost any other imaginable) talks about a "thin transference." *A transference to a therapist can be considered a form of attachment.* Let's repeat what Frank says. "In the consulting room, one characteristic of psychotic functioning is when a patient immediately develops an intense set of feelings about the therapist – an intense attachment whose thinness" (the patient barely knows the therapist) "is of marked contrast to the tenacity with which it is maintained. This intense *attachment* (the italics are my emphasis) stems from a need for comfort and safety, protecting against deep inarticulate fears of annihilation." (Frank J. 2016, *supra*). I am positing that the incredibly "intense" and blind attachment to Trump by a large portion of his base is a *"thin attachment."* This does not mean that the base is psychotic. It simply means that the base members' "fears of annihilation" (poverty, illness, loss of identity and self-esteem ("greatness") produced an *intense and thin* immediate attachment to Trump.

How can an attachment be both "thin" and intense? The thinness is due to the fact that the attachment is not one based on the normal development of a relationship over time. (In transference, this can take a long time building between therapist and patient.) Thin attachment is starkly different from gradual attachment (transference) based on mutual familiarity and interaction between patient and therapist.

It is not based upon the *exchange* of ideas about religion, politics, and values. It is a one-way relationship, with the idolizer, partisan, or base voter giving up his or her own judgements, and internalizing those of the leader. It is intense because of the neediness of the attacher. (I can't help thinking of the relationship of the relatively tiny Remora which attaches itself to the huge shark for a free ride. It is appropriately called the "sucker fish"

11. Now to return to the question, why do people in large numbers tend to vote against their best interests (for example, when they voted for George W. Bush?) Specifically, why did Trump's base vote for him against their self-interest, when he and his choice of party clearly represented the wealthy, as the GOP has done lately to such extremes? To extend the fish metaphor, they swallowed his slogans and memes "hook, line and sinker." This thin, or blind attachment involves an internalization and substitution

of the leader's issues and platform for any personal issues or independent political philosophy. Any fears of the loss of much of the social safety net are banished.

The clearest form of "blind attachment" can be seen in the tendency of children to bond with an abusive parent, and repress their anger. Bill Clinton is an example.

"'This sounds crazy but I never hated my stepfather, Roger Clinton. Even after he pulled the trigger in here, when he was drunk, even after he beat my mother—even after I got big enough to stop him from beating my mother,' says Mr. Clinton." (Rather, D., 1993) [Dan Rather interview. Bill Clinton: His Life" *CBS, 60 Minutes, 3/27/1993]*]

Another classic example is the case of Ms. Beauchamp, a patient of Dr. Morton Prince. She blamed herself for her mother's lack of affection for her. Despite her mother's obvious rejection, she clung to the hope that she could improve herself and thereby win her mother's affection. (This is described in some detail later.)
(Prince M., 1906) [Prince, M. (1906) *The Dissociation of a Personality"* 2md edition. 1969, is a reprint of 1906 original. Westport, CT: Greenwood press.]

Neither Bill Clinton nor Ms. Beauchamp were in a position to leave home and flee the abominable behavior of one parent. A young child is dependent on the parents for financial support and protection. The attachment to the abusive parent is" blind," due to the dependency of childhood. It is perhaps not "thin" because it usually has been built up over time, but it parallels the abandonment of the child's goals and needs in favor of those of the abuser. This is analogous to the relation of the "base' to the president. Both abused child and base are needy; they desperately need help from parent or leader, and neither will provide it.

About a month after the inauguration, Trump started to campaign for the 2020 election! As he gives his stump (strump) speech, there are still cries of "lock her up!" from his followers. Incredibly, they are able to ignore the choice of cabinet members. My previous discussion of the cabinet shows that it is composed not only of millionaires and former CEOs, but many members have actively participated in cutting wages, outsourcing, closing public schools, and "vulture capitalism" that immediately affects the well-being of the base.

They say that "love is blind." Maybe she is also deaf and dumb (in the sense of cognitive impairment, not impaired speech.) An interesting parallel comes to mind. In *The American Soldier* (Stauffer et al., 1949, *supra*) the problem of the loyalty of enlisted men to their officers was discussed. I have not been able to locate a quotation in the three-volume work. However, the topic stuck in my mind, because I was an officer during WWII and often wondered about it. The researchers found that loyalty to officers, indeed the strong attachment to them, remained intact until the mortality rate reached a high percentage of the platoon or company. After that percentage, some officers were "fragged" with hand-grenades. The authors gave an explanation of this phenomenon in social-psychological and psychoanalytic terms. They suggested that the soldier would initially give up his superego to his officer. This meant in cognitive terms that the executive functions of the soldier were handed over to the officer. These functions are governed mainly in the prefrontal region of the frontal lobes. They are a set of cognitive processes involving reasoning, planning, problem solving, working memory, cognitive flexibility, attentional control, and inhibitory control. Handing these functions over to an officer, or to Trump, means that you let *him* think and plan for you. If you have problems (and surely the base has a full load of them) Donald will solve them for you. You are "in his hands," reassured and comfortable about the future, about jobs, and all those things that used to worry you. It is like handing control over to your father, or to God.

So the shouts of "lock her up" during and after the Trump campaign rallies are analogous to the cries of religious fervor in a backwater church meeting. Ties to a glory-shouting minister or an incendiary presidential campaigner are "thin" in terms of a fully developed two-way relationship. They *are strong one-way relationships,* not reciprocal or egalitarian) with the power all in the hands of the preacher or the president. Neediness is the glue that binds.

There is a concept in social psychology that is relevant to the attachment of the base to the leader. It is called "internal versus external locus of control." Tests have been devised to assess the locus and its strength. For example people who blame "bad luck" for their problems have an external locus. They believe in fate. They feel they are the "little guy" and are powerless. The "Invictus" lines, "I am the master of my fate, I am the captain of my soul" exemplify the internal locus of control. The external locus seems to fit the "base," for indeed it is made up chiefly of lower-educated white males. The captains of industry are actually much more the masters of their fate, because of their wealth and power. Those with external locus of control believe in fate, and thus in an all-powerful god. Many, but not all religions, believe in preordination. Why does the base take *any* political action if it believes fate has condemned it to poverty or a smaller share of worldly goods and pleasures? Perhaps because they are told over and over that Satan is out there promoting evil. God and Satan are locked in a struggle. Satan (external locus) sends his forces against you. They are the "other." Trump uses the term "enemy" for the liberal media, and Muslims, who must be banned from the country. Mexicans are "rapists," and are a good alternative target for the base. It is clearly a campaign to redirect the base's legitimate anger at the wealthy and powerful to other targets.

Interestingly, external locus of control, especially when the "enemy" (Satan) is seen as a controlling, rather than a kindly shepherding god, is associated with projection of the various unconscious conflicts of the paranoid individual. In Germany, the sexual stereotype (he rapes your daughter) and the economic stereotype (the "Jewish World order," Jewish bankers, selfish exploiters) were both projected onto Jews. In the U.S., the sexual stereotype migrated to African-Americans, while the Jews retained their age old reputation as "Christ-killers" and misers.

The phrase "Get thee behind me, Satan" is a quote from the Bible (King James Version, Matthew 16:23.) The devil offers Jesus worldly power and glory if he agrees to worship him, and Jesus turns him down in no uncertain terms. The phrase gained wide popularity anew with the song written by Irving Berlin (1935) and sung by such luminaries as Harriet Hilliard, Ginger Rogers, Ella Fitzgerald, Woody Guthrie and Pete Seeger.

> Get thee behind me, Satan
> I want to resist
> But the moon is low and I can't say "No"
> Get thee behind me.

Get thee behind me, Satan
I mustn't be kissed
But the moon is low and I may let go
Get thee behind me.

It must be obvious, even to the Freud-denier (distantly related to the global-warming or climate-change deniers?) that Satan in this song is a projection of the repressed wish for a kiss, or more. Similarly, all kinds of socially tabooed activities are blamed on the devil, but come from within the individual's own head.

Sex and aggression are basic biological drives, and are integrated by the amygdala. They are triggered by various hormones, chiefly testosterone and estrogen in mammals. The process of arousal is complicated, involving various organs. It is a *generalized response*, and can be set off by fear, pain, drugs, visual and auditory stimuli, in addition to a "love object" (otherwise known as a lover.) What is the location of these drives? For lack of the advanced neurology of today, Freud used the term "Id" as the location for the sexual and aggressive drives, while the "Superego" was the voice of society, controlling those two drives. The Superego is sometimes referred to as the "introjected parental image," but it could be a teacher, the preacher, the cop on the corner, or any handy authority figure. When Trump says Mexicans are "rapists." it makes us wonder if he has that subject in the back of his mind. His famous line on tape, "Grab 'em by the pussy. You can do anything," was by definition in the front, not the back, of his mind. If all Muslims are "terrorists," maybe Donald has terrorist tendencies; for example, separating millions of immigrant parents from their U.S.-born children? Those who criticize him are tweeted to be "sick," "bad, or "losers," all qualities he is terrified of. His various quotes, shown previously, fall into the Dark Tetrad areas of narcissism, Machiavellianism, psychopathy and sadism. He has chosen advisors with some of the same tendencies. How "SAD!" (a common Trump tweet) for our country, and especially for the "base" he promised to help.

The current "state of the union" under Trump is so deteriorated that steps must be taken by people who wish to live in a democracy. Because of the immediate dangers to life, limb and liberty, I am suggesting that short-term efforts should take priority. Long-range planning, such as the reduction of inequality, building of infrastructure, or improving public education must take a back seat to what individuals and organizations can do to effect regime change in the U.S. If this cannot be accomplished-by the FBI and CIA releasing their information concerning the Russian connection and hacking of the 2016 election, then preparation for winning the midterm elections and the 2020 presidential election by a landslide should be a goal. The Democrats won the House majority at mid-term, but did not win back the Senate. Winning the House of Representatives promises to curb some of Trump's power. The House Democrats can investigate the Russian affair without presidential interference, even if Mueller's investigation is blocked by Trump's biased attorney general appointments.

On 3/20/2017, there was a hearing on Russian attempts to influence the U.S presidential elections in 2016 by the House Select Committee on Intelligence. F.B.I. Director James Comey and National Security Agency Director Mike Rogers, a U.S. Navy Admiral, served as witnesses, and members of the House questioned them for about five hours. The extent of Russian activity to influence the election in favor of Trump and to defeat Hillary Clinton was revealed in more detail than ever before. I have previously reviewed most of what was made public up to the hearing date, but some interesting new information came up. More recent events can be found in the Timeline, which has my comments on the events as well.

This chapter continues with discussion of the "Russian Connection," the "dark money" from U.S. billionaires financing Trump, the personality of a U.S. tycoon, Howard Hughes, the non-existing vetting of presidential candidates, the billionaires, the origins of the anomic personality, why people vote against their best interests, and a review of some people who would score high in the dark tetrad.

In 2008, a Russian billionaire, Dmitry Ryboloviev bought an estate in Florida, from Trump for $95 million. Donald had purchased it for only 41 million. Dmitry was going through a bitter seven year divorce, and he needed to unload cash to keep it from his wife. She finally won 4.8 billion. Why did Dmitry buy it for over twice Trump's original purchase price? Perhaps it was a present from Putin, who seems to have come to the rescue every time his American puppet went bankrupt. "Beware Putin when he is bearing gifts!" A word from Putin to Dmitry, who had served a jail sentence and was not in Putin's good graces, and Donald probably got his gift pronto.

More information came to light about Trump team members who have had contacts with Russians. Paul Manafort had been Trump's de facto campaign manager. In March, 2017 he was in Russia, safe from FBI questioning. "A Ukrainian lawmaker released new financial documents Tuesday allegedly showing that a former campaign chairman for President Trump (Manafort) laundered payments from the party of a disgraced ex-leader of Ukraine using offshore accounts in Belize and Kyrgyzstan." (Roth, A., 2017) [Roth, A. "New documents show Trump aide laundered payments….." *The Washington Post,* 3/21/2017.] There is more discussion about the ongoing investigation and trial of Manafort. As of March, 2018, Manafort had been under house arrest, since he may still have access to hidden funds, and might flee to avoid further prosecution and imprisonment. He was later imprisoned as a high risk defendant, who tried to influence witnesses while still free. On money-laundering charges alone he faces 30 years' imprisonment. Pressure on Manafort and Gates is a means of obtaining evidence of collusion or obstruction of justice against Trump by Special Counsel Mueller.

There is evidence pointing to a bargain between Putin and Trump. Obama put those sanctions in place to punish Russia for the hacking of the 2016 elections. Putin badly wanted the Obama sanctions against Russia lifted, because they were hurting the economy. Flynn, Trump's National Security Adviser, was fired, because he lied to V.P. Pence about meeting with the Russian Ambassador. It is suspected that during that meeting he discussed the lifting of the sanctions. Trump is believed to be beholden to Putin, not only because of possible Russian videotaping and wiretapping of his earlier 2013 visit to Moscow, but also because the President may be in deep debt to Putin or his fellow-billionaires. Trump got a loan from Deutsche Bank (run by Russians) for $300 million. It seems the bank has been laundering billions of illegally-gained rubles by buying stocks in rubles and selling them simultaneously in London for dollars. The Deutsche Bank is being investigated by the U.S. Department of Justice. Who is heading that department? None other than Jeff Sessions, a Trump appointment and supporter. No wonder the bank is not calling that loan. The real wonder is that the bank would ever have made a loan to someone who has a history of bankruptcies, and has used *force majeure* [worldwide financial failure in 2007-8] as an excuse to refuse to repay a huge bank loan previously. During the campaign period it looked as if Trump was going soft on criticizing Russia for invading and annexing Crimea, but since then, and through March of 2017 so far, he has changed his tune. Instead he has accused Obama of being soft on Crimea.

A remarkable article in the *New Yorker* by Jane Mayer (Mayer, J., 2017) [Mayer, J. "Trump's Money Man." *The New Yorker,* 3/27/2017.] reveals how Trump's road to the presidency was financed, and who brought the financier and Trump together. Robert Mercer, aged 70, made his billions by designing trading algorithms for a hedge fund, Renaissance Technology. (Mercer and his Renaissance Technology contributed massively to the Brexit revolution in the United Kingdom, leading to Britain's leaving the European Union!) He eventually became its CEO. "During the 2016 campaign, Mercer gave $22.5 million in disclosed donations to Republican candidates" (quotes are from Mayer's article) and PACS (political action committees, and probably much more in undisclosed donations, now possible due to the Citizen's United decision.) He is a libertarian, and has some very contradictory political positions because of it. "Several former colleagues of Mercer's said that his views are akin to Objectivism, the philosophy of Ayn Rand. Magerman told me, 'Bob believes that human beings have no inherent value other than how much money they make. A cat has value, he's said, because it provides pleasure to humans. But if someone is on welfare they have negative value.'"

The Mercer family, Mayer tells us, was responsible for bringing some of the central figures of the Trump team into the campaign. One of them was Patrick Caddell, a political operator and contractor for Mercer. Others were Steve Bannon and Kellyanne Conway. As far back as 2012, Bannon was the Mercers' de facto political adviser.

"In 2014, Bannon began hosting a radio show that often featured Patrick Caddell, who effectively had been banished by Democratic Party leaders after years of tempestuous campaigns and fallings-out. On the air, Caddell floated dark theories about Hillary Clinton, and often sounded a lot like Bannon, describing "economic nationalism" as the driving force in American politics. Under Barack Obama, he said, America had turned into a 'banana republic.'"

Caddell reviewed all the Republican presidential candidates, with a goal of finding a potential "Mr. Smith" (referring to the 1939 movie about a naïve populist). He focused on Trump. "He was the only one with the resources and the name recognition. As Bernie Sanders's campaign showed, the populist rebellion wasn't partisan." (Mayer, J. *supra*.)

Roger Stone and Caddell spoke to Trump, and told Mercer about him. Soon after this, Paul Manafort, 67, Trump's campaign manager, was fired. He "resigned" on August 19th, 2016, after it was revealed that he had taken $12.7 million in cash payments from Viktor Yukanovych, the former Ukrainian President and ally of Putin. In addition, he had run a pro-Russian-Ukrainian lobbying campaign in the U.S., but had not registered as a foreign agent.

The vacuum made by Manafort's firing was quickly filled with Mercer henchmen under the guidance of Mercer's daughter, Rebekah. "Bannon became the campaign's C.E.O., Conway its manager, and Bossie its deputy manager." Robert Mercer has not only paid salaries for Trump's campaign. He has given $10 million to Breitbart News, formerly headed by Bannon. It is an alt-right Pandora's Box, spewing racist, anti-Semitic, and anti-Muslim hatred. It was the source for much of the anti-Hillary propaganda during the campaign. The fact that just a few men, like Mercer and the Koch brothers, can determine the course of our country is frightening. These are our home-grown oligarchs. They are anomic personalities, who have no limits to their ambition or their power.

The pace of events casting a shadow on the Trump Presidency accelerated. Comey's announcement on 3/20/2017 that the FBI was investigating possible Trump campaign collusion with Russian agents to defeat Hillary and help Trump win the election was a tremendous setback for Trump. He countered by tweeting that Obama had wiretapped the White House, which Comey refuted.

Then an attempt by the House to pass a health bill that would have gutted Obama Care and left 24 million people without medical insurance failed to get to a vote. "Seven years of Republican efforts to eradicate President Barack Obama's proudest domestic achievement ended Friday before a single vote was cast. House Speaker Paul Ryan sensationally pulled his Obamacare repeal bill from the floor Friday afternoon, a day after President Donald Trump had threatened to walk away from health care reform if he didn't get a vote." (Collinson, M. 2017) [Collinson, M. et al. "Health Care Bill Faces Bigger Challenge in the Senate." *CNN, 3/25/2017*] Trump said that Obamacare will explode, and then we can have a great health plan.

The failure to get to a vote was due primarily to the stance of the Freedom Caucus Conservatives, who felt that the bill was just "Obama lite." It was not draconian enough for their taste! On the other hand, some moderates feared the wrath of millions of constituents who would lose their insurance, and/or see their premiums rise. Well, as I noted before, the bill to "repeal and replace Obamacare" barely passed the House on 5/2/2017, but it has a long road ahead through the Senate and back again to both House and Senate before final approval.) Trump is planning to go on to the next item on his agenda, tax reform, which may not be much easier to push through, due to this schism in the Grand Old Party. It looked for a while as if Trump and Bannon were ready to throw Paul Ryan, Speaker of the House, under the bus. (However, Bannon seemed to have been demoted by being removed from the National Security Council at the behest of General H.R. McMaster.) Then Bannon had a victory over the Kushners, when Trump opted to withdraw from the Paris Climate Agreement on June 1st, 2017).) As usual, someone else has to be the fall guy, not the boss. This is a basic tenet of Machiavellianism. Trump could have started his agenda with infrastructure, not health care or taxes. That might have been more acceptable to both the DEMS and the GOPS. Bannon's eventual firing was triggered by a book suggesting that Bannon, not Trump, was calling the shots. Motto: "never upstage a narcissist."

The next political spasm arrived because Paul Manafort (Trump's fired campaign manager) Roger Stone (former campaign manager and adviser to Trump) and Carter Page, (a foreign policy adviser to Trump during the campaign) all agreed to testify about the Russian connection to the House Intelligence Committee. Of course, if their lawyers will not let them testify under oath, they can lie as much as they please. It would be in the power of the Justice Department to subpoena them, but Jeff Sessions is the Attorney General, and he will no doubt be called to testify, even though he has recused himself from an investigation of the Russian connection.

Twenty-three people in various states have hired a lawyer and are asking the Justice Department to start a criminal investigation into Sessions. Will this administration survive all the suspicion that these investigations arouse? How will there be time to govern if all the major White House players are under investigation, and busy preparing their defenses?

House Intelligence Committee chairman Devin Nunes (R, CA) clearly tried to derail the investigation. He bypassed his own co-chairman, Rep. Adam Schiff (D, CA) and the members of the Committee by reporting information he had received from the FBI to the press and to Trump without also informing his own Committee members. This left the Committee "in the dark," and caused Schiff to say that the House investigation had been compromised. Further interference in the progress of the investigations by Nunes makes it clear that he is acting as a shill for Trump.

"Chairman just cancelled open Intelligence Committee hearing with former Director of National Intelligence James Clapper, former CIA Director John Brennan and former deputy Attorney General Sally Yates in attempt to choke off public info," Rep. Adam Schiff, the top Democrat on the committee tweeted moments before going to speak to the press Friday morning." (LoBianco, T. & Raju, M. 2017) [LoBianco, T. & Raju, M. "Partisan split at House intel committee over canceled open hearing." *CNN*, 3/24/2017.]

It is clear that the wrangling over the Russian influence on the elections and the role of Trump and his various helpers in that scandal will go on for some time. At this point it is impossible to predict the outcome. It looks bad for the President, since so many of his appointees have been involved in suspicious or even criminal activities. Rather than continue to follow the incredibly complex intrigue, which makes the Teapot Dome scandal and the Nixon impeachment over Watergate seem like child's play, *I think it best to explore how we can avoid the ascension to power of so many flawed leaders.*

Not all of our tycoons are seriously flawed. The three top current philanthropists, Warren Buffet, Bill Gates, and George Soros, seem well-balanced and have made massive contributions to our society The fourth, Howard Hughes, (deceased) made a fortune as a movie producer-director, and businessman. He also designed airplanes, and broke coast to coast speed records piloting them. His father was an inventor, and as a pre-teen Howard built a radio transmitter. He rivaled the sexual anomics I described previously, in quality if not in quantity having "dated" many famous movie stars, including Billie Dove, Faith Domergue, Bette Davis, Ava Gardner, Olivia de Havilland, Katharine Hepburn, Ginger Rogers, Rita Hayworth and Gene Tierney. He showed early signs of obsessive-compulsive disorder that gradually worsened. He created a special fork for sorting peas, a favorite dish, by size. He suffered severe injuries due to several near-fatal plane crashes, and became addicted to codeine because of the pain. During his last two decades he became a recluse. Watching films while sitting naked, due to allodynia, a painful hypersensitivity to stimuli, he avoided bathing and normal hygiene a year at a time. Concerned about residual radiation from the atomic bomb tests scheduled at the Nevada test site, he offered million dollar bribes to both Presidents Nixon and Lyndon Johnson. What if he had offered more? Would we have won the war against Japan? Hughes was no doubt of genius-level intelligence. His abilities were scattered over too many divergent endeavors. Aside from the OCD, he seems self-destructive. His net worth at death was 1.5 billion, equivalent to 6.3 billion today. As a philanthropist, his major contribution was the founding of the Howard Hughes Medical Institute, which was dedicated to basic research. Its endowment, as of 2007, was worth 16.3 billion, making it the fourth largest private organization in the U.S.

Hughes' accumulation of wealth and achievements in so many fields suggests the tantalizing effect of personal deregulation. There seemed no level of satisfaction with Hollywood's most glamourous and talented movie stars, or with each level of attainment. Trump's favorite song, "Is that all there is," seems as if it might fit all of our anomic exemplars. The obsessive-compulsivity seems to be part of the striving picture, as in the case of Bernie Madoff and Donald Trump. The concern with contamination shows up in Trump (he hates those multiple political handshakes) but is much more extreme in Hughes. Perhaps you need an obsession to be the very best, richest, and most powerful in our society. And you need to be grandiose. Imagine trying to bribe two presidents, not because of your concern with fallout affecting the millions living in the Southwest, but because of your personal fear of contamination! (Howard Hughes, Wikipedia) [Howard Hughes, Wikipedia. The biographical material on Howard Hughes' life is paraphrased from *Wikipedia*, "Howard Hughes."]

How difficult would it be to pick candidates for the presidency who are of sound mind and body? When looking for potential *vice*-presidents, there is extremely careful vetting. I mentioned the huge questionnaire that Cheney used to vet half-a-dozen V.P. candidates. (He took the job himself!) Why should the *presidential* candidates be excused from such a thorough examination? Certainly a small panel, consisting of a well-known internist, a respected psychiatrist, and a political scientist who has specialized in presidential history and biography, could do a better job of protecting our country from a potential dictator than the present system.

There were sixteen candidates in the Republican primary election. Of these, I would have thought that perhaps five were presidential timber; Jeb Bush, Lindsey Graham, Carly Fiorina, John Kasich, and George Pataki. Of the other ten, I would say they could never pass a proper vetting. Whether due to extreme alt-right positions, obvious cognitive damage, or activities verging on the anti-social or criminal, they would not pass. As for the democrats, Clinton, Sanders, Lessig and Chaffee would pass if I were on the panel. I would have skipped Jim Webb, a good candidate, but who carried a loaded gun. A president who is armed? What kind of model would he have been for our youth?

It is clear that people attracted to certain professions ae more likely to partake of one or more of the traits of the Dark Tetrad. It is almost a stereotype that actors are given to narcissism, though it is hopefully not often of the "malignant" type. And who among us would not like to be able to see ourselves on screen or TV as a handsome lover, a dashing hero, a sultry seductress? Athletes, as reviewed previously, are stars not only on the courts, golf links, or playing fields, but also in bed. Politicians love to hear the sound of their own voices reverberating in the foul labyrinths of their outer ears. Pastors, priests and rabbis are our designated "gentle shepherds" who are stand-ins for the Lord. But quite a few of them have delivered harsh Philippics on topics like abortion and LGBTQ. Politicians and lawyers have a reputation for lying and manipulation going back centuries.

So what's new? It is the narcissism, Machiavellianism, psychopathy and sadism magnified by the financial and political power of a burgeoning number of multi-billionaires in the U.S. and worldwide. It is a frightening new inequality, and it is growing rapidly. We read about the Koch brothers, who have pushed for conservative legislation and supported right-wing candidates. Robert Mercer (who was the chief financial backer of Trump, Bannon and Miller) has been the *eminence grise* who has turned our democracy topsy-turvy. Mercer's world-view makes the Koches look like Mother Teresa. After the Citizen's United decision in 2010 unlimited amounts of "dark money" can be given, without the identification of the donor.

Is it possible to have a cap on the amount of income an individual (or family) can acquire in a year? The most frequent argument against an income cap is that it would reduce, or even eliminate, incentives for some of the most creative people. What about a cap for net worth? After the first billion, what do you need? How many yachts can you buy? More important, how many politicians can you buy? Let's look at Mercer again. His annual earnings from his hedge fund, Renaissance Technologies, are $150 million. His net worth is not known, but he is the fourth largest contributor to right-wing PACS and causes.

We can't compare Mercer's net worth directly to those of other wealthiest U.S. individuals, because Mercer's is unknown, but his hedge fund is worth in the 30 billion range, of which he is a part owner. Here are a few of the wealthiest U.S. Americans, their net worth, and their political leanings:

Billionaires

Name	$Billions	Corporation	Political leaning
Bill Gates	81	Microsoft	D
Jeff Bezos	67	Amazon	D
Warren Buffet	65.5	Berkshire-Hathaway	D
Mark Zuckerberg	55.5	Facebook	D
Larry Ellison	44.3	Oracle Corp.	D
Michael Bloomberg	45	Bloomberg LP	R/D
Charles Koch	42	Koch Industries	R
David Koch	42	Koch Industries	R

The first impression is that five of the eight wealthiest are, or "lean," democrat. Of course, that is pleasing to me, and good for the country, since they are more likely to donate dollars to the social safety net which is being torn by Trump and Company. Another impression is that creativity is involved in all eight enterprises, but especially in Gates' and Zuckerberg's ingenious use of computers to change (improve?) our lives in major ways. Jeff Bezos' Amazon and other on-line sellers are soon going to make the American Shopping Mall a thing of the past. Whether this is good or bad in the long run I don't know. Bezos is investing one billion a year in the development of "space tourism" rockets. (Tourism for the .01% wealthy?) Bloomberg has revolutionized information on corporate trading and news. Fred C. Koch, one of the two founders of Koch Industries, invented an innovative crude-oil refining process, which jump-started that huge organization. This conglomerate is involved in many industries and is the second largest privately-held industry in the U.S. The creativity of these billionaires is a major argument against setting a cap on income or wealth.

Despite the fact that these top five wealthiest men give primarily to the Democrats and to liberal causes, the power they each have should not be embedded in a single individual. We can now see, as in a dystopian horror film, what one Libertarian billionaire, Mercer, can do to change the direction of our entire nation. He is a climate change denier. That could affect the planet we live on. He wants to go back on the gold standard. That might affect the U.S. and the world-wide economy. He is a racist and anti-Semite, and his promotion of his longtime henchman, Bannon, to be Svengali to Trump's Trilby brings with it an alt-right vision. The three legged stool of Bannonism is "Capitalism, nationalism, and Judeo-Christian values." (Guilford, G., 2017) [Guilford G. "What Bannon really wants." *Quartz*, 2/3/2017.]

Fortunately, Bannon has been removed from the National Security Council (4/5/2017) at the behest of General H.R. McMaster, who was appointed head of the NSC after General Michael Flynn was ousted from that position due to his various Turkish and Russian connections. (Bannon was later fired by Trump, purportedly over the allegation in the book *Devil's Bargain*. that Bannon was running the show.)This move by McMaster is meant to remove "political elements" from the NSC, and bring back individuals with specific expertise, including the military. At a time when Syria and North Korea pose potential military emergencies, this was a good move, but it was also overdue because of the politicization of the NSC. Bannon still had a full portfolio, and he was still Trump's closest advisor, until he was "fired." The rise of McMaster and the partial curtailing of Bannon's power diminished the influence of Mercer, who had been the principal supporter of Trump, Bannon, and Breitbart News. In an apparent power-struggle between Bannon and Jared Kushner and his wife, Ivanka (Trump's daughter), Jared Kushner was gaining the upper hand until his meeting with Russian bankers made him subject to investigation. Bannon's continued strength was shown on 6/1/2017, when Trump announced he was withdrawing from the Paris Climate Agreement.

The various demonstrations against Trumpism have been successful, but there needs to be continual pressure on the White House, the senators, and representatives to curtail the gradual slide toward dictatorship. Access to personal data from telephones and computers is already in progress. The government can get data from providers, such as Verizon, and from there hackers can get bank accounts, credit information, etc. Political preferences and activity can be monitored by data from i-Phones and TV program preferences. The Trump assault on the press and "leakers" has intensified.

The President, true to his anomic personality and narcissism, does not take responsibility for any tragic event or mistake during his watch. The April 2017 massacre of innocent Syrian civilians was triggered directly by our announcing the abandonment of any anti-Assad involvement on our part. Here is the brief timeline:

On Thursday, March 30th, 2017, Rex Tillerson, Secretary of State, said "I think the longer term status of President Assad will be decided by the Syrian people." This was a 180 degree reversal of the longstanding U.S. position on Syria of "regime change."

On Tuesday, April 4th, only five days later, an Assad government Syrian army jet bombed the town of Khan Sheikhoun, using sarin gas, which killed at least 72 civilians, including 20 children.

`On Wednesday, April 5th, Trump said "When you kill innocent children, innocent babies, babies, little babies, with a chemical gas that is so lethal, people were shocked to hear what gas it was, that crosses many, many lines, beyond a red line. Many, many lines."

It is so obvious that Assad got the signal from Tillerson that the U.S. was no longer going to try to overthrow him, and he now had *carte blanche* to use poison gas, starvation, and any other methods needed to keep himself in power. Trump has repeatedly said that he likes to be noncommittal in order to keep our enemies guessing. In the case of Syria, why didn't he just leave the old policy of regime change in place, to avoid tipping Assad off that the U.S. wouldn't intervene? One reason is just plain stupidity, either by Trump or by Tillerson, or both. Another is that Trump, although he has often said that we should not meddle in Syria, is plainly beholden to Putin in many ways, and therefor doesn't want to expose himself to blackmail, or worse.

Political Update, 5/18/2017

As of this writing, 5/18/2017, events have taken a dark turn for the Trump White House. Without going into great detail, they are as follows:

1. Trump has fired two Attorneys General in succession; Preet Bharara, and Sally Yates, and also James Comey, the Director of the FBI. Each of them was capable of testifying against him concerning the Russian Connection. By firing them, he has shown he has something to hide, and has also put them in a position where they can testify against him. 2. After much outcry from some Republicans and from all the Democratic Senators and Representatives, Rod Rosenstein, Deputy Attorney General, appointed Robert Mueller, former FBI Director, as Special Counsel for the independent Russian Investigation. This is the turn of events that was eagerly awaited, since the FBI, House and Senate investigations have been either compromised or slowed down. 3.Trump has unwittingly given highly classified information to the Russian Ambassador and Foreign Minister during a meeting at the White House the day after he fired Comey. The information concerned ISIL, and was given the U.S. by Israel. This jeopardizes our sharing of secret information with our allies, who may not trust us to guard their secrets.

Well, the arcane convolutions of the Trump presidency will go on for some time. They are so mysterious and happen so rapidly that to keep abreast of events, one has to visit CNN, MSNBC, read the New Yorker and the Washington Post, go to various websites on one's computer, including the Daily Kos, listen to Robert Reich every night, and occasionally tune in on Fox News to see who is being accused of wife abuse, statutory rape, or sexual harassment.

I hope there are some explanations in this book of how we got to this stage of proto-Fascist kleptocracy. Why are the 1 percent or the .01 percent accumulating wealth at such an increased rate? What can be done about it? Morris Berman, Thomas Picketty, and Joseph Stiglitz come up with different explanations, different predictions, and different solutions, as discussed lateer. Their solutions are based on the field of economics. If it's very rich people who are causing such destruction, why not tax them, and create strict regulations that limit their wealth and power? Even assuming that heavy taxation of the wealthy would solve the problem, there is the obvious drive for more, that has its roots in the DNA of survival. New plutocrats are being created every day, and new technology is helping this surge.

There are two major areas of discussion in this book that I think might make a contribution to our well-being. First is the investigation of the origins of the anomic personality, and the accompanying cut-throat competition and feelings of tantalization that are its hallmark.

Second is the set of hypotheses concerning the widespread adult attachments of our modern cultures, and the explanation it affords, of the fact that people (particularly those who comprise the "base" of demagogic leaders) consistently vote against their own interests.

Origins of the Anomic Personality

To start, I will try to address the first topic, which is the central thesis of this book. How did we come to have a sudden burgeoning of billionaires? Millionaires are now a "dime a dozen." Of all the 7.3 billion people in the world, there are "only" 1826 billionaires. (These figures vary wildly, according to the definitions involved. I have chosen reasonable figures, particularly those of Forbes)) Of those 1826, some 540 are from the U.S. or 29.5 per cent. Considering the relatively small population of the U.S. (318.9 million in 2014) compared with 7.3 billion worldwide, there are a lot more billionaires in the U.S. than you would expect from an even worldwide distribution.

Even more startling is the number of millionaires in the U.S., 13.5 million as of 2016, or 4% of the population. In 2014 alone, there were 920,000 new millionaires made. The movement of wealth from the many into the pockets of the few is escalating, and with the advent of the Trump administration and its extremely wealthy cabinet, there is no end in sight to this tectonic shift.

Not only do we have a U.S. social character that is made up heavily of upward striving narcissistic individuals, but we have a plethora of outliers, both millionaires and billionaires, who as we saw in our few exemplars, are prone to be Machs, and show traits of psychopathy and sadism. There seems to be an over-representation of the Dark Tetrad in these very wealthy individuals. Is it because they are preselected because of their upbringing, parenting, schooling, or a high testosterone level, or some genetic factor? (Don't forget that identical twins separated at birth tend to vote almost identically. The Pearson correlation, R= .56!) *The Dark Tetrad levels of these outliers make us think, once again, that these antisocial traits are the major adaptation to a zero-sum culture, and one must have them or develop them in order to "get ahead." And getting ahead means getting ahead of, and necessarily stepping on, others.*

Let's look again, briefly, at our four outliers' traits. Dick Cheney, nicknamed "Darth Vader" formerly the CEO of Halliburton, became the most powerful V.P. in our history. For seven years, to a great extent, he was running the country. During the 9/11attack on the U.S. he was calling out the Air Force, while George W. was reading the book, "The Pet Goat," to second-graders at the Emma E. Booker School in Sarasota, Florida. Cheney got the V.P position by stealth, and had a dark view of the world. He was the main instigator of the invasion of Iraq and the "WMD's". (Iraq supposedly had "weapons of mass destruction," the excuse for the invasion.)

Donald Trump a (former?) real-estate mogul and TV personality, became president under suspicious circumstances (ties to Russia) and to my view, has brought about the dawn of the "Dark Ages America" (my classic oxymoron). This collapse of the U.S. was predicted by gloomy Morris Berman. I am afraid he may be right.

Other anomic outliers have risen to positions of wealth and power by cheating others, and have crashed due to hubris and grandiosity of one kind or another. Bernie Madoff thought he could hold off paying his Ponzi scheme victims forever. Another example of hubris and grandiosity is Eliot Spitzer, former Governor of New York State. Spitzer was having trysts with prostitutes. Roger Stone, a GOP political activist, hired reputation-assassin and longtime friend and advisor to Donald Trump, (the small world of "deplorables!") "tipped off the FBI about Spitzer's use of prostitutes and helped bring about his downfall.")Meek, J.G., 2008) [Meek, J.G. et al. *NY Daily News*, "Spitzer Scandal never Fades" 3/12/2008.] Stone recently threatened to expose all he knew about Trump and Russia, when he (Stone) was being investigated by the FBI. My impression? I opened a Chinese fortune cookie years ago, which said "He who lies down with dogs gets up with fleas."

Hubris and the false armor of a belief in one's own invulnerability can be dangerous for the sons of the ultra-rich, such as Spitzer and Trump. The belief in one's invulnerability (one type of grandiosity) usually diminishes after the teens. That's why the car driver's insurance rates go down sharply after age 25. We write about those who have flown too high, like Icarus, because the media know that there is no limit to the public's *Schadenfreude*, the joy at seeing somebody successful or famous fail, or "come a cropper" (to fail badly, originally to fail to stay on your horse.) Tiger Woods must have known that there was a risk in visiting prostitutes, because when the "John" is rich or famous, there is always the temptation to "out" him for payment by scandal magazines, or to threaten blackmail. "Pride goeth before a fall" and so do narcissism and grandiosity.

While Tiger, Bernie M, Dick and Donald are current anomic outliers, a whole generation of children are potential *extreme* anomics That is because the accumulation of great wealth by a small portion of the nation, (the 1 percent or the .01 percent) as noted by Picketty and others, has made the struggle for wealth and "success" that much harder. I already discussed in some detail the high teen suicide rate in some Silicon Valley high schools. The parents, when interviewed, claimed to avoid pushing their children to succeed, but they typically asked daily about school grades and exams.

Now (2017) a new approach is being tried in schools like the ones in Arlington, Mass. In preparation for a suicide prevention meeting, the Arlington High School Patch put out some statistics. Eighteen percent of high school students and 15% of middle school students reported having thoughts of suicide in the past thirty days. [Arlington Patch, 2/5/2016.] It also noted that opioid abuse and other substance abuse was directly connected to the rising suicide rate.

Of course it is helpful to intervene *before* depression and anxiety overwhelm our striving teens. Suicide is destructive to parents, siblings, and fellow students too. As I said before, today's parent's anxiety about their children's future is well founded. Paid internships are hard to find. Public school budgets are being cut under the battle-axe of Betsy DeVos. In 2016 Obama issued two memos directing the Federal Student Aid Office to help borrowers manage and discharge their debt. DeVos has withdrawn those memos. (Nasiripour, S., 2017) [Nasiripour, S. "Trump's education secretary wants to limit costs…" *Bloomberg News*, 4/12/2017.]The Trump campaign against public schools has found its champion. The Democrats' platform promise to fund two year public colleges is a dream long gone. I often wonder if the wealthy want to preserve an underclass of uneducated people to act as servants and manual laborers.With automation and robots taking over most of those jobs; factory production, store checkout, online sales and mailing by Amazon, what work will be left for even the high-school graduate without further education?

Before we can expect parents to be less anxious and pushy about their children's school performance, we need to have many more full-time jobs available, and job training in new skills associated with new technology. We need to curb outsourcing. The Trump administration has made only feeble efforts in these areas The "Carrier Corporation" event was really a staged "photo-op," part of the White House lip service and promises to "support the base."

Why do people in the "base" vote against their best interests?

This brings us to consider some hypotheses about why people in the "base" almost always seem to vote against their own best interests. Is it mass stupidity of the base? Lack of education? Getting all your news from a single biased source, such as Fox News? Is it genetic in origin? While I have previously discussed many possible factors, two hypotheses seem most plausible. The first is based on the history of great disparity between reforms promised during presidential campaigns (and most other political campaigns) and the legislation which follows the inaugurations. There are several common names for this disparity; *"bait-and-switch," "lip-service,"* and *"head-feint."*

Trump promised a surge in jobs, but so far only the failed attempt to stop the Carrier Corporation from outsourcing jobs to Mexico is in evidence. Talk of a major infrastructure program has yet to become fact. Wealthy banks like Goldman Sachs were a target during campaign speeches, but Steven Minuchin, a second-generation Goldman Sachs millionaire, was appointed Secretary of the Treasury. Tariffs of 35% were touted during the campaign, but post-election, Commerce Secretary Wilbur Ross is emphasizing an increase in U.S. exports, not tariffs. (In 2018, however, the administration did radically raise taxes.) Promises to lower taxes meant lowering them for the rich, not for the middle or working class.

The Trump proposed "discretionary" budget for 2018 made major cuts to most departments, and a large increase for Defense and School Choice. The following table shows major percentage increases or decreases, and shows where the hearts of the President and his Cabinet lie. It's G.O.P. and selfish all over again. The cuts are scheduled for safety net items. "Defense" takes up half of all discretionary spending. This is a gift to corporations that make military supplies, tanks, planes, ships, jeeps, food rations, tents, uniforms, oil, gas, and munitions.

Environmental Protection	-31%
State Department	-29%
Agriculture Department	-21%
Labor Department	-21%
Health & Human Services	-18%
Department of Commerce	-16%
Department of Education	-14%
Housing& Urban Developm't	-13%
Transportation	-13%

Energy	-6%
Small Business Admin.	-5%
Veterans Affairs	**+6%**
Homeland Security	**+7%**
Defense	**+9%**

Noteworthy is the huge *new* budget item for "school choice," private (religious) schools, and charter schools, of $1.4 billion. Betsy DeVos has a lot of clout! The Department of Defense 9% increase from the 2017 to the 2018 budget brings it to a total of $639 billion. This overshadows all other discretionary spending. It reminds one again of General-and-President Ike Eisenhower, who told us to "guard against the acquisition of unwarranted influence......by the military-industrial complex." With Trump's decision to bomb the Al Shayrat airport near the city of Homs in Syria, there may be an excuse for all-out war production, depending on the Russian reaction to the bombing. Since we warned the Russians one hour ahead of the bombing, it all seems very gentlemanly, except that the U.S. strike killed nine, including four children. Were some of them Russian soldiers?

Bait and Switch

The bait-and-switch explanation for why the "base" voted for "the Donald" against their own interests certainly accounts for some of the mystery. A cabinet composed of millionaires and billionaires will not have the best interests of the masses at heart. Advisers like Bannon had an alt –right agenda that is hardly proletarian, but consider the fact that Trump openly promised to get rid of Obamacare during his campaign, and only failed to get House approval later on because his "reforms" of health care were not conservative enough for the members of the House Freedom Caucus! How could half the electorate go along with promises to destroy their health-care plans? How could working-class and middle-class people vote for Trump when he had consistently criticized Social Security? Moreover, he was running as a Republican, and the Republicans have tried for years to replace Social Security with various investment plans, seeking to make all Americans into conservatives because they owned a few shares of stock. For this apparent blindness to self-interest, we have to turn to a second hypothesis, that of *blind attachment to a leader or authority figure.*

Rick Perlstein asks the same question that I and so many others have asked. "If Donald Trump was elected as a Marine Le Pen-style — or Hiram Evans-style — *herrenvolk* republican, what are we to make of the fact that he placed so many bankers and billionaires in his cabinet, and has relentlessly pursued so many 1-percent-friendly policies? More to the point, what are we to make of the fact that his supporters don't seem to mind?"(Perlstein, R., 2017) [Perlstein, R. "I thought I Understood the American Right. Trump Proved Me Wrong." *The New York Times Magazine,* 4/11/2017.] Perlstein does blame the obvious bait-and-switch, but the undiminished fervor of the base after several months of post-election betrayal still puzzles him. His answer is that the show-business charisma and skills of Trump, and before him Reagan, can account for this apparent loyalty in the face of betrayal.

Charisma

"The often-cynical negotiation between populist electioneering and plutocratic governance on the right has long been not so much a matter of policy as it has been a matter of show business." (Perlstein, op cit.) These theatrical skills no doubt contributed to the popularity of both Reagan and Trump. But does every presidential candidate have to be charismatic, a skilled actor? Looking back, we can see George W. Bush and his father hardly able to get through a sentence without a blooper. George W.'s "I know you all want to put food on your family" is a classic, among many. A family of dyslexics was elected to the presidency, despite their verbal gaffes. Truman was hardly overloaded with charisma. He emanated strength and determination during wartime, but he was not a showman. Nixon was hardly a movie star, in contrast to Reagan. Very early presidents were by and large not charismatic. That was before radio and television. Roosevelt, Kennedy, Johnson, Bill Clinton and Obama were all skilled speakers, and attractive personalities. But good leadership has not always depended on charisma, though it may seem so because we are not familiar with presidents of the past.

Blind Attachment

I have discussed two of many explanations of why people vote against their best interests; "bait and switch" on the part of leaders pre-and-post-election, and charisma, which applies to some, but not all leaders who mislead their base. A third possible explanation, among several others, and one that has particular relevance to the loyalty of Trump's base, even after what seems like a betrayal, is the hypothesis of a *"thin or blind attachment."* Though I have explained it in detail previously, a brief review of the genesis of the hypothesis is due here. First, the Cro-Magnons, our ancestors, lived only twenty years, on average. During that short time there was a demand for constant surveillance to protect the helpless child from the wild predators of that period, particularly bears who wanted the same lodgings as these cave dwellers. Due to natural selection, the survivors had to have strong parent-child attachment, which is now carried in our DNA. We now see emotional attachment to a leader (and to stars, athletes) which overrides any personal needs or political issues. The goals, issues, and values of the leader (president) are substituted for the goals, issues and values of the members of his "base." This type of attachment is similar to what Justin Frank, a psychiatrist, has called a "thin transference. There is no normal and gradual attachment formed between patient and therapist over time. "This intense attachment stems from a need for comfort and safety, protecting against deep inarticulate fears of annihilation." (Frank, J. *supra.*)

We have inherited that strong need for attachment, but we live in a world with few animal predators, and we live for at least an extra sixty years. We attach to movie stars, to the likes of Kim Kardashian, to star athletes, and to leaders, seemingly without much regard for their individual characteristics.

Now we come to the specific question of why Trump's "base" continued to exhibit this extreme attachment to him, despite the fact that he was clearly reneging on his promises of jobs, lower taxes for the middle-class, and the Mexican wall. In addition, the reality of massive cuts in medical care and possibly in Social Security were being revealed. These issues, and their leader's spendthrift lifestyle at tax-payer's expense, disorganization, and possible ties to Russia did not diminish their devotion.

Paul Krugman's recent article is about what he feels is the fantasy of restoring the coal industry to its former glory. Between 1950 and 2017, the number of employees in the coal industry plummeted from about 500,000 to about 50,000. Trump promised to bring back coal jobs. During the presidential election, he got 67.7% of the West Virginia vote, compared to Hillary's 26.2%, while nationwide she won the popular vote by several million votes! Krugman's suggestion "is that coal isn't really about coal — it's a symbol of a social order that is no more; both good things (community) and bad (overt racism). Trump is selling the fantasy that this old order can be restored….."(Krugman, P., 2017) [Krugman, P. "Coal Is A State Of Mind." *The New York Times, The Opinion Pages,* 3/1/2017.] Krugman is right.

But in addition to the shift in the social order, there is the stark reality of a scarcity of jobs, and that is always threatening. Nursing accounts for the about one sixth of West Virginia jobs, and nursing is not yet a "male" job. Who are the miners and loggers who have been "left behind?" They are the white high-school-or-less-educated males who have shown a recent nation-wide spike in alcoholism, opioid addiction and suicide; in contrast to all other demographic groups, which have shown improvement in these and other health statistics. We are possibly looking at a picture of desperation. Job loss and poverty, combined with loss of self-esteem, make for "deep inarticulate fears of annihilation" and can lead to seeking a *blind* attachment (a synonym for a "thin" attachment) to an uncaring figure who gives the illusion of caring.

Any phenomenon as complex as political allegiance and voting has to be of multifactorial origin. I hope that reviewing three possible factors, "bait-and-switch," "blind attachment," and the more occasional role of charisma in the candidate, has helped to unravel a bit of this mystery.

More reasons why the "base" voted against its own self-interest.

No doubt, different factors play different roles in the various demographic sub-groups. People in the rust belt, in Appalachia, in large cities and in the suburbs have different motivations, and tend to have special interests and issues, from LGBT and ghetto life to power and inheritance taxes in the gated community. If they are *not* "blind", then the issues matter to them. Moreover, blindness is not limited to Appalachia. The billionaires who blindly backed Trump rather than a more stable and politically experienced candidate, must have second thoughts about their choice. If Trump starts a war with nuclear North Korea to take attention away from his Russian dalliances or his failure to gut Obamacare or to create a surge in jobs, they will be as sorry as the rest of us.

Racism: The Trump campaign used the eternally effective method of attacking people of color in order to gain favor with whites. The "Southern strategy" (Nixon and Goldwater) worked so well that it changed the solid Democrat South to Republican. Trump started his "birther" campaign in 2011, and clung for it for years, even after Obana produced his U.S. birth certificate. I've already mentioned the dog-whistle message of "Make America great (White) again." The general principle is to redirect the anger of the base over their grievances (jobs, health care, schools, etc.) onto minorities. This process sifts the blame from the conservative government to the "other." In his campaign and in later attempts at legislation, Trump railed against Mexican "rapists" and banned Muslims from seven countries (later only six) because they would harbor terrorists. He has used the term "radical Islamist terrorism" to stoke fear and redirect base anger away from the loss of the safety net and onto a world population of 1.5 billion. Immigrants in general are a target, similar to the right-wing parties in Europe (e.g., Marine le Pen.)

Anti-elitism: The "elite" are a tried and true target of the right. V.P. Spiro T. Agnew attacked federal judges and bureaucrats as "pointy-headed intellectuals." Past GOP presidents have used intellectuals or "snobs" as the whipping boys, to make a closer bond with the base. That base has historically contained the "basket of deplorables" unfortunately so labeled by Hillary.

Sexism: When Trump's 2005 rant on videotape was made public; "Grab them by the pussy. You can do anything (when you're a star.)," the public had already been exposed to his attacks on various women. Those included Alicia Machado, Rosie O'Donnell, Arianna Huffington, Megyn Kelly, and dozens of others he called pigs, dogs or slobs. Because Elizabeth Warren has claimed some Native American ancestry, he calls her "Pocahontas." Similar to the attacks on "elites" the denigration of women seems particularly suited to attract the less-educated white male base. When Trump and his minions use the targets of elites, women, minorities and immigrants, they are appealing to the base's anger at the college-educated, and the women, minorities and immigrants who are competing with them (or are believed to be competing with them) in the work force, At deeper levels it is clear that the "locker-room" buddy talk of Joe-Six-Pack is part of what Trump is mirroring. The appeal of a pussy-grabbing macho president who can have any woman he wants is not to be discounted, because our society is still sexist, and assertive women

(Hillary, Elizabeth Warren, and Carly Fiorina) are a threat to male dominance. So women-bashing may have secretly become part of the male-to-male bonding process. Don't forget that for the first six or seven years, boys are attached to mothers, not fathers, and to gain male identification, they need to use what Talcott Parsons called the "sissy-complex." This disengagement from mother-identification is termed "compulsory masculinity." (Parsons, T. 1954) [Parsons, T. "Certain Primary Sources and Patterns of Aggression in the Social Structure of the Western World. 1947, in *Essays in Sociological Theory,* Glencoe, IL: Free Press, 1954] The male rebellion against his mother is often incomplete. We see it in adults, in the shouts of "wicked Hillary!" and the tweets against successful or assertive women. The fact that "pussy" refers to female genitalia and to boys or men who lack machismo is hardly a coincidence. Girls, in contrast have no developmental need to dis-identify with their mothers.

This mother-son struggle and its side-effects in anger, fear and discrimination against women is not new. The seductress has power over men. Think of the Rhine-maidens, the "Lorelei" who comb their golden hair while the poor sailors crash their ships on the rocks. Similarly, the sirens tried to entice Ulysses with their song. The seductress Salome danced with seven veils, and demanded John the Baptist's head on a plate. Eve tempted Adam with an apple given her by a serpent. Cleopatra seduced both Julius Caesar and Mark Antony. Mata Hari used her wiles as a spy for Germany in World War I, and was executed by a firing squad. The list goes on; Catherine the Great, Delilah, Medea, temptresses real and imagined.

Election Fraud: Both political parties have used illegal means to win elections. Recently the GOP has outdone its past record of dirty tricks. When Richard Nixon gave his approval for the Watergate break-in, the purpose was to obtain information about the Democrats' election strategy, donors, and voters. The Russian hackings of the DNC (Democratic National Committee) Headquarters and the laptop of John Podesta (Chairman of Hillary Clinton's 2016 presidential campaign) were an attempt to obtain and release information that would undermine American's faith in their government and in Hillary Clinton and the Democratic Party. The "Russian Connection" of the Trump operatives (Flynn, Manafort, Page and Stone) is still being investigated as of this writing, but the resultant favoring of Trump and denigration of Hillary surely prevented the base from voting in its own best interests. Gerrymandering has been used by both parties to increase their electoral vote. Gerrymandering helped the GOP to win the 2016 election, because they lost the popular vote. Preventing specific demographic groups (e.g. African-Americans) from voting Democratic or from voting at all was done by legislation requiring driver's licenses or other identification difficult for poor people to obtain. You can't vote in your own best interests if you can't find a local voting booth—that is, if you can't physically vote. The minority vote was heavily for Hillary, but not as strong as it was for Obama, for which there may be many reasons. In the end, the electoral votes won the election. Especially in this 2016 election, the role of illegal manipulation in preventing the base and other voters from voting in their best interests should be emphasized by the media, and not diminished by delays in investigations and major obfuscations on the part of the White House, the FBI and James Comey, and the House and Senate Investigations Committees.

Russia and North Korea Update

After discussing several hypotheses to explain why Trump's base, and other voting bases in the past, have voted against their own self-interests, it may be time for a brief update on the deterioration of U.S. relations with Russia and North Korea.

A meeting between Rex Tillerson, U.S. Secretary of State, and Vladimir Putin on 4/12/2017, during which they discussed Syria, North Korea and the Ukraine, turned out badly. They agreed to create a working group to discuss U.S.-Russian problems, which have severely escalated recently. Trump's apparent 180 degree reversal on his previous attitude toward Putin and Russia has diplomats' heads spinning worldwide.

Tillerson said after the meeting that U.S.-Russian relations had reached a "low point." He also said that "There is a low level of trust between our two countries. The world's two foremost nuclear powers cannot have this kind of relationship."

Of course, the "elephant in the room" is the ongoing investigation by the FBI and a Senate Committee of the probability that Russia influenced the presidential election, and made it possible for Trump to win, by hacking various computers and by enabling Julian Assange to transmit damaging misinformation about Hillary Clinton, his avowed enemy. The links between Trump, Putin and Russian interference are found mainly between Trump's helpers, allies and political operatives and the Russian ambassadors, agents, Russian oligarchs, etc., during the campaign, and shortly after the election. These allies, helpers and operatives were Julian Assange, Paul Manafort, Carter Page, Michael Flynn, Roger Stone, and Jeff Sessions (to name a few prominent members). Trump's turnabout, suggesting a split with Putin, was made plausible by the 4/6/2017 firing of the 59 Tomahawk missiles on a Syrian air base. It remains to be seen if there is further deterioration in U.S. –Russian relations. If Trump does carry the split further, it will suggest that he has nothing to fear from any blackmail by Putin. If this is just an angry (staged?) prelude to another détente, it will suggest that a deal has been struck between the two leaders. You, Putin, keep your mouth shut about my peccadilloes in Moscow during the beauty pageant, or about how you helped me win the election, and I will not attack Assad in Syria again, nor complain about your annexing Crimea. I'll also go soft on pushing for a NATO buildup, and maybe soften or lift those sanctions that Obama imposed on you for annexing Crimea.

Our presidents have long been threatening North Korea in an effort to stop their development of nuclear missiles. In a recent annual parade in Pyongyang celebrating the birth of Kim Il Sung, North Korea's founder and the grandfather of Kim Jong-Un, huge ICBMs (intercontinental ballistic missiles) were displayed. These may have been empty fakes, but the saber-rattling between two extreme narcissists, Trump and Kim Jong-Un, makes it more dangerous than under previous administrations. Can this very aggressive stance be a conscious move on the part of Trump to push through his gigantic defense budget? Or to make sure he stays in power? Remember the meme, "You can't change horses in mid-stream."

Just when you think we are on the verge of nuclear war, the Donald makes his 180 degree reversals. On April 30th, 2017, he said in an interview on CBS "Face the Nation", "So, obviously, he's (Kim Jong Un) a pretty smart cookie" (to have gained power at age 27). "I'd be honored to meet with Kim Jong Un under the right circumstances." I sometimes felt sorry for Sean Spicer, Trump's generally confused spokesman, who had to address so many confusing reversals in policy. The explanation may be that the boss thinks secretly that "My confusion will confuse the enemy, and keep him off balance." (See the relevant Trump quote.)

Since North Korea had announced that it would test a missile during the parade, it was assumed it might be an ICBM. If fitted with a nuclear warhead, such missiles could reach Japan, South Korea, and even the West coast of the U.S. On April 10th, a U.S. 3rd Fleet Public Affairs site posted this announcement: "USS Carl Vinson, At Sea —Adm. Harry Harris, commander, U.S. Pacific Command, has directed the Carl Vinson Strike Group to sail north and report on station in the Western Pacific Ocean after departing Singapore April 8."

April 11, 2017, Trump tweets, "North Korea is looking for trouble. If China decides to help, that would be great. If not, we will solve the problem without them! U.S.A."

April 11th: Defense Secretary says "she's (the Vinson) just on her way up there (the Sea of Japan and South Korea"

April 11th, (airing April 12th:) Trump: "**We are sending an armada**, very powerful. We have submarines, very powerful, far more powerful than the aircraft carrier. That I can tell you."

April 13th: NBC News reports that the United States is prepared to launch a preemptive strike if it thinks that North Korea is about to launch a nuclear weapons test.

April 17th: Defense News deduces that the Carl Vinson isn't, in fact, headed up to the Korean Peninsula — at least not yet. A Pacific Fleet spokesman, Cmdr. Clayton Doss, confirms that the Carl Vinson is not in the waters around either South Korea or Japan.

April 18th: The Carl Vinson strike force was at that very moment of tweets and announcements, April 11th, *sailing in the opposite direction*, to take part in joint exercises with the Australian Navy in the Indian Ocean, 3,500 miles southwest of the Korean Peninsula! There have been many reversals of statements and goof-ups made during the first few months of the Trump administration, but none that could have had such dire results as the Carl Vinson armada mix-up. It could have triggered a missile response from Kim Jong-Un, who made open threats to the U.S. during the "show-of-force" parade in Pyongyang. It undermines the trust that allies like South Korea and Japan, both possible targets of North Korean artillery, place in the power and military protection of the U.S. The warring factions within the White House, and competition between or lack of communication between the various armed services and between the various departments, (Justice, FBI, CIA), can lead to serious consequences.

James Comey testifies before Senate Intelligence Committee, update.

On 6/8/2017 James Comey, former director of the FBI, testified before the Senate Intelligence Committee. As is usual, he was questioned by both Republican and fellow Democrat Senators. This was an historic occasion, at a level reminiscent of the battle between Nixon and prosecutors over Watergate. Comey said that Trump on several occasions, using veiled threats about firing him and demanding his loyalty, had tried to stop him from continuing the Russian investigation. When Comey refused, he was fired, but not until the next day. Comey said the Trump administration had lied. They claimed Comey was fired because of his mishandling of the investigation of Hillary Clinton and the classified documents on her personal server. The next day Trump himself declared, in a typical reversal, that he himself wanted Comey to stop the investigation "because of pressure on the administration" (i.e. pressure on Trump because of his own involvement with Putin and his representatives).

Comey accused President Donald Trump of firing him to try to undermine the agency's investigation of possible collusion by Trump's campaign with Russia's alleged efforts to influence the 2016 presidential election. Comey said Trump had defamed the FBI. He also said Trump had suggested to him in February that he stop an FBI probe into former NSA advisor, Michael Flynn. Flynn is still facing charges of being on the Russian radio station payroll, and not revealing that he was acting as a foreign agent for Turkey. Fl;ynn was later convicted of multiple charges.}

His revelations could reflect badly on Trump, who has similar connections (Deutsche Bank, etc.)

When asked if he thought Trump's actions toward him amounted to "obstruction of justice," Comey said that Robert Mueller, now Special Counsel, would "have to sort that out." The implication is clear; that Trump faces possible obstruction of justice charges. The question remains; will the Republican majority Congress ever throw Trump under the bus, (impeach him?) while he is doing all their dirty work for them? Trump gets the blame for their drastic safety net cuts. So far his "base' is still loyal. (June, 2017). (The mid-term Democrat majority in the House will initiate its own investigation of Trump, that cannot be derailed by a firing of Mueller by a Trump District Attorney minion.)

A summary of who's in each Dark Tetrad:

Any individual can fall into one or more of the four Dark Tetrad personality trait categories. Trump, for example, based on his tweets and quotes, shares in all four of the tetrad. This is due partly to the fact that his tweets and quotes are extremely accessible, compared to most other individuals. He also exhibits other traits that are well worth mentioning, but are hard to document in non-tweeters, such as "Anti-Intraception." and "Anomic Striving." I have added a few individuals, such as Eliot Spitzer, Jack Welch, Steve Jobs, Donald Rumsfeld, Betsy DeVos, and others who seem to exhibit these various clusters of traits and symptoms. The category of Idée Fixe is exemplified by Rumsfeld, but several in the White House also present this phenomenon especially Bannon and Miller. Sexual Anomics are described in Chapter Three, and there are many of them, but Tiger, Wilt the Stilt, and Charlie Sheen are among the outstanding examples.

It should be remembered that these tetrads and symptom groups are not diagnoses, and we are talking about the subclinical population. None of the four anomic avatars, Tiger, Bernie M., Dick Cheney or Donald Trump, has been in psychiatric treatment, to my knowledge. Bernie M. might possibly qualify as a clinical case, since he is in jail, but that would be stretching a point.

TETRAD CATEGORIES

NARCISSIST: (both "everyday" and "Aggressive Narcissist," Factor One)

Aggressive Narcissist: Trump, Bernie Madoff, Stephen Bannon.

Everyday Narcissist: Tiger Woods, Lloyd Blankfein (grandiose) Most movie stars and performers.

MACHIAVELLIAN: ("kiss up, kick down")Trump, Dick Cheney, Bernie M., Stephen Bannon, Steven Paul "Steve" Jobs, and probably John Francis "Jack" Welch.

PSYCHOPATHY: Bernie M., Trump.

SADISM: Trump, Steve Jobs? (Mistreatment of his daughter? Slave-driver with workers?.)

ADDITIONAL CATEGORIES

SEXUAL ANOMICS: Wilt the Stilt, Magic Johnson, Charlie Sheen, and Tiger Woods.

ANOMIC STRIVING: Trump: (workaholic, sleeps four hours, skips lunch, lacks satisfaction at any level of achievement, and tweets in the wee small hours. "Hypomanic").

(Jobs and Welch might qualify, but no clear evidence is available.)

AUTHORITARIAN: Trump, Dick Cheney, Steve Jobs.

FEELINGS OF INVULNERABILITY: Eliot Spitzer, Tiger Woods (An aspect of grandiosity).

IDEE FIXE: Donald Rumsfeld, Steve Bannon, Betsy DeVos, Dick Cheney (the "Imperial Presidency").

If these people were characters in a play or movie, would you go and see it? If your son or daughter wanted to marry one of the above-mentioned individuals, would you approve or disapprove? If these same people were running the country, heading many corporations, and imposing their goals and values upon you and your family, would you vote for or support them? If you would say "No," then you must do all in your power to defeat the current occupants of the White House, support Democrats and moderate Republicans in the Senate and House mid-term election, and join in efforts to turn back the tide of racism, sexism, war-mongering, and kleptocracy. If you value the planet earth, and hope your grandchildren can still drink pure water and breathe clean air, then vote for people who are not climate deniers. There's not much time left! Elect people who will deliver jobs, not just promise them. Support public schools and colleges, not religious-affiliated "privatized" charter schools. The country, in fact even Planet Earth, is in your hands!

TRUMP TIMELINE, JUNE THROUGH DECEMBER, 2017

(Selected "events" are from www.onthisday.com/events/date/2017/ and 2018.)

My comments are (mostly) in parentheses. This 16 page Timeline document was added to the previous text to update pertinent events relevant to understanding Trump's behavior. I show how Trump's personality traits and political and other events, interact. Unlike the previously flowing text, the Timeline devotes a relatively short paragraph to each event and its date.

JUNE

1 U.S. leaves the Paris Climate Accord. (This confirms that Trump favors coal and oil development and profits over the environmental future of the planet. Extreme narcissism.)

8 Ex-FBI-Chief James Comey testifies to Senate Committee that Trump told "lies plain and simple." (A trait of psychopathy.)

12 Attorney General Jeff Sessions denies meeting Russians before the Senate Intelligence Committee.

14 Senate imposes new sanctions against Russia for meddling in the 2016 election. (This triggers huge Russian effort to get rid of the sanctions, via Trump.)

JULY

2 Trump tweets fake wrestling video of himself attacking a "fake news source", CNN. (Cunning, sadism.)

4 North Korea tests first successful ICBM. (This is followed by many tests, ending in an ICBM capable of attacking all of the U.S.)

19 U.S. Senator John McCain is diagnosed with brain Cancer. (Though a Republican, McCain has often stood up to Trump in his crucial voting with Democrats. (Trump said "He's *not* a war *hero*. He's a war *hero* because he was captured. I like people who weren't captured." Lack of empathy, sadistic criticism of many public figures.)

21 White House Press Secretary Sean Spicer resigns after opposing Trump appointment of Anthony Scaramucci, a wealthy former hedge fund manager, as Communications Director. (Opposition to Trump's decisions is likely to lead to the exit door. Reince Priebus also opposed Scaramucci's appointment, and "resigned" soon after. [July 27]. Trump's harsh public criticism of Spicer is in keeping with his sadism and authoritarian character.)

24 Jared Kushner, Trump's son-in-law, said he did not collude with Russia after meeting with Senate investigators. (Subsequent testimony brought out that there was collusion at the Trump Tower meeting, including promise of information damaging to Hillary Clinton.)

26 Trump issues policy to ban the transgendered from the military, thus overturning Obama changes. (Criticism of others' sexual practices is often vehement, when the critic is involved in some societally disapproved sexual behavior him-or-herself. An example is J. Edgar Hoover's war on homosexuals, when he himself was actively homosexual. This policy change also appeals to Evangelicals and Trump's "base.")

27 Reince Priebus resigns as Chief of Staff. (After siding with Sean Spicer, Priebus was due for firing. He resigned, but had endured months of public criticism by the boss. Machiavellians like Trump kick down, but kiss up to the powerful, such as Putin.)

28 General John Kelly is appointed Chief of Staff. (Kelly has shown some strong conservatism. He failed to criticize, and in fact supported, Trump's response to Myeshia Johnson, the grieving widow of La David Johnson, one of four soldiers killed in an ISIS ambush in Niger. Democratic Congresswoman Frederica Wilson blasted Trump for telling Myeshia, "I'm sure he knew what he signed up for but, when it happens, it hurts anyway." "He knew what he was getting into when he joined" the military. "Kelly said. "That's what the president tried to say to the four families yesterday." (Trump has shown his prejudice against Muslim soldiers and their parents [the Khans] previously. His fear of the "other" plays well with his base. His sadism dominates, even when he is trying to play the role of supporting father-figure/President. He also selects staff who share his anger and prejudice.)

30 Putin cuts number of U.S. diplomats in Russia by 755, in retaliation for the U.S. sanctions.

31 Anthony Scaramucci is fired as White House Communications Director after less than two weeks. (Maybe Spicer, Priebus and Bannon were right. Scaramucci, known as "the Mooch," used extreme profanity in long public rants. He was rewarded by Trump for his large campaign contributions, not selected for his political skills. Machiavellians like Trump typically leave a trail of "fired" spouses and associates.)

AUGUST

2 Trump signs legislation imposing sanctions on Russia>5 U.N. Security Council imposes sanctions on North Korea for continued missile program.

8 (In response to North Korean threat to attack Guam) Trump warns N. Korea that he would unleash "fire, fury and frankly power, the likes of which have never been seen before." (Narcissistic grandiosity. Verbal skills of a manipulator typical. Unfortunately his grandiosity is not controlled by legal safeguards to stop him from "pressing the nuclear button.")

9 North Korea says it plans to fire rockets on Guam.

10 Trump declares U.S. opioid addiction a national emergency. (But typically, he does not ask Congress to allocate money for a "war on drugs" waged by previous presidents.)

12 At "Unite the Right" march in Charlottesville, Virginia, a car mows down pedestrian counter-protestors, killing one woman, and injuring at least a dozen.

12 Trump; tweets "There is blame on both sides" (His reaction to a deliberate attack on the part of White Supremacists is widely criticized in the media. His lack of empathy appears again. There is no concern for the death of the young woman. She is the "other," the "enemy." His response to the death or illness of others verges on psychopathy. Psychopaths have no empathy at all. Destroying the lives of the "Dreamer" children causes him no guilt or remorse.)

14 The president condemns racist violence in Charlottesville. (Only in response to a huge public hue and cry.)

18 White House Chief Strategist, Stephen Bannon, is fired by Trump. (Bannon, Miller and Sessions compiled the "Travel Ban", denying U.S. entry to citizens of [eventually] six Muslim countries. This was the first big move of the new administration. It was a catastrophe. Instead of starting a massive and popular new infrastructure program, Trump was immediately losing the support of over half the country. The ban was extreme. It led to hundreds of detentions, massive protests, and lawyers from ACLU and other groups defending immigrants at airports.

Bannon was in the spotlight. Many assumed that he, not Trump, was calling the shots. When the book, *Devil's Bargain,* about the Trump/Bannon relationship, came out, it focused mainly on Bannon, and his political philosophy of "nationalism." It was widely read—a best-seller. Soon after publication, Bannon was fired.

Trump is extremely "thin-skinned." This hypersensitivity to any insult or negative comparison stems from his underlying feelings of inferiority, and early narcissistic injury, discussed at length previously. The thought that Bannon was upstaging him was probably too much for this star of the television show "The Apprentice." He has continually undercut any of his appointees who show the slightest sign of intelligence or political skills.

A prime example is his *publicly* telling [tweeting] Secretary of State Rex Tillerson [formerly CEO of Exxon-Mobil] that he should forget about his diplomatic efforts with North Korea, since it would be "wasting his time." Tillerson called Trump "a fucking moron" in front of other officials. Tillerson was replaced by C.I.A. Director Mike Pompeo, on March 18th,

2018. Tillerson didn't agree with Trump on many major issues, such as leaving the Paris Accord, and about how to approach Kim Jong Un of North Korea. Tillerson had established several "back channels" with North Korea, and foresaw only lengthy negotiations ahead. Trump undercut Tillerson, tweeting "I told Rex Tillerson, our wonderful Secretary of State, that he is wasting his time trying to negotiate with Little Rocket Man. Save your energy, Rex, we'll do what has to be done!" In November, 2018, there were signs of secret nuclear installations in North Korea. Trump's diplomatic "triumph" proved to be a failure.

When John Kelly replaced Priebus as Chief of Staff in July, his mission was to clean up the contentious White House staff struggles that had made many enemies. He was a center of power in his own right who could possibly challenge problems that had taken place in the first six months of the new administration. In November, 2018, he is about to be fired.

Of all the ideologues in the administration, Bannon was perhaps the most dangerous. He was more extreme than Trump, and more educated and intelligent. His move back to being the editor of Breitbart News, the voice of the alt-right, seemed appropriate. It did not, however, give him enough voice to get Roy Moore [Rep.] elected over Doug Jones [Dem.] in the 12/12/2017Alabama election for U.S Senator. The Black vote and the millennials high income and highly-educated women, spelled doom for Moore, whose sexual assaults on teen girls did not stop Trump and company from supporting him for Senator. Maybe Bannon had lost some of his much vaunted political powers.

(1/4/2018.)Trump's lawyer said the book, *Fire and Fury: Inside the Trump White House*, by Michael Wolff, is libelous, and demands of the publisher "that you immediately cease and desist from any further publication, release or dissemination of the book." The book quotes Stephen Bannon saying that Donald Trump Jr. had been "treasonous" and "unpatriotic" for meeting with Russians during the 2016 campaign and that Ivanka Trump was "dumb as a brick," among other slurs. Mr. Trump retorted, saying that when Mr. Bannon was fired, "he not only lost his job, he lost his mind" and he has "nothing to do with me or my presidency." So ends another Trump relationship, confirming his membership in the Machiavellian club. Bannon's apparent political demise will rid us of a fascistic, anti-Semitic, anti-Muslim ideologue, whose program consisted of "capitalism, nationalism, and Judeo-Christian values." It will be no great loss, and sadly there are many others of the same ilk ready to replace him.

25 Trump pardons Joe Arpaio, even though he was convicted of racial profiling. (The President clearly supports the alt-right and racists. His labeling of Mexicans as "rapists" is just one of many outrageous slurs against various ethnic and religious groups. See his quote, wanting "Jews in yarmulkes, not Blacks, handling my money!"

28 North Korea fires another missile over Japan.

SEPTEMBER

4-5 Trump denounces Dreamers program. (Deferred Action for Childhood Arrivals, or DACA) allows children born in the U.S. to illegal immigrants to stay in the U.S. Again, the lack of empathy of Trump and the Republican Congress is evident. If you don't have a soft spot in your heart for children who will be torn from their homes and friends they grew up with, then you are hard-hearted.—at least a narcissist, at worst a sadist.)

7 Cyberattacks on Equifax affect 143 million in the U.S. (Cyberattacks and cyberwarfare have entered a new era. The U.S. has had little defense against the Russian cyber incursions that clearly helped Trump win the presidency.)

11 The U.N. places new export sanctions on North Korea. (In response to ICBM tests.)

12 Hope Hicks is appointed White House Communications Director. (Hicks, a former model, has been close to Trump and his inner circle since before the inauguration. She replaced Scaramucci in that position. She is scheduled to testify to Mueller in mid-October. She is expected to give important information to protect herself from perjury. On February 8th, 2018 she left the White House. She had picked the wrong boyfriend, Rob Porter. He was fired as a security risk. He had not received a security clearance because he had been accused of abusing two ex-wives. He had been allowed to stay on the job, though Trump, Kelly, and Hicks knew about his violent record. Unfortunately, he had access to all the information flowing in the White House, including top secret material. The accusations against Hillary Clinton for having classified information on her personal computer pale before this example of deliberately sloppy security.

13 Trump at the U.N. vows to "totally destroy North Korea if it threatens the U.S." (Part of a stream of incendiary statements causing consternation among world diplomats. This is due to his grandiosity, which may well be compensation for underlying inferiority feelings. His use of exaggeration in describing himself or his accomplishments as "The best. the greatest, the smartest, Huuge, the best looking," and his attack on Cruz as "Little Rubio" when Cruz mentioned Trump's small hands, all suggest part of his motivation to attain the presidency. He publicly declared he was of proper size in the penis department. Has there ever been a U.S. president who publicly discussed his genitals?)

23-24 NFL players stay in dressing room during the national anthem, and some kneel on the field, in a widespread campaign to protest racial oppression and inequality. *In response, Trump said to a rally for Luther Strange for Alabama U.S. Senator* "Wouldn't you love to see one of these *NFL* owners, when somebody disrespects our flag, to say, 'Get that *son* of a bitch off the field right now, out. He's fired. He's fired!" Trump was expressing his hatred of blacks [for example, his seven years of claiming that Obama was not born in the U.S., not wanting black CPAs to "handle his money," and keeping blacks out of his housing projects] But he was also cannily using anti-black sentiment to fire up his base and get them to vote for Luther Strange, in this contest for U.S. Senator from Alabama.

He switched his support to Roy Moore, accused of sexual misconduct with a fourteen year old girl, and four other young women. Moore lost to Doug Jones, a Democrat, which was a severe blow to Trump, the GOP, and Bannon, who put much effort into the Moore campaign. Sexual misconduct by a candidate (or the President) seems to pose no problem for U.S. voters on the right, and perhaps for those on the political left as well, when it means winning a Congressional seat.

25 Ex-N.Y. Congressman Anthony Weiner is sentenced to 21 months in jail for sexting a teenage girl. {Weiner was married to Huma Abedin, Hillary Clinton's right-hand aide. He shared a computer with his wife. The existence of thousands of emails on that computer involving some of the confidential memos sent to Clinton as U.S. Secretary of State were announced by James Comey before the presidential election. He said Clinton's use of a private computer was "careless and negligent," but not criminal. His announcement of the discovery of a second batch of emails

shortly before election day is believed by many to have supported the Trump cries of "crooked Hillary" and "Lock her up,", and to have cost her the election.

OCTOBER

1 Stephen Paddock kills 58 people and injures 489 at a Las Vegas concert. This was the largest mass shooting by a single gunman in U.S. history. (Paddock was a retired accountant, a gambler, a poker player for high stakes. He was affluent, though money losses may have been a "trigger." Although there were cries of outrage on the left, and demands for stricter control of guns, especially those used in combat, the National Rifle Association did not call for any controls, nor did Trump. He said the quick response of law enforcement was "in many ways, a miracle. We'll be talking about gun laws as time goes on. But I do have to say, how quickly the police department was able to get in was really very much of a miracle." As time goes on- and on and on. The President typically kicks the can down the road, when it comes to legislation helping people other than the National Rifle Association and his right-wing or corporate friends.)

5 Accusations of sexual assault by Hollywood producer Harvey Weinstein surface, (A tidal wave of accusations follow. Most are by women who report they have been harassed, assaulted, and even raped, usually by men in the workplace. There are also some reports of sexual assault by older men recalled by younger men, as in the case of actor Kevin Spacey. Since the early years of Hollywood, the "casting couch" has been a road to a successful career for young actresses, but only recently has it gained the status of a crime. Much of this change can be attributed to the women's movement, and the willingness of the harassed women to come forward. It is no longer a joke. Surprisingly, the current president seems to be forgiven by his base for his "Hollywood Tape" gropings and assaults. The excuses, "It's just locker-room talk," and "boys will be boys" begin to pale against the onslaught of accusations, firings, and resignations in high places. Trump's quotes about "a piece of ass" and Megyn Kelly's bleeding "whatever" show that he too is still living in the Dark Ages with respect to women's status, their intelligence, their choices about their bodies, and their unequal pay.)

18 Trump says to the bereaved family of Sergeant La David Johnson, one of four soldiers killed during an ISIS ambush in Niger, "I'm sure he knew what he signed up for but, when it happens, it hurts anyway." (See July 28 for details. The soldier was black, and his black family criticized Trump for his heartless response and forgetting the name of their son over the phone. The phrase "it hurts anyway" shows that the President knows that what he said is unacceptable. It is an afterthought, hoping to excuse his blatant cruelty and sadistic tendencies in attacking the grieving parents. He attacked the Khans whose son also died in combat, because they criticized him. His stated rule is "Get even with people. If they screw you, screw them back 10 times as hard." This is virtually a direct quote from Machiavelli's *The Prince*, and it puts Trump squarely in the second group of the "Dark Tetrad." Of course, he shares in the other three dark trait clusters; Aggressive Narcissism, Psychopathy and Sadism. He is a "winner" not a "loser", even when it comes to darkness.)

20 Pollution is linked to one in six deaths; a million in 2015 [published in *The Lancet]*. (Trump and his Environmental Protection Agency {EPA]} appointee, Scott Pruitt. deny global warming. Trump signed an executive order telling Pruitt to repeal the Clean Power Plan. Pruitt seeks to delay the imposition of rules limiting mercury pollution.

Remember the outbreak of Minamata disease {mercury poisoning} in Japan, discovered in 1956? Human, cat, dog and pig deaths continued for 32 years. The symptoms are muscle weakness, loss of peripheral vision, damage to hearing and speech, often followed by insanity, paralysis, coma and death. Children and human fetuses are particularly vulnerable. Is choosing Pruitt another instance of Trump's concern for children similar to his treatment of the "Dreamers?" Pruitt is a self-described "leading advocate against the EPA's activist agenda." Worse yet, the President's choice of Betsy De Vos for Secretary of Education bodes ill for our millions of public school-children.)

30 Paul Manafort, Trump's former campaign chairman and an associate, Rick Gates {Manafort's former business partner} are indicted on fraud charges and surrender to Special Counsel Mueller. (They plead guilty to conspiracy against the U.S., money laundering, making false statements, and acting as an unregistered foreign agent, among other guilty pleas. Over seventy-five million dollars flowed to them through offshore

accounts. George Papadopoulos, Trump's Foreign Policy Advisor during the campaign, pleads guilty to lying to the F.B.I. All this news is the first evidence that Mueller is hitting hard at the White House, and sends shivers through its occupants, who rush to hire private lawyers.)

30 Federal judge blocks Trump's ban on the transgendered in the military. (This ban is more evidence of the President's fear and hatred of the "other," which includes other races and religions. Although there has been some acceptance of sexuality once called "deviant," the U.S. has a long way to go, and Trump has set back the progress made over a one hundred year period.)

31 John Kelly, White House Chief of Staff, says in speech that "lack of ability to compromise led to the Civil War." (He was widely criticized as sounding racist, since his statement completely ignores the central issue of slavery. His military background and training may have preselected him to be conservative, but there have been politically liberal generals, such as Joseph Stillwell. During World War II he famously said "Illegitimi non carborundum" which roughly and comically translates into "Don't let the bastards grind you down.")

31 In New York City, a terrorist in a truck mows down people in a bicycle lane in Manhattan, killing eight and injuring ten. (Trump blamed the Democrats for the immigration law, saying that they made the attack possible." Governor Andrew Cuomo suggested Trump was "playing into the terrorists' hands" and said the attack should not be politicized.)

NOVEMBER

2 Jerome Powell is nominated by Trump to chair the Federal Reserve. (He is the first investment banker to chair the Fed. The post is usually held by an economist. Trump overlooked Janet Yellen, although a second term is usually offered the incumbent chair. Powell's policy is reportedly close to Yellen's, but Powell may go easier on the banks, because of his background and the White House ties to bankers through Trump's appointments. For example, Jay Clayton, Steve Bannon, Steven Minuchin, and Gary Cohn all worked at Goldman Sachs at one time or another. Only time will tell how Powell will treat the banks.)

5 Trump begins twelve day trip to Asia, starting in Tokyo, Japan. ("Prime Minister Abe is called 'a trainer of wild animals,' said Fumio Hirai, a commentator on a morning news show on Fuji TV. "And the world is watching how he does with President Trump.")

5 Gunman shoots 26 dead and injures 20 at church in Sutherland Springs, Texas. (Trump's response, in part; "We have a lot of mental health problems in our country, as do other countries, but this isn't a guns situation." Well, if it wasn't a guns situation, how did those 26 people get shot and die?)

7 U.S. Democrats win in off-year elections. (Ralph Northam wins governorship of Virginia and Philip Murphy wins governorship of New Jersey. These are upsets, and are viewed by the Democrats as a sign of a Trump slump in popularity.)

9 Five women detail sexual misconduct by comedian Louis C.K. (There is an avalanche of dismissals, firing, and apologies by sexual abusers, and a tidal wave of accusations by women who have been abused.)

9 Alabama GOP Senate candidate Roy Moore is accused of sexual misconduct with teenage girls by the Washington Post. (He was backed by Trump, regardless of the accusations, and he lost.)

16 U.S. Senator Al Franken is accused of groping and forcibly kissing a woman. He apologizes, and resigns under pressure from fellow Senate Democrats. (Trump bashed Franken for his sexual misconduct, but did not say anything similar about Roy Moore, who abused teen girls, not mature women like Franken did. While all these revelations and accusations and firings are going on, what about the 19 women who accused Trump of sexual assault or other misconduct? Some of them have been interviewed by Megyn Kelly. They are Jessica Leeds, Ivana Trump [his first wife], Kristi Anderson, Jill Harth, Lisa Boyne, several Miss Teen USA contestants, Temple Taggart McDowell, Cathy Heller, Karena Virginia, Mindy McGillivray, Natasha Stoynoff, Jennifer Murphy, Juliet Huddy, Rachel Crooks, Samantha Holvey, Ninni Laaksonen, Jessica Drake, Summer Zervos, and Cassandra Searles. Apparently a king can do no wrong.)

21 Television host Charlie Rose is fired after allegations of sexual harassment by eight women. (How does Donald T. get away with it, when established and trusted figures like Charlie Rose and Al Franken get fired or forced to retire? How does The Donald get away with claiming that the

Hollywood Tape is not authentic, after having publicly apologized for it, and calling it "just locker room talk?")

DECEMBER

1 Michael Flynn, Trump's former National Security Advisor, pleads guilty to lying to the F.B.I. (A light sentence is expected in exchange for testifying and providing evidence against the White House. Mueller can use Flynn's testimony to persuade other White House members to come forward. Many of them are hiring lawyers for their own future defense.)

4 The U.S. Supreme Court allows Trump's travel ban to people from six predominantly Muslim countries to come into effect. (The President's fear and hatred of Muslims is finally successful in banning them from entry. By building a wall along the U.S.-Mexican border, he has tried to ban Mexicans, whom he previously called "rapists. His xenophobia plays to the fears and prejudices of his "base.")

4 The President scales back two Utah national parks. Bear's Ears National Monument is scaled back 85%, and Grand Staircase Escalante National Monument is scaled back 50%. (This opens huge tracts of land to oil, lumber, and minerals development. In contrast to most previous presidents, who tried to preserve the land for future generations, Trump's focus is on profits for himself and corporations. This is the grand scheme of the Machiavellian, who takes from the people, and gives to the rich.)

4 New York Metropolitan Opera suspends famous conductor James Levine after allegations of sexual misconduct. (Where will it end?)

5 Democratic Representative John Conyers resigns after allegations of sexual misconduct. (Will there be any leaders left after the accusations stop?)

6 Trump recognizes Jerusalem as Israel's capital, announcing plans to move the U.S. Embassy there. (This announcement has raised a storm of protest, and a general strike in the West Bank and Gaza.)

11. U.S. Senator Kirsten Gillibrand calls for Trump's resignation, given that nineteen women have accused him of sexual harassment.

11 Attempted suicide/terrorist bomb attack in New York City subway wounds five. Bomb fails to fully explode. (The terrorist says "Trump, you

failed to protect your nation." The 27 year-old US-.born Muslim pledged allegiance to ISIS.)

12/13 Deputy Attorney General Rod J. Rosenstein defends the character and impartiality of Robert S. Mueller III, the special counsel appointed to investigate the "Russian Connection" and possible collusion by White House members, including the President. (The Republicans got a boost from the release on 12/12/2017 of text messages exchanged between an F.B.I. agent, Peter Strzok, and an F.B.I. lawyer, Lisa Page. These two described an election victory by Trump as "terrifying," and said that Hillary Clinton "just has to win." The right-wing press and the White House spokespeople claimed that the *entire* investigation and its staff were politically biased, so the Mueller investigation should be stopped. Mueller quickly removed Strzok from the Russia investigation. Page was not part of the investigative team.

The GOP used the Strzok/Page messages to attack Mueller, and called for the appointment of a *second* special counsel to investigate the "biased politics" of the Mueller team.

Seizing on a pre-election message between two obviously Democrat-biased people only shows the desperation in the Trump camp, as Mueller flexes his muscles, thereby threatening legal action against Trump and the White House staff.)

29 Trump is interviewed by the New York Times. (When asked if he would possibly reopen the investigation of Hillary Clinton's email server, he said "What I've done is, I have absolute right to do what I want to do with the Justice Department. But for purposes of hopefully thinking I'm going to be treated fairly, I've stayed uninvolved with this particular matter."

If Trump orders the department to end an investigation into his own conduct, such as collusion with the Russians or his financial dealings, he could open himself to charges that he is obstructing justice. His repeated statements that the continuing investigation is harmful to the country, if taken at face value, *seem* to be the concern of a president who cares about the reputation of his country. "The only thing that bothers me about timing, I think it's a very bad thing for the country. Because it makes the country look bad. It makes the country look very bad, and it puts the country in a very bad position. So the sooner it's worked out, the better it is for the country." And of course, the better it is for Trump.

In Trump's case, the confounding of his own interests with those of his country is obvious. No previous president has used his position to profit financially. Trump has asked Comey, and no doubt others, for their loyalty. That is the demand of an emperor or king. In the U.S., loyalty is due the government and the Constitution. The merging of himself and his country in Trump's mind is evidence of extreme grandiosity, a major trait in narcissism. Louis the XlV of France said *"L'etat c'est moi."*, or "I am the State." That may be true in a monarchy, but not in a democracy.)

31 So ends a most disastrous year for the United States, the world, and the Planet Earth. The Greeks believed disasters were predictable by the position of the stars (dis "bad," and astron "star"). In Shakespeare's *Julius Caesar*, Cassius says "The fault, dear Brutus, is not in our stars, but in ourselves that we are underlings." And the fault is in ourselves that we are under Trump.

TIMELINE, 2018

JANUARY 2018

Jan 9 Former White House strategist Steve Bannon leaves Breitbart News after his criticism of the White House in *Fire and Fury* book. (Good riddance and farewell to the most ideological alt-right and dangerous member of Trump's cabinet. His smarts were a threat to Trump's ego.)

Jan 11 U.S. President Trump causes worldwide controversy when it is reported he called African countries "shitholes" during immigration meeting. (Aside from the crudity of his remark, it shows his utter contempt for people of color. Don't forget his father Fred was jailed briefly. In 1927, 1000 KKK Klansmen marched through Queens, Jamaica, starting a massive brawl. Seven men were arrested including Fred Trump, a resident of Jamaica and a Klan member. The apple doesn't fall far from the tree.)

Jan24 President Trump withdraws the US from the Trans-Pacific Partnership (Trump has consistently damaged our relations with other nations, both East and West.)

Jan 31 Trump administration formally suspends the Clean Water Act. (He has consistently done everything in his power to destroy the environment, and protect the gas, coal, oil, mining, and lumber industries. While G.W. Bush did a lot of environmental damage, Trump exceeds him by far. We have a president who "doesn't believe in global warming," and pulled the U.S. out of the Paris Accord. The U.S. under Obama used to be the leader in international environmental agreements. No more.)

FEBRUARY

Feb 7 White House aide Rob Porter resigns in wake of physical abuse allegations by ex-wives.

(Proper vetting of personnel in this administration has been notable by its absence.)

Feb 14 Ex-student Nikolas Cruz guns down 17 people at Marjory Stoneman Douglas High School, Florida, before being captured. (Trump's and the GOP's protection of the Gun Lobby has been notorious. Is it now possible (2018?) that Congress will OK the production of plastic guns whose parts can be downloaded from a home computer? Moreover, these guns have no serial numbers or markings, and cannot be traced!)

MARCH

Mar 1 Hope Hicks resigns as White House Communications Director to President Trump.

(Hicks, a former model, had been dating Rob Porter, a lawyer and a "golden boy" favored by Trump. Hicks had previously dated Corey Lewandowski, one of Trump's early campaign managers, and also a lobbyist, political operative and political commentator on television. He, like Porter, had a record of spousal abuse. Either Hicks had a predilection for abusers, or more believable, most of the available White House male staff were abusers, which left her little choice.

According to Michael Wolff, in *Fire and Fury*, Trump told Hicks when she started dating Lewandowski that she was "the best piece of tail Lewandowski will ever get." This once again shows Trump's extreme narcissism, even when speaking to Hicks, someone who had been his faithful assistant for years. One of the marks of the narcissist is treating people as objects. Then again, in some circles, being called a "piece of ass" may be a compliment.

Mar 1 US President Donald Trump says he will impose 25% steel, 10% aluminum import tariffs, raising fears of a trade war. (This decision has hurt many U.S. interest groups, especially the farmers. Many countries have raised their tariffs on U.S. goods in retaliation. Donald T. does not seem to care who gets hurt by his decisions, many of which are off the cuff, or tweeted. His foreign relations record is a shambles of conflicts, insults, and claims of "America First.")

Mar 6 "Highest overdose death rates ever recorded in the US", 142,000 overdoses in 2016-17 period according to US Centers for Disease Control and Prevention. (There are many demographic categories by gender, age, ethnicity and education level. Strikingly, the death rate for white males between 45-54 with grade-school or high-school-only education has shown a 20% increase between 1994 and 2013. This sharp increase did not occur in the other demographic groups. These excess deaths have been due to drugs (opioids) alcohol, and suicide. The connection between the major composition of Trump's "base" and the white-male-less-educated age 45-54 leap in death rate seems tragically clear. They are the people in Montana mining towns, the coal miners of Appalachia, and men displaced by machinery in a digital-service economy. Trump claims to have helped them, but has done little to retrain them or start up new industries.)

Mar 13 U.S. Secretary of State Rex Tillerson is fired by a tweet from President Trump. This is after months of undercutting Tlllerson. (The Narcissist thinks he alone is capable, thus grandiose. The Mach has big plans, which often fail. The Sadist undercuts others' endeavors and belittles them. Trump's Dark Tetrad membership is clear in his tweet to Tillerson. "I told Rex Tillerson, our wonderful Secretary of State, that he is wasting his time trying to negotiate with Little Rocket Man." Note the sarcasm in "our wonderful Secretary of State," for Trump clearly wants to replace him. The denigration of the man he wants to negotiate with, Kim Jong Un, seems both self-defeating and sarcastic. Trump finally comes away from the meeting on North Korea without any commitment by Kim to actually reduce or inspect his nuclear missile capability. Tillerson later calls Trump "a moron.")

Mar 14 U.S. students across America commemorate Florida high school shooting with mass walkouts across the country.(This next generation of outspoken high-school and college students seems to me the last hope for our Democracy, and indeed for our planet. They will have to win the benefits that students in many countries poorer than the U.S. are now afforded. Trump is their enemy, and they know it. Cuts in education (via Betsy DeVos) Social Security, and Medicare impinge directly on their future.)

Mar 18 Vladimir Putin is elected to a new six-year term as Russian President with 76% of the vote, his fourth term.

(Given Trump's admiration for Putin, perhaps he will ask for six years instead of four? Our compliant House of Representatives might even comply!)

Mar 22 President Trump imposes $60 billion of tariffs on Chinese imports. (The Chinese respond with tariffs on $60 billion of U.S. goods, with levies of 5% to 25%, 8/4/2018. The Trump trade war continues.

Mar 24 Tens of thousands attend "March for Our Lives" rallies held in Washington D.C. and around the world to protest gun violence. (The close ties between the President and the NRA have become clear. A Russian spy (Mariia) even joined the NRA and some religious groups in an effort to influence U.S. voters, particularly those against gun control, to be more favorable to Russia. She even founded an anti-gun-control organization in Russia. Meanwhile, plastic guns by the millions may soon make gun control virtually impossible unless there is swift action by Congress.)

Mar 26 Porn star Shera Bechard, a.k.a Stormy Daniels and born Stephanie Clifford, claims she had an affair with Donald Trump in an interview with CBS's 60 Minutes and was later threatened to keep quiet. (Stormy and her present 2018 attorney, Michael Avenati, have been a big thorn in Trump's side.) Michael Cohen, Trump's long-time attorney until Cohen was raided and his records seized, had been Mr. Fixit for several other Republicans involved in lawsuits by former models, strippers, and high-priced call-girls. RNC deputy finance chairman, Elliott Broidy, a venture capitalist, "confessed" that he paid a $1.6 million settlement to buy the silence of Stormy Daniels. He publicly apologized, and resigned from the RNC co-chair.

It turns out that Broidy was probably a stand-in for Trump. The twists and turns of this story seem confusing and incredible. According to Karen McDougal, Trump had simultaneous affairs with Stormy and McDougal that started with a four day golf tournament in Lake Tahoe. McDougal expressed amazement at the level of Trump's sexual activity during the four days, and his ability to keep the two models from knowing about each other's involvement.

Aside from all the escapades involved, the legal maneuvering must be explained. Cohen and Broidy were co-chairs of the RNC. They probably put their heads together in a scheme to save Trump's face just before the 2016 ele ction. Broidy would very publicly "confess" that he got Daniels pregnant, and would pay the $1.6 million hush money. Was he a martyr, a saint? Apparently not. It has been suggested that through his ties to Trump, and his regular large contributions to the GOP, he got contracts with the Saudis and the UAR (United Arab Republic) that yielded millions. The term "vulture" capitalist, not venture capitalist, seems to apply to him, despite his apparent sacrifice and public shame.

Campos, a law professor, says "I've argued that a great deal of circumstantial evidence points to the affair being between Donald Trump and Bechard/Daniels. that Broidy entered into the NDA (non-disclosure agreement) to silence Bechard as a favor to Trump. Trump, according to this theory, repaid Broidy by agreeing to at least two Oval Office meetings, at which Broidy lobbied for the interests of the United Arab Emirates against the UAE's Gulf state rival Qatar. The UAE then rewarded Broidy's firm with a $600 million defense contract." (Campos, P., 2018)

[Campos, Paul. Here's a Theory About That $1.6 Million Payout From a GOP Official to a Playboy Model. *New York Magazine*, Updated 5/8/2018]. Because the revelation of the payoffs of hush money just weeks prior to the election would have cost Trump the presidency, an elaborate scheme with many players was initiated. The latest revelations of this cloak-and-dagger operation are too complex for inclusion here, but can be found at (Palazzolo, J. et al. 2018) [Palazzolo J.et al. "Donald Trump Played Central Role in Hush Payoffs to Stormy Daniels and Karen McDougal" *The Wall Street Journal*, 11/9/2018.]

It now appears that Trump directed Cohen and others to cover up his dalliances with large amounts of hush money using campaign funds, and these directions were taped by Cohen. This puts Trump in danger of prosecution for illegal campaign contributions. Clearly, the hush money was politically motivated. Immediately after the mid-term elections, Trump fired Attorney General Jeff Sessions. He avoided the logical promotion of U.S. Deputy Attorney General Rod Rosenstein (not a Trump loyalist) and appointed Matthew Whitaker as Acting A.G.

Whitaker has been outspoken in support of Trump, and can be expected to shut down or greatly curtail the Mueller investigation by drastically cutting its funding. He is currently facing charges concerning a fraud scheme. He may not be *legally* appointed by the President, since he has not been confirmed by the Senate. The Democrats' retaking of the House majority means that there will be additional investigation of the Russian connection, and possibly the hush-payments. Trump's presidency is in danger, and he is fighting back, using unlimited presidential powers of appointment which seem to be a very weak spot in our system of checks and balances.

What of "the Donald's" character? After all, we are now anxiously concerned with the President's current extreme behavior. He has praised a violent supporter for doing a "body slam" agaainstg a protester. His constant stream of invective against national liberal figures has finally resulted in a series of attempted bombings. The intended victims were the Clintons, Joe Biden, George Soros, Maxine Waters, Tom Steyer, Barack Obama, Earl Holder, John Brennan, Robert De Niro, Corey Booker, James Clapp and Kamala Harris. The bomber, Cesar Sayoc, is 56, and has a criminal history. His truck is plastered with political messages. With "lock her up" chants and "Democrat mobs" our leader cotiunes to elicit violence from his base.

This story of peccadilloes and cover-ups alone might cost him the presidency, if proven in court, or confessed under oath. Starting affairs with two models in four days, attempting to involve two other models and strippers in a failed effort to double his pleasure, conniving with Cohen and Broidy to conceal this activity from the public before an election, and continuing this extramarital activity during the second year of his marriage to Melania, his third wife, a few months after Barron was born. It is not a pretty picture. Yet a substantial portion of the American public has chosen to overlook all his faults, in favor of their White Republican identity.)

APRIL

Apr 9 The FBI raided the office and hotel room of Trump's longtime lawyer, Michael Cohen, on Monday, seizing records including those related to Stormy Daniels. Cohen has made at least twelve tapes of phone conversations he had with Trump. (Cohen has "flipped"" and testified against Trump. After being the President's confidante and "fix-it-man" for years, he might well have expected a lucrative appointment to the White House staff, but none was forthcoming. The Trump/Cohen relationship exhibits the symptomatology of the Machiavellian, as well as the other three members of the Dark Tetrad. The typical Mach leaves a stream of catastrophic relationships behind during his lifetime. "You're fired!" applies to his business partners, friends, wives and cabinet members. As a full-blown Narcissist, he never takes responsibility for these blow-ups.)

Apr 14 U.S, U.K., and French forces carry out airstrikes on sites associated with Syria's chemical weapons program, in response to Douma gas attack. (The U.S. role in Syria is not yet clear in 2018. However, Trump has apparently accepted the dominant role of Russia in Syria. Russia consistently supported Bashar al Assad, Syria's President. Now that ISIS has been defeated in Syria, Russia needs Syria to encourage the sale of its arms to other Middle Eastern countries. It also fears Muslims in Syria, who would be a threat to Russia. Trump's attachment to Putin, for reasons complex but as yet not fully understood, {huge loans, blackmail?}have weakened the U.S. position on Syria, which was once "regime change.")

Apr 27 Historic Korean summit: the North's Kim Jong Un and Moon Jae-in of South Korea agree to officially denuclearize the Korean peninsula. (After months of hurling insults at each other, Kim and Trump finally meet at the "summit" in Singapore, June 12, 2018. The meeting of the two Koreas had paved the way for the Trump/Kim meeting. Though Trump boasted of a good "deal" there was actually no firm commitment by Kim to denuclearize, to stop testing small nuclear weapons that could hit the U.S., nor did he make any moves to allow inspection of the underground nuclear facilities in N. Korea. Trump promised to stop joint war games with South Korea. Kim has made promises before. Without some evidence through inspection, nothing has been accomplished. Kim actually won this "deal.")

MAY

May 2 Iowa passes U.S.'s strictest abortion ban, based on a fetal heartbeat. (The Trump administration has done everything in its power to curb women's rights. It has limited access to birth control, and has started abstinence-only sex education. In addition, Trump's tweets and verbal attacks on individual women, such as Megyn Kelly, Carly Fiorina, Representative Maxine Waters, Nancy Pelosi, and Mika Brzezinski, among hundreds of others, are not acceptable discourse even in such parlous times as today.)

May 7 Vladimir Putin is sworn in as Russian President for another six years. (Ouch!)

May 8 Trump pulls the U.S. out of the multilateral Iran nuclear deal.

JUNE

Jun 4 Trump tweets "I have the absolute right to pardon myself." (If the President can pardon himself he is then clearly above the law. Let's call him Emperor or "His Highness," but not President. This legal controversy could lead to the loss of our democracy. It has been called a "constitutional crisis.")

Jun 5 Harvey Weinstein, film producer, pleads guilty to rape and sexual assault charges in court in New York. (Hundreds of politicians, CEOs, authors, television and Hollywood personalities have been demoted, fired, publicly shamed or even jailed because of inappropriate sexual advances, "groping" and forcible sexual attacks. Weinstein used the age-old "casting couch" to gain sexual access to young actresses eager for work. The outcry from women's groups, and the "me too" parade with its red pussy hats, has helped turn the tide against male sexual predators. As in all revolutions, there have been some excesses, but remember, women only got to vote in 1920!. "You've come a long way, baby!" shouted an ad for Virginia Slims cigarettes in 1968. Phillip Morris was hard at work, increasing the women's lung cancer death rate all over the world.)

Jun 5 Trump's administration policy of separating immigrant children from their families violates international law, according to the UN. (The bipartisan hue and cry over the treatment of the immigrant children and the government forced separation of parent and child has already been described. This attack on the family as an institution finally created such a worldwide condemnation of Trump and his administration that "the decider" had to give in.)

Jun 20 Trump signs Executive Order ending family separation at the border for illegal immigrants. (It took one act, the separation of immigrant parents and children, that was more outrageous in the public's mind than cutting medical benefits, Social Security, women's right to abortion, gutting environmental protection, privatizing the public schools, to force Trump to back down. Is parent-child separation the only issue that will make for bipartisanship? The world recognizes sadism when it sees it.)

Jun 20 U.S. ambassador Nikki Haley announces the U.S. is leaving the UN Human Rights Council. (The Trump administration's policy clearly follows the ideology of the President, who has no interest in human rights, or in the cooperation between nations called the U.N.

Jun 27 Supreme Court Justice Anthony Kennedy announces he will retire July 31st.

JULY

Jul 3 U.S. Justice and Education Departments rescind Obama affirmative action policies in college admissions.

Jul 5 U.S. Environmental Protective Agency head, Scott Pruitt, resigns amid allegations of misconduct. (Farewell to an extreme anti-environmentalist, a fox protecting the henhouse).

Jul 9 Trump names Brett Kavanaugh as his Supreme Court nominee to replace Anthony Kennedy. (Kavanaugh has a record of consistent conservative voting on issues before the U.S. Court of Appeals for the D.C. Circuit over a twelve year period. He was also Staff Secretary to George W. Bush. The Democrats demand records from those years, for his take on Bush's surveillance program and the CIA's torture program.

Kavanaugh helped Kenneth Starr impeach Bill Clinton, who of course was eventually acquitted. His confirmation, if not blocked by the Democrats, will have moved the Supreme Court far to the right for at least a generation, since Kavanaugh and Neil Gorsuch are both relatively young. The fact that Supreme Court justices vote along party lines, and not according to the law, should be common knowledge by now. Trump's greatest damage to our democracy may be his two appointments to SCOTUS. Short of a nuclear war or a life term for the presidency, following the footsteps of the dictators he so admires, these two appointments by Trump may be his most lasting contribution to a dark future.)

Jul 12 Trump arrives in the UK for a four day visit amid protests. (Trump is straining ties with nations that have been our most trusted friends. He criticized PM Theresa May over her Brexit policies. "May has wrecked Brexit." He sat in Churchill's chair. What nerve, and lack of respect! Tens of thousands protested his visit in London and in Scotland, where he owns a golf course. His grandiosity knows no limits. He also exhibits his authoritarianism and Machiavellianism, by "kissing up"{the Queen and "kicking down" {May}.This hierarchical view of the world accounts for some of his scorn for the poor, and worship of the powerful and rich {Putin}. As he wrote, there are only "winners and losers" and he can't afford to be a loser. What action will he take if he does lose and is impeached or indicted? Losers often want to take others with them when they commit suicide, be it political or actual.)

Jul 13 U.S. Dept. of Justice charges 12 Russian intelligence officers with cyber-attacks against Democratic officials during the 2016 election. (There's no disputing this evidence. The U.S. has been attacked in this instance by men in the Russian cyberforce. They are cyberspies. FBI head, Mueller, releases information that takes attention away from the Trump-Putin one-on-one meeting; a carefully timed release.)

Jul 16 Trump appears to accept the word of Putin denying meddling in the U.S. 2016 election, in an interview at the summit meeting in Helsinki. (A great hue and cry is raised by U.S. leaders across party lines, sensing a sellout to Putin. Some examples: James Clapper, "an incredible capitulation," John Brennan, "He is wholly in the pocket of Putin. Nothing less than treason," Joseph Biden, "Flattering dictators.....makes us less safe," John McCain," Trump—unwilling to stand up to Putin,"

Newt Gingrich, "The most serious mistake of Trump's presidency," Mitt Romney, Trump's behavior is "disgraceful," Paul Ryan, "Russia…..remains hostile to our most basic values and ideals."

Jul 16 Mariia Butina, a 29 year old Russian, was arrested after twelve Russian intelligence officers (spies) were indicted on charges of hacking Democratic computers during the 2016 campaign. (Butina tried to arrange a secret meeting between Trump and Putin during the 2016 campaign. She made contacts through the NRA (National Rifle Association) and National Prayer Breakfast., trying to steer the GOP toward a more pro-Russian policy. The arrest was clearly timed to counter Trump's assertion that he had no reason to disbelieve Putin's denial of Russian interference. "I have President Putin, he just said it's not Russia. I will say this. I don't see any reason why it should be" {Russia}." Of course, Trump quickly recanted under public pressure.

This was the statement that finally raised as bipartisan howl, other than separating immigrant children and their parents.

In fact, all seven U.S. intelligence units publicly blame Russia for meddling. Direct payments by Russians belie Trump's denial. For instance, there was the Russian oligarch's overpayment for Trump's Florida mansion, netting Trump a fifty-five million dollars' profit. That's not chump-change, and demands reciprocal political payment through support of Russian goals.

Narcissists, Machiavellians, and Psychopaths all lie. Trump has consistently lied about his dealings with Russia, with women, with his cabinet and co-workers. He even says that he likes to confuse people so they don't know what he's planning. That paranoid trait has made it extremely difficult for his staff to function.

Jul 22 Trump threatens Iraq in all caps text (tweet) of "consequences" in response to a speech by President Hassan Rouhani of Iran. (Trump thought the Iran agreement was a "bad deal." But the chief wheeler-dealer has no better solution to the Iran nuclear threat than other US. Presidents had.

The U.S. and other nations had an agreement with Iran to halt nuclear development for ten years, but Trump called it a bad deal. All the other signing nations did not resign from the agreement. Actually, this was the best deal we could get, because it involved strict inspections of nuclear facilities. The author of *The Art of the Deal* is so grandiose he thinks he alone can make major decisions, as he did in real estate, where he went bankrupt four times.)

Jul 26 About 711 immigrant children separated from their parents are still in custody for various reasons. Approximately 1242 children under 5 have been reunited with their parents. As many as 1425-1720 over 5 years of age have not been reunited. (The general outrage over using these separations to terrify potential immigrants into staying out of the U.S. prompted Trump and his administration to allow reunification of families to proceed. A U.S. Court imposed a deadline for reunification for children under five. Breaking up families to achieve political goals is direct evidence of Trump's sadism. His quotes state that he enjoys hurting people's feelings, and his public denigration of hundreds of people also supports his membership in the Sadism group of the Dark Tetrad. Yet his attacks on women and minorities have **not** caused a similar outcry on *both* the right and the left.)

Jul 27 House Freedom Caucus leaders Jim Jordan and Mark Meadows introduced articles of impeachment against Deputy Attorney General Rod Rosenstein. (Another attempt to derail the Mueller investigation!)

Jul 30 Trump has repeated the same refrain: There was "no collusion" between his campaign and Russia. But on Monday, his personal attorney, Rudy Giuliani, took a different tack, saying that "collusion is not a crime." (So even if there *was* collusion with Russia, Trump is innocent of any treasonous behavior? The twists and turns of some lawyer's arguments are truly laughable, and show their desperation.

Jul 31 The first day of the trial of Paul Manafort. He and his business partner, Rick Gates, have been charged with twelve counts, among them money laundering, acting as an unregistered agent of a foreign country and making false statements. The indictment has been described briefly under Timeline December 30, 2017.

(Manafort worked as a lobbyist for Viktor Yanukovych, President of Ukraine. Yanukovych was strongly pro-Russian, and he and several oligarchs looted the Ukrainian government coffers. After a massacre of Ukrainians by armed pro-Russians, Yanukovych was ousted in the "Euromaiden Revolution." Russia had its eye on Crimea, part of Ukraine, for some time. Soon Russian-oriented Crimeans and Russian Troops helped annex Crimea to the Russian Federation.

Now Manafort had lost his golden goose, Yanukovych, and the 60 million dollars he earned for his work in Ukraine. His spendthrift ways needed more cash. He had bought a $300,000 season ticket to the New York Yankees games. He sported a $15,000 ostrich leather jacket, and wore cashmere pants. He had bought six homes His cupidity outdid even Bernie Madoff, one of the most extravagant consumers of our time. By 2016 he was reportedly broke.

Then he got a $16 million loan by supposedly offering a banker a job in the Trump administration. With Machiavellian cunning, he had offered to work for Trump without pay, knowing he could get a lot of money by dangling his connections. The banker never got the job. Mueller added bank fraud to his charges against Manafort.

Given Manafort's incredible criminal career, you would think that Trump would avoid hiring him, even without pay. Yet his choice of cabinet members, described previously in detail, included several people who used their government positions for outrageous personal gain, or had records of interpersonal violence. Birds of a feather? {flock together}.

Why is this trial so important? Because it is the first test of the incriminating material Mueller and his team have dug up. If they are successful in putting Manafort away, it will bode well for the eventual moves against Trump.)

AUGUST

Aug 1 "FBI Agent Peter Strzok (on the Mueller team) should have recused himself on day one. He was out to STOP THE ELECTION OF DONALD TRUMP..." (This Trump tweet is one of many attempts to smear the Mueller investigation, the FBI, and draw attention away from revelations showing obstruction of justice and collusion. Peter Strzok a member of Mueller's FBI investigating team, and Lisa Page, an FBI lawyer, were lovers. In successive emails, Page wrote "{Trump's} not going to become president, right? Right?!" Strzok replied "No. No he won't. We'll stop it." The Inspector General found no evidence that their personal political beliefs influenced their work. Mueller fired Strzok post-haste.

Page left the FBI. These lovers were hardly criminals, yet they gave Trump another chance to try to derail Mueller's investigation of Trump's blatant Russian connection.)

Aug 1 ""This is a terrible situation and Attorney General Jeff Sessions should stop this Rigged Witch Hunt right now, before it continues to stain our country any further, Bob Mueller is totally conflicted, and his 17 Angry Democrats that are doing his dirty work are a disgrace to USA!" (This Trump tweet seems to be an escalation of his usual attacks on the Mueller investigation. Here he is clearly directing or ordering Sessions to fire Mueller and his 17 prosecutors. Matthew Axelrod, a prosecutor serving under Obama, said "He is asking Sessions to subvert the law" and that "there's no one who ought to be able to investigate his actions and if necessary hold him accountable for those actions." Trump's direct request shows that he knows the investigation is a real threat to his presidency and to the freedom of himself and his family

CHAPTER TWO

DEFINING THE ANOMIC PERSONALITY

Homeostasis is a term used in physiology. It describes the metabolic equilibrium maintained by an organism or cell by means of regulatory systems. But the regulation of society is merely analogous to the body's regulation, (only roughly comparable, and not homologous, or not having the same *structure*.) If the body's mechanisms get imbalanced, the system usually adjusts automatically. If it does not, symptoms appear, and trigger adjustments. If these don't work, the organism can get very sick, or even die.

A society doesn't have automatic homeostasis. Checks and balances have to be written into law. There has to be societal action to control excesses, and hopefully to achieve the best life for the greatest number of people. In a dictatorship, the "balance" is obtained by force and violence. In a democracy, the goal is to obtain a balance of the interests of different groups through the election of their representatives. As we now see in the United States, this can be a disputatious process, with the Democrats and Republicans espousing seemingly irreconcilable goals, values, and agendas.

The regulation of wealth and power is handled in many different ways. The potlatch ceremony of the Pacific Northwest Native American tribes (including the Kwakiutl, Haida, Tlingit, Salish and Tsimshian) was a means of leveling wealth and power by giving gifts to guests, who acted as witnesses to this largesse. Food, music and theater were provided, at the expense of the family hosting the potlatch. The tithing of the Christian church is an ancient form of redistribution, meant to support the church and its charities.

The redistribution of wealth by means of a progressive tax system is the bane of the Republican Party. An attack on the Welfare System, another major means of redistribution, was launched by William Clinton, (a Democrat!) in his 1992 campaign promise to "end Welfare as we know it." In 1997 Temporary Assistance for Needy Families (TANF) replaced Aid to Families with Dependent Children (AFDC). This introduced the concept of "workfare" as opposed to welfare, and cut jobs training programs. The U.S. Chamber of Commerce was elated. Taxing the wealthy to level the playing field has been a mantra of liberal Democrats, while cutting taxes (especially for the wealthy) has been the Holy Grail of the Republicans. The Democrats support a safety net, while the Republicans railed against "Welfare Queens." The Tea Party now focuses its attacks on immigrants, perhaps because "illegals" are a more acceptable target than the poor.

Other forms of redistribution are nationalization (for example, of failed banks), and property redistribution, such as eminent domain, land reform, and inheritance tax. The GOP has consistently fought against the inheritance tax, labeling it as theft. Interestingly, they labeled it the "death tax." In a similar move, the term "death panels" was popularized by Sarah Palin on her Facebook page. To fight the health reform bill, the right wing invented the big lie, "Obama wants to kill your grandmother." Numerous studies have shown that conservatives are more hypervigilant, more sensitive to threat and more physiologically aroused by thoughts of death than liberals. Some research suggests that the Bush/Rove emphasis on WMD's (Weapons of Mass Destruction) helped Bush win reelection.

During two G.W. Bush years, (2001 and 2003) the inheritance taxes were reduced, and the capital gains tax on the sale of investments was also cut. This overwhelmingly benefited the top 1% of income earners. In January 2010 the inheritance tax was suspended for one year. The 2016 estate and gift tax exemption is $5.45 million per individual. The income tax rate for the highest bracket is 39.6% for single taxpayers earning more than $415,050.

A question about redistribution arises. Why do the poor often not support Welfare and higher rates of taxation at upper income levels? One explanation is that they have hopes of upward mobility, either for themselves or for their children. Another is that they lack "class consciousness," a Marxist concept. I suggest another explanation; how a pattern of uncaring parenting (cold, punitive or labile) can set up each generation to vote and generally act against its own interests. They relate to an uncaring leader (G. W. Bush or Trump) as they previously learned to relate to their uncaring parents. If Bush wanted tax cuts for the rich, why would the poor vote for him? Perhaps because they never opposed their own parents who were more likely to be authoritarian, like Bush. Trump is not just an uncaring leader. He is vindictive, and his policy is to take from his base even what little security they now have. Rampant inequality has not changed over the ages. "For to everyone who has will more be given, and he will have an abundance. But from the one who has not, even what he has will be taken away." (Matthew 13:12).

Whatever the multiple factors involved in this apparent contradiction (the poor support the policies of the rich) they keep the poor, and now even the middle class, in a state of perpetual inequality.

THE BUBBLES

The anomic personality arises partly through child-rearing and parental practices, and partly through societal states of anomie or deregulation. There have been periods of great financial anomie, or bubbles, when the usual turmoil and lawlessness of the market becomes exaggerated. (Emile Durkheim, the French sociologist, considered the financial world in a state of *perpetual* anomie.) One of the most striking bubbles was the deregulation of the price of tulips, resulting in the Tulip Mania of Holland in 1636. Since the bulbs were sold by weight in the winter for digging up ("lifting") and delivery in the summer, a speculative market arose. The bulbs could have grown a lot, or just a little, by the time of lifting. This was, in effect, just like the futures markets. Investing in tulip bulbs was one great big gamble. The promissory notes for future bulbs were traded to other buyers. In two months the price increased twenty times. In February 1637, the tulip market collapsed. Buyers tried to default on their promises to purchase bulbs which had fallen sharply in value. Sellers demanded their money at the originally promised prices. Finally a commission was created, and payments were made at less than 5% of the original price. This scenario is strikingly similar to the U.S. housing bubble, which burst in 2006-7. Many home owners who were "under water" (owed more on their mortgages than the depressed value of their houses) simply abandoned their homes. This in turn further depressed the value of houses in the neighborhood, as homes were looted and deteriorated.

Only a relatively small segment of the Dutch population engaged in the speculation; merchants and skilled craftsmen. The mania occurred during a period of social disorganization. The bubonic plague killed one seventh of the population of Amsterdam. The Thirty Years War was raging. To put this in perspective, one rare bulb sold for 5,500 florins, equal to $133,650 in gold (at $900 per ounce.). Conspicuous consumption was widespread among the wealthier Dutch. A rare tulip was, for a short time, a mark of esteem, just as the McMansions were during our housing bubble. (See Mike Dash. *Tulipomania,* New York, Crown Publishers, 2001).

About eighty years after the tulip mania, another famous bubble burst, this time in England. In 1711 England had raised a huge debt, due to the expenses of the War of the Spanish Succession. A brief timeline shows how devastating this crash was, how gullible and greedy people were, and how a whole society was thrown into a state of anomie. In 1711 a South Seas Company was set up, with the supposedly lucrative feature that enabled it to trade with Peru, Ecuador and Mexico, exchanging British cloth and garments for gold. King Philip of Spain would allow only one ship a year to trade, and demanded a good share of the profits, but this did not deter British investors!

The trade actually performed consisted largely of selling 34,000 Africans into slavery in the Spanish colonies. The British Government debt was reduced by converting it into South Seas stock. The initial investors took the profits, while later investors were stuck with worthless paper, a typical Ponzi scheme. In 1720 the bubble burst. Both rich and poor gathered outside the Bank of England, demanding their money. In one year the stock had gone from 100 pounds to almost 1000 pounds per share, and then became almost worthless. (See Wikipedia, South Sea Company.) Interestingly, the South Sea bubble investors cut across social class lines, while the Tulip bubble was mostly limited to the merchant class.

Inspired by the South Sea stock rising prices, numerous joint stock companies sprang up in England and in other European countries. These companies were largely scams or Ponzis, and in 1720 the "Bubble Act" was passed by Parliament outlawing unauthorized stock initiatives. In the

U.S. we had the dot.com bubble, the Enron bubble, the real-estate bubble, and even in 2010 control over such volatile investment vehicles was still being considered. In July, 2010, a financial regulation bill was passed by the Senate, and signed by the President. It is the most sweeping regulation of the banks, the markets, and the brokerage houses since the Great Depression. Indeed, it is the first reversal of the trend toward deregulation in about seventy years. It narrowly passed the Senate, with only three Republicans voting for it. Here are a few of the features of this bill:

A Systemic Risk Council. Made up of major financial regulators, it would try to identify financial risks to prevent bubbles and busts.

Non-bank Resolution Authority. Empowers the council to tell the FDIC to shut down non –bank financial firms when they are in danger of failing.

Consumer Financial Protection Bureau. Empowers a regulator to see that consumers are treated fairly by banks and finance corporations. Credit cards will be regulated, but auto dealers are exempted.

Regulation of Derivatives. Through the process of "securitization," packages of sub-prime mortgages were sold, leading in large part to the housing meltdown. Derivatives like these will now be put on exchanges, and banks will be forbidden to sell some of them.

Regulation of Bond Rating Agencies. Moody's and Standard and Poor's were paid by the banks for their ratings. Unfortunately, "he who pays the piper calls the tune" (and the rating). The new Office of Credit Rating Agencies at the S.E.C. Commission will create new rules for independence from the banks whose bonds they are rating, and increase transparency and internal controls.

There are many other features of this Dodd-Frank Bill too numerous to mention. It barely passed the Senate, and lacks many controls desired by liberals, but it is a huge step in the right direction; toward financial regulation.

Were all the people involved in the Tulipmania, the Southseas Bubble, and the various bubbles in the United States true anomic personalities? I think not. We don't know what the personality structure of the Dutch in 1637 or the English in 1720 was like, nor were psychiatry and psychology sufficiently advanced at that time to use the terms we now use to describe psychopathology. However, we have a good idea of some of the historic leaders who exhibited extreme narcissism, hubris, grandiosity, a need for adulation, excessive fear of dying (for example, Hitler), the manipulation of people for their own benefit (people treated as objects), exploitation of others, anger at any criticism, preoccupation with fantasies, and exhibitionism. We also see some of these traits in our four anomic models; Donald, Tiger, Bernie, and Dick. But what makes the anomic personality different from all the other categories? It is the limitlessness of their desires and activities.

Let's look briefly at some of the leaders of the past, for clues to the psychology of the anomic personality. In historic times, only the behavior of the powerful and wealthy was recorded. (anon.) In my writing I reviewed the lives of several famous leaders. Alexander the Great had limitless ambition, and indeed conquered most of the civilized world at that time. He had a drunken swordfight with his father, and this father-son conflict was present in almost all the leaders I surveyed.

Genghis Khan was captured by rival tribesmen, tortured, and forced to wear a wooden collar. At age seven he escaped, avenged his parents' death, and became a warrior.

Napoleon, a Corsican, suffered from strong feelings of inferiority due to his rejection by the cadets at his French military school. He was also very short, and called "The Little Corsican." He soon made up for his shortcomings.

Stalin was savagely ridiculed by his father, and became a brutal killer. Hitler was continually beaten and ridiculed by his father. He also had doubts about his father's origins. His grandmother worked in a Jewish household, and was reputed to have borne a child by the master. Again, abuse, ridicule, and identity conflict seem to produce a monster with the overwhelming need to prove himself, at ther expense of six million Jews and millions of other victims in the Siberian Gulag.

Bill Clinton never knew his father. He had to fight his drunken stepfather to protect his mother. His need for adulation, his treatment of women as objects leading to his impeachment by the House in 1998, and his manipulation of others for his own reelection benefit (ending "Welfare as we know it" in order to win a second term) mark him as a relatively benign narcissist.

George W. Bush had poor self-esteem. He suffered from dyslexia, was shorter than his younger (and favored) brother, had a star athlete and war hero for a father, and a "drill sergeant" for a mother. He manipulated the public for the benefit of his privileged social class, and he was grandiose (claiming victory in Iraq, dressed in a green flight suit and holding a white helmet after landing on the deck of the aircraft carrier USS Abraham Lincoln). He was preoccupied with fantasies about receiving instruction directly from God, when making political decisions.

Obama shows the identity problem so often marked in leaders. Abandoned by his African father at age two, he lived for periods with his white mother, but was primarily raised by her parents. His father, though a Harvard graduate and an economist, had already abandoned a previous wife and child. He returned to Nairobi, to become a chronic alcoholic. Imagine the young Barack's strong motivation to compensate for his father's failure. His repeated reaching out to the Republicans in a continually rebuffed effort at bipartisanship may well be a learned behavior stemming from his need to get along with both whites and blacks during his early years. His grandiosity is suggested by his attempt to save the economy, reform health care, regulate the excesses of the financial world, stop global warming, reduce dependency on oil and coal, and escalate a war in Afghanistan, all at the same time. That he has succeeded in several of these initiatives makes us the beneficiaries of his grandiosity. It is probably true that any candidate for the presidency or other very high office has to be a bit grandiose.

It seems at times that movie stars have cornered the market on narcissism. Perhaps they simply reflect what is going on in the lives of the general public, but *their* dirty laundry is laid out for view by the media. If Joe Blow beats his wife, nobody much cares.

Henry Fonda, Joan Crawford, and Bing Crosby were all movie stars. It is logical that people with a strong need for adulation would be attracted to the stage & screen. These three stars were narcissistic parents, and two of them physically abused their children.

Joan Crawford's adopted daughter, Christina, wrote that *Mommie Dearest* beat her with clothes hangers. Bing Crosby's son Gary wrote (*Going My Own Way*), that his alcoholic father beat him and his brothers with belts and canes. Two of Gary's three younger brothers (Dennis and Lindsay) committed suicide by gunshot.

Henry Fonda was given to rages and was extremely cold and rejecting, according to his daughter Jane. She tried all her life to please him and even bought the rights to a film script, *On Golden Pond*, so *he* could win an Oscar, which he finally did. He never thanked her for this effort, and publicly said that he resented the fact that she had won an Oscar before him. (Are movie stars pre-selected for abuse of their children, or are the abused children of celebrities more likely to get published?)

Mel Gibson, movie actor and producer/director, was labeled a narcissist by David Brooks (Brooks, D. "The Gospel of Mel Gibson." *The New York Times,* July 15. 2010, Op-Ed.) He is known for his dictatorial manner and his rages. His most recent gaffe was beating up his former girlfriend, Oksana Grigorieva, and then telling her over the telephone that the beating was justified. Unfortunately for him, she tape-recorded their conversation, and he was charged with assault.

But why did David Brooks tackle Gibson, when there are so many other narcissists in the news? For example, he could have quoted Lloyd Blankfein, the CEO of Goldman Sachs, who said "We are doing God's work." If he can say that after the banks, through creative securitization, caused a worldwide financial meltdown, then he and God are putting the Devil out of business.

We've seen the narcissism of some political leaders, star athletes, movie stars, Wall Street bankers, and corporate CEOs. Their hubris, lack of empathy, manipulation of others, and drive to acquire power, wealth and sexual dominance have been briefly reviewed. What are we to call them? Where do they most typically fall in the various diagnostic categories and popular labels used over the years?

The terms narcissist, character disorder, personality disorder, psychopath, paranoid personality, and neurotic all have overlapping symptoms and behaviors.

With the regional, class, and ethnic variation found in the United States, it is harder to describe a national character than in more homogeneous societies. However, at the time Alexis de Tocqueville visited America, (1831), it was much more homogeneous than it is today. Although de Tocqueville visited many cities and the Michigan wilderness, his description of the New Englander seems to be a general assessment of American character.

"…..in his face, lined by the cares of life, reigns an air of practical intelligence, of cold and persevering energy, which strikes one at once." (Quoted in Ledeen, Michael A.*Tocqueville on American Character,* New York: St. Martin's Griffin, 2000.)

This young Frenchman also noted the anomic quality of American life;

"…..The desire of prosperity has become an ardent and restless passion…. and it soon becomes a sort of game of chance, which they pursue for the emotions it excites as much for the gain it procures." (In Ledeen, op. cit.).

The Westward expansion probably contributed a great deal to the persistent limitlessness of American goals. In old countries, there was no land to expand into, and people generally had to stay put, (or in some cases, migrate to America). The foundations of anomie, then, may not be all due to the striving for salvation, (as described by Max Weber in *The Protestant Ethic and the Spirit of Capitalism*) (Weber, M. 1905. Translated by Talcott persons 1958, Scribner's) but to additional factors such as geography, climate, raw materials, (plants, animals, minerals) and even to the genetic endowment of the settlers.

If de Tocqueville described the early New Englanders' striving and restless passion for more, Margaret Mead emphasized their practicality. The title of her book, *And Keep Your Powder Dry,* (1942) comes from the expression, "Put your trust in God, and keep your powder dry," (spoken by Oliver Cromwell to his troops before crossing a river). In other words, religion, philosophy and ethics are O.K., but self-reliance is the key to survival. (Gunpowder for the frontiersman's rifle was kept in a powder-horn.) Mead also wrote that the challenge to a fight was often started by saying "Just knock this (wood) chip off my shoulder." The characteristic reluctance to *start* a fight was in contrast to the readiness for combat once the challenger made a move. In Owen Wister's *The Virginian,* the hero's famous phrase was "When you call me that, (son of a bitch) smile!" This became "Smile when you say that." through popular usage. It calls forth an image of a frontier youth with a "chip on his shoulder," or the inner-city youth who gets angry at being "dissed." Aggression has to be controlled, but the hypervigilant individual is always ready for action.

Practicality, hypervigilance, and a "restless passion" for more, found in Americans 180 years ago, and exhibited by the early settlers, form a base from which the excessive behavior of the anomic personality could grow. The mythic figures of the American West are all larger than life. Paul Bunyan, Pecos Bill, Wyatt Earp, John Henry, Buffalo Bill Cody, Jesse James, and Wild Bill Hickok embodied the dream of unlimited male potency. There is no limit to their physical strength, their marksmanship, or their practical skills. When cowboys became dominant among movie heroes, these same traits persisted. Independence, hair-trigger response to attack, and a grandiose self-confidence in the face of Indians, railroad magnates, or cattle rustlers were their hallmarks, as well as a laconic and taciturn streak.

It is interesting to speculate why these heroes, in contrast to the more recent male figures in the movies, seem relatively uninterested in sex. Roy Rogers, in his films, was clearly more attached to his horse Trigger than to any woman. In real life, he married twice. His second wife, Dale Evans, sang along with him in twenty-seven films. She could ride and shoot as well as sing. While Roy could shoot and ride, his primary skill was singing. A joke of that period suggests that his film contracts always included a paragraph about his singing.

A bedraggled messenger rides up to Roy's cabin. "Roy, Roy! There's rustlers stealing cattle on the Jones Ranch." Another messenger rides up. "Roy, come quick. Bandits are holding up the Leadville Bank!" A third horseman cries "Roy, jump on Trigger and save Jud Hawkins. A posse is stringing him up from a Joshua tree!" Roy grabs his guitar, and replies, "I'll catch them rustlers, I'll shoot those bandits, and I'll save Jud Hawkins, but first I'm going to sing you a little song."

What happened to those uncommunicative he-men of the Old West, who grabbed a gun, not a guitar, in an emergency? They got changed into musical performers. Except for their horses, they were similar to Mickey Rooney's early Andy Hardy, Donald O'Connor, Gene Kelly, the early Dick Powell, Nelson Eddy and Mario Lanza. Gene Autry and Tex Ritter were singing cowboy stars similar to Roy Rogers. The singing cowboys, especially Roy, appealed to children as well as adults. Trigger was a beloved horse with many tricks, and was stuffed and put in a Roy Rodgers museum upon his death.

A new type of hero developed after the silent films, and was popular alongside the singing cowboy types in the 1930's. They embodied the pioneer traits of independence, hypervigilance, and hubris. No enemy was too numerous for them to tackle. Errol Flynn was a typical swashbuckler. He was reckless and impetuous. With some slight variations, all the following male movie heroes were similar; James Cagney, John Wayne, Humphrey Bogart, James Stewart, Charlton Heston and Kirk Douglas. Cagney and Bogart often played anti-heroes. Bogart and Stewart were typically laconic, and had to be coaxed into a fight (knock the chip off my shoulder). While these were all accomplished actors with a wide range of roles, they frequently played action heroes. Wayne, Stewart and Douglas were often cast as cowboys or Western constables and sheriffs, (for example, Wyatt Earp). Cagney and Bogart were perfect in gangster roles.

These film heroes and anti-heroes were anomic, because they had the pioneer traits to an extreme. They were unregulated, because they knew no law (out West) or because they were justified in mayhem and killing because of being outnumbered or fighting vicious perpetrators. The actual gunfighters fought as *both* sheriffs and as criminals. Wyatt Earp, Billy the Kid, the Dalton brothers, Doc Holliday, Jesse James, Bat Masterson, and other gunslingers often wore two hats as outlaws and lawmen.

The popularity of these early mythic figures and action heroes gives us a look into the values, character structure, and fantasy life of the current American male. Secretly, many men would want the physical and sexual prowess of a Tiger Woods, the financial (though illegal) skills of a Bernie Madoff, the supreme power of a Dick Cheney, and the tough charisma of Donald Trump. Not many are capable of such physical, financial or political feats. Many who *are* capable would not risk everything to succeed as these four men did. They had inhibitions, inner controls, or simply abstained from such excessive behavior because of fear of punishment or failure. The difference between internalized controls (conscience, moral values) and external or societal controls (fear, police) is most important. Poor internalization of societal norms could be the fault of narcissistic or abusive parenting. In contrast, the society itself may not offer regulation for the parents to teach to, or model for, their children. Both situations can give rise to the anomic unregulated personality.

Merton (*Social Structure and Anomie,* (see Chapter 4) made a fourfold typology based on whether a person (represented by four "ideal types") internalized the goals and the means of achieving those goals. An "innovator" would be someone who has internalized the societal goal of achievement, but has not internalized the proper means of achieving that goal. An example would be a Mafia don, who claims to be just an ordinary businessman. It's good for your boy to grow up to be a businessman, to achieve, but not through monkey business; graft, money laundering, prostitution, drugs, and murder. Bernie is an "innovator;" a high level thief and con man. To some extent, Dick is also, for he used his position for personal gain, for enriching his inner circle of corporations, and for almost unlimited power. Tiger's achievement by athletic prowess is totally legitimate. He's not an innovator, but he is a sexual anomic. Donald is a champion innovator. His mokey business is on a grand internatonal scale.

We have looked at some famous leaders who could be considered anomic personalities due to their unlimited ambition and narcissism, to see if they shared some aspects of childhood experience. Severe physical punishment or abuse, extreme ridicule, conflict with fathers, identity confusion, and a poor self-image due to being compared to other ethnic groups or more capable siblings or fathers seem typical of these famous strivers and overachievers. In addition to early family experience and parental behavior, the culture (tribal, warlike, capitalist) also plays a great part in producing anomics. De Tocqueville's characterization of Americans as having "an ardent and restless. . . desire of prosperity" still fits us like a glove after two centuries.

Can anomic personalities be classified as personality disorders, as in DSM IV and V? (Diagnostic and Statistical Manual of Mental Disorders, DSM V, 2013.American Psychiatric Association.) Are they psychopaths (now labeled "antisocial personality disorders"?) Are they "character styles?" Are they paranoid, borderline, or narcissistic (now all considered to be personality disorders)? Are they neurotic? While they may partake of some or all of these diagnostic labels, their prevalence in so many cultures, and particularly in the United States, strongly argues for not considering them to be pathological in the ordinary sense.

A brief discussion of our conflicting views of human nature may be helpful here. Extreme striving, selfishness, instrumental values (manipulation of others), lack of guilt and empathy, lying, etc., are considered by perhaps a majority of people to be fixed, God given, and the essence of human nature. Great thinkers such as Freud, Hobbes, Durkheim and Voltaire held this view.

In *Leviathan*, (Hobbes, T. 1651.) Thomas Hobbes pictured man in his original state of nature as being in constant fear of violent death. Freud saw man's fear of death as being due to an instinct of aggression, which pitted man against man. Durkheim saw loss of social control over man's nature (our label is "personal deregulation" at the individual level) leading to a societal state of "anomie," which showed itself in individuals as anxiety, fear and sometimes suicide. (Durkheim used the term "anomic" to describe one type of suicide, prevalent in the deregulated world of finance.)

For Freud, the ideal of "brotherly love," "love thy neighbor," or even more so, "love thine enemy" involved a tremendous sacrifice. Reining in the aggressive drive, in his view, was a major "discontent," necessary for civilization. He saw man's view of the neighbor as: "...a temptation to them to gratify their aggressiveness on him, to exploit his capacity for work without recompense, to use him sexually without his consent, to seize his possessions, to humiliate him, to cause him pain, to torture and to kill him. *Homo homine lupus*; (man is a wolf to man), who has the courage to dispute it in the face of all the evidence in his own life and in history?" (Freud, S. 1929, pp. 50-51)

Freud felt that in order for societies (civilization) to survive, aggressive and sexual instincts had to be controlled by repression and by reaction formation.

"Culture has to call up every possible reinforcement in order to erect barriers against the aggressive instincts of men and hold their manifestations in check by reaction formations in men's minds. Hence its system of methods by which mankind is driven to identifications and aim-inhibited love-relationships; hence the restrictions on sexual life; and hence, too, its ideal command to love one's neighbor as oneself..." (Freud, op. cit., p. 51)

The opposite view of man's nature is exemplified by Wordsworth, In *Intimations of Immortality*, he said that we come at birth "trailing clouds of glory... from God, who is our home." Jean Jacques Rousseau, 1712-78, in *Discourse on the Arts and Sciences*, contrasted man in a "state of nature" (the "noble savage") with man in society, which corrupted him. In his *Social Contract* Rousseau famously said "Man is born free, but everywhere he is in chains." This view of the child as basically moral until society drags him down contrasts with the deterministic view of instincts in the newborn that must eventually be controlled; a sort of psychoanalytic infant damnation. In the days of Margaret Mead, Ruth Benedict, Abram Kardiner, Ralph Linton, and Gregory Bateson, we graduate students used to call this "pisspot determinism," because nursing, weaning, and toilet training explained everything.

Granted that there are some cultures where competition is kept to a minimum (the Pueblo Indians), and some cultures where sharing is endemic (the rapidly disappearing hunter-gatherer societies), but by and large mankind struggles to survive, and individual and family survival take precedence over concern for others. The origins of altruism and caring for others outside the immediate family are now attributed to preserving the genes of the larger group. This, in effect, helps the survival of the common gene pool, though not necessarily the survival of the individual.

Karen Horney, in *The Neurotic Personality of Our Time*, noted that the quest for power, prestige and possession is widespread in our culture.

"The irrational quest for possession is so widespread in our culture that it is only by making comparisons with other cultures that one recognizes that it is not a general human instinct, either in the form of an acquisitive instinct or in the form of a sublimation of biologically founded drives. (Horney, K, *The Neurotic Personality of Our Time*, New York, W.W. Norton & Co., 1937, p. 173.)

Horney saw compulsive striving for power, prestige and possession as neurotic, and said "Even in our culture compulsive striving for possession vanishes as soon as the anxieties determining it are diminished or removed." (op. cit. p. 173.) But our fears of "impoverishment, destitution, and dependence on others" can only be assuaged in the case of the wealthy who can afford psychotherapy. For the masses; the poor, the ill, the aged, the minorities, and even the middle class since the current recession/depression which struck worldwide, there seems no alleviating their anxieties, nor fixing the cause of their legitimate fears. In our country the Tea Party rage and fear of joblessness, foreclosure, and even destitution enabled the GOP to co-opt that angry energy in support of the very policies that impoverish the angry ones. I have focused on the question "What makes people vote against their own self-interest?" If the financial elite can pin the elitist label on the academic or liberal elite, (the "pointy-headed intellectuals" of former Vice-President, Spiro Agnew) the *ressentiment* is redirected away from those in power to intellectuals, minorities, immigrants, Muslims, etc.

The riots in France in 2010 over adding two more years to the retirement age are a sign of the general retrenchment and the ressentiment of the masses (feelings of inferiority and a moral code used to attack the sins of the privileged, or "elites") The reduction of the social safety net in England has been drastic. The economies of Spain, Portugal, Greece, Ireland and many other countries have hit a wall.

Striving for survival, which becomes more salient during times of economic depression in wealthy nations, and is continuous in impoverished nations, is part of man's nature. Unlimited striving, or survival gone wrong, is what I would call "anomic," using a narrow definition of Durkheim's term.

If a set of behaviors and attitudes (narcissism, excessive striving, limitless goals, lack of empathy, grandiosity, etc.) is very widespread in a culture, we could call it "statistically normal," but it could be considered abnormal or pathological from a psychiatric or psychological viewpoint. Richard Brickner, in *Is Germany Incurable,"?* (Brickner, R. 1943. Philadelphia: J.B. Lippincott.) labeled Hitler's Germany a paranoid culture. Attributing a psychiatric diagnosis to a nation or culture raises alarm bells, for it smacks of "labeling" use by bigots to denigrate those of other persuasions or groups.

When Horney labeled our culture "neurotic," she was well aware that striving for prestige, power and possession was an earmark of U.S. culture. Since these behaviors are endemic in our culture and in most developed countries, it is hardly a neurotic symptom to strive, covet money and other's wives, etc. It is evident that what we are talking about is a personality type, not a personality disorder.

Since this personality type is so common, at least in the U.S., it could be labeled a "socially patterned defect." This term was introduced by Erich Fromm. (Fromm, E., 1954) [Fromm, E., *The Psychology of Normalcy*, Dissent, New York, Vol. 1, (Spring 1954), pp. 139-143.] The individual with this type of defect does not suffer the usual consequences of his behavior (suspicious, withdrawn, aggressive, compulsive, etc.) because he is living in a culture where almost everybody exhibits these same behaviors. He is not ostracized and does not suffer opprobrium for behaving in this way. Quite the contrary, these traits and behaviors may help him gain wealth and power. Later we will talk about the conscious selection of "psychopaths" for high corporate positions.

"There is, however, an important difference between individual and social mental illness, which suggests differentiation between the two concepts: that of *defect* and that of *neurosis*. If a person fails to attain freedom, spontaneity, a genuine expression of self, he may be considered to have a severe defect…If such a goal is not attained by the majority of members of any given society, we deal with the phenomenon of *socially patterned defect*." (Fromm, op. cit., p. 2)

The intense competition for prestige, power and possession was spelled out by Horney, (op. cit. p. 186). But the motivation she attributes to these neurotics are the same motives that humans have for survival. All humans have anxiety when in need of food, shelter, and the possessions needed to stay alive and healthy, and possibly to reproduce. Thus her distinction between healthy and unhealthy aggression and healthy and unhealthy accumulation of goods, power, and money is problematic.

Horney said that anxiety is what motivates the neurotic, especially those neurotics who seek power prestige and possession. However, anxiety and fear underlie all of our behavior. We all have a drive to survive. (I will talk later about primary narcissism, which is early and healthy self-love and self-preservation.)

Anxiety is a preparatory response. It prompts us to prepare for tasks and threats we may face. If the anxiety doesn't lead to direct action (which it seldom does in complex civilized societies) then the anxiety may be crippling rather than helpful. This harks back to Cannon's "flight or fight." response, part of a general stress response. (Cannon, W.B., 1953, 1915) [Cannon, Walter B. *Bodily Changes in Pain, Hunger, Fear and Rage.* [*ed.* 2] Boston. Mass., Charles T. Branford Co., 1953, first ed. 1915).] When there is a perceived threat, adrenaline and norepinephrine are released. These catecholamines result in increased heart rate, sweating, rapid breathing, constriction of blood vessels and muscles, shutting down of the digestive system (dry mouth), and pupil dilation, among other changes. There is also a general increase in vigilance, presumably hard-wired to protect us (and our fellow mammals) from attack by predators. (Anon.)I have found several studies that showed hypervigilance to be more typical of political conservatives than liberals, especially when exposed to threat stimuli. If you can neither flee nor fight, as in most civilized societies, you are stuck with the preparatory response symptoms, which are indeed often incapacitating.

If anxiety is endemic, and part of the general response to life's conditions and demands, then it alone is not the hallmark of neurosis, or of the personality disorders. Is anxiety a key to the anomic personality? Actually, the anomic individual is less apt to evidence overt anxiety than other personality types. The classical picture of the neurotic is one of repeated self-defeating behavior that is "ego-dystonic." This means that difficulties he faces and even his behavior in those situations are unacceptable. to him. He may seek therapy for the resolution of this conflict. The antisocial personality and the anomic personality have no conscious conflict over their behavior. On the contrary, they revel in it.

A major difference between the neurotic and the anomic is that the neurotic (for example, the dependent or obsessive compulsive personality disorder) takes a few steps forward and then takes some steps backward in a self-defeating scenario. There is little or no backsliding by the anomic personality. He or she is usually well organized, and embarked on a straight trajectory of success unless he has some fatal flaw, an Achilles heel that derails him. Tiger had to exercise and compete in many tournaments, a demanding schedule. Bernie had to juggle his books using "creative accounting," and keep up a front with numerous charitable activities. Dick was the former CEO of Halliburton, the largest U.S. contractor in the war in Iraq. During the 9/11 attack on the World Trade Center he virtually took over command of the country. His rise to the vice-presidency took extraordinary executive functioning (frontal cortex). These three were far from neurotic. They showed no guilt or remorse, and used people as objects. They all had charisma, were superficially charming, and each lied about some topic, (\ sex, money and Weapons of Mass Destruction).

The narcissistic element in the anomic man includes an inability to take a long view, despite his careful planning. This may be due to deliberate risk taking or to denial. Bernie must have known at some level of consciousness that a Ponzi scheme inevitably fails, and that Ponzis are eventually caught. When the base of the pyramid of scammed investors becomes too large to pay everybody back, only the early investors get paid, and the jig is up. Tiger must have known that cocktail waitresses and highly-paid call girls are out for money, and that one of his chickens would squawk. At some level Dick must have known that the character assassination of Joseph C. Wilson and the "outing" of his wife, Valerie Plame, as a CIA analyst would backfire. He knew the report that Saddam Hussein sought yellowcake uranium from Niger was false. He let Scooter Libby, his right-hand man, take the rap (another trait of the anomic man).

Another example of seemingly deliberate risk-taking, despite careful long-term planning in a brilliant career, is Eliot Spitzer, the ex-New York Governor. The use of a credit card to pay for illicit sex is far from street-wise. In addition, call-girls and prostitutes nowadays all seem to want publicity. The continual withdrawal of sums over $10,000 is also a no-no, and will act as a red flag. If you have political enemies, these three goof-ups can get you in deep trouble. Are these careless mistakes, or unconsciously self-destructive (i.e., neurotic)? I think that in this case, the narcissism of an anomic personality created a cloak of invulnerability. Growing up very wealthy and privileged could also create this feeling of invincibility. It is more likely to be seen in an adolescent than in an adult.

The anomic man shares behavior and traits with the antisocial, narcissistic, paranoid, and possibly the borderline types. He is less likely to exhibit the violence of some of the antisocial types. These personality types and personality disorders lie on a continuum, as with most measures of mental health and pathology.

The anomic man is suspicious, and often hypersensitive, traits in the paranoid category, DSM-IV personality disorders, as summarized by Masterson. (Masterson, J.F. 2000) [Masterson, J.F. *The Personality Disorders.* Phoenix, AZ: Zeig, Tucker & Co., Inc., 2000.] The following listed personality disorders show the listed traits often found in the anomic personality, based on the models I have chosen and discussed.

Antisocial; irresponsible, criminal activities, aggressiveness, financial difficulties, impulsivity, recklessness, lying (but not juvenile delinquency).

Borderline: impulsivity, anger, identity disturbance, self-damaging acts [eventually], (but not idealization/devaluation of others), affective instability, intolerance of being alone, or chronic emptiness/boredom).

Narcissistic: grandiose, preoccupied with fantasies, exhibitionistic, poor response to criticism, manipulative, exploitative.

The anomic personality is least likely to exhibit the characteristics: of the following personality disorders: Schizoid, Schizotypal, Histrionic, Avoidant, Dependent, and Obsessive-Compulsive.

Another clue to the nature of the anomic man is the cluster of traits based on factor analysis of the Hare Psychopathy Checklist ("Psychopathy," *Wikipedia) and Hare, R.D. 2003)* and(Hare, R.D. 2003) [Hare, R.D. 2003*Manual for the Revised Psychopathy Checklist.* Toronto, ON, Canada: Multi-Health Systems, 2003.] While these factors are not used in diagnosis, they give us an idea of how anomic personalities are related to psychopathy, and especially how they are *not related.* The PCL-R has twenty items. Based on the case history and a "semi-structured" interview, a score is given which measures traits and behaviors that fall into two factors.

Factor 1 is labeled "aggressive narcissism." It is much closer to the anomic types I have described than it is to Factor 2, "Socially deviant lifestyle."

Factor 1: Aggressive Narcissism

  Glibness, superficial charm
  Grandiose sense of self-worth
  Pathological lying
  Cunning/manipulative
  Lack of remorse or guilt
  Emotionally shallow
  Callous/lack of empathy
  Failure to accept responsibility for own actions

Factor 2: Socially deviant lifestyle

  Parasitic lifestyle
  Poor behavioral control

Promiscuous sexual behavior
Lack of realistic, long-term goals
Impulsiveness
Irresponsibility
Juvenile delinquency
Early behavioral problems
Revocation of conditional release

It is clear that Factor 1 resembles the anomic man in every respect. Narcissism is dominant, but aggression in the physical sense is strikingly absent. Factor 2, in contrast, is clearly comorbid with criminality. The only overlap of Factor 2 with the anomic personality is the "promiscuous sexual behavior," and the lack of *realistic* long-term goals. (Poor planning ("executive") functions are often attributed to criminals and delinquents, but it has been pointed out that they are fully capable of planning their thefts and scams.)

The goals of the "anomic triumvirate" were unrealistic, but they were long-term. Bernie's scheme was bound to fail, Tiger's philandering was sure to get him in trouble eventually (though his goal of golf champion was not unrealistic), and Dick's goal of creating an imperial presidency was bound to create a backlash in the legislative and judicial branches of our government, as well as in the general public.

Since the traits in Factor 1 are found to varying degrees in almost all ranks and facets of our society, it is no wonder that as early as 1979 Christopher Lasch wrote *The Culture of Narcissism: American Life in an Age of Diminishing Expectations.* (Lasch, C. 1979) [Lasch, C. *The Culture of Narcissism: American Life in an Age of Diminishing Expectations.* New York: Norton, 1979.] While he reviews the same traits found in Factor 1, he mentions another very important component. The clinical narcissist exhibits an exaggerated fear of dying. Our culture is so youth-oriented that an eighty-year-old woman had a facelift. In my book, (anon.) I discuss this American preoccupation. Obsession with health and diet, cosmetics, memorials, legacies, and artistic and literary productions to outlast the author is rampant. (Author, speak for yourself!)

What do Tiger, Bernie and Dick, Fall, Tweed, Nixon, Blankfein, the famous leaders (Alexander the Great, Stalin, Hitler and many others) have in common that makes them eligible to claim membership in the anomic personality hall of fame?

Anomic PersonalityTraits

1. They pursue their goals relentlessly.
2. Their goals are limitless.
3. They are grandiose. Trump says he is the smartest, has the highest I.Q. Alexander conquered the world. Hitler killed six million Jews and millions of others. Tiger becomes the wealthiest athlete ever. There were 793 billionaires in 2009 according to Forbes Magazine. The wealthiest three were Bill Gates (Microsoft, 43 billion), Warren Buffet (37 billion, Berkshire Hathaway) and Carlos Slim Helu (35 billion, Telmex, América Móvil). Lloyd Blankfein, CEO of Goldman Sachs, made a bonus of $68 million in 2007. And he is only the 73rd richest man in the world! Dick tried to create the Imperial Presidency.
4. They treat other people as objects; Tiger treated numerous women as objects. Bernie stole from his own synagogue members. Trump says you can "grab women by the pussy."
5. They are cunning and use language to justify their acquisitive or aggressive behavior. Trump uses tweets: "SAD!" "Digusting!" "Drain the Swmp" etc. In 2009, Lloyd Blankfein, when asked about the huge incomes of members of his firm, Goldman Sachs, says that "I don't want to put a cap on their ambitions. As the guardian of the interests of the shareholders and, by the way, for the purposes of society, I'd like them to continue to do what they are doing." He says "I am just a banker doing God's work." The wordsmiths who dreamed up the "Clear Skies Initiative," "No Child Left Behind," "family values," "axis of evil," "Weapons of Mass Destruction," and "death panels" were cunning propagandists, intent on disguising their true objectives.
6. They are often pathological liars, and deny their offenses and predations when these are discovered.
7. They are usually charismatic, and use their charm and interpersonal skills to gain power and possession. Many politicians (as well as

con artists) are smooth talkers. They have to be in the age of television. John Kennedy, Bill Clinton, and Barack Obama all have or had superb verbal skills and physical appeal. These three over-achievers also had to have the energy and drive to attain the presidency.

8. They often show a lack of empathy. George W. Bush had a certain homey charisma that appealed to at least half the nation. He was definitely not a post-marital philanderer. However, he exhibited very little concern for the common man, and signed off on the largest number of executions in Texas history. He made fun of Karla Faye Tucker, who was about to be executed for murder, saying in mock sympathy that she would plead "Please don't kill me". As Governor, he let her be executed.

9. Often exhibit sexual hyperactivity. Sexual hyperactivity is not necessarily part of the anomic personality (vide Cheney), but is so often linked to it that it is worth examination. John Kennedy and Bill Clinton presaged Tiger Woods' extracurricular activity, but Kennedy did not suffer the consequences, while Clinton was impeached by the House of Representatives. This trait of sexual hyperactivity is more likely to arise in a societal state of sexual anomie; that is, a sexually permissive society. But anomic high-achievers in many more traditional cultures have also been very active sexually: for example, Mohandas Gandhi.

10. Theuy are often overachievers.

What we have come to know posthumously about the personal conduct of many of history's most extraordinary political leaders suggests that a combination of charismatic personality, a drive to attain power, and sexual compulsivity is a common pattern among heads of state. How might we understand the psychological connection between sexual addiction, charisma, and the quest for power?" (Bloland, S.F.) [Bloland, S.E. Bill Clinton and John Kennedy: The Dark Side of Charisma. Psychoanalytic Dialogues, Vol. 10, Issue 2, 2000 pp. 285-289).]

Bloland points out that both Clinton and Kennedy, as compulsive womanizers, "risked their political careers (if not the welfare of the country) in the addictive pursuit of sexual gratification." She states that

Mao Zedong, Mahatma Gandhi and Martin Luther King "qualify as sexual addicts." Both the power of such leaders, their charisma, and their access to money may have made philandering easier and made them attractive to women.

Given their limitless goals, manipulation of others as objects, cunning use of language to disguise their true goals, their lying, and their lack of empathy, you would think that they could never be hired for an executive job.

"One might think that conning or bullying traits in a job applicant would be so obvious to employers that such candidates would not be hired for important jobs, especially those where the ability to get along with others is critical/" (Babiak, 2006) [Babiak, P. and Hare, R.D. *Snakes in Suits; When Psychopaths Go to Work.* New York, HarperCollins, 2006]

On the contrary, Babiak and Hare found that rather than firing these difficult types, they were sought after, and often achieved high positions in the corporate world. They cite several reasons for this seeming paradox. Smooth-talking psychopaths with charisma can fool interviewers. Also, attributes of leadership such as taking charge, decision making, and getting others to perform may emerge as "coercion, domination, and manipulation." In addition, the business model morphed from the structured bureaucracy to a rapid innovative style. The grandiosity and lack of empathy in the psychopath could easily function well in this new business world.

It is hardly news that psychopaths are often selected for leadership roles, whether in business, the military, government or other institutions. Who has not experienced a domineering boss, a crooked politician, or a bank president who pushes sub-prime loans? This behavior is pervasive in our culture.

In the United States, and in capitalist societies in general, the greed and competition reaches new heights. It has become more extreme during recent Republican administrations. Way back in 1939 the sociologist Edwin Sutherland coined the term "white collar crime," and defined it as "a crime committed by a person of respectability and high social status in the course of his occupation." Since the spoils system of the Jackson administration laid the foundation for American graft, governmental scandals have been rife in our history. Boss Tweed moved furniture into New York's City Hall, charged the taxpayers, and then moved it out the back door.

The oil fields of the Teapot Dome scandal were in Wyoming and California. They were reserved for the Navy, but Senator Albert Fall, a Republican, got himself appointed Secretary of the Interior, and leased the fields to two big oil companies. In return he got huge personal loans and expensive gifts. Fall was sent to prison for a year and fined $100,000.

Former President Richard Nixon had full knowledge of the Watergate caper (1972). Government "plumbers" broke into Democratic campaign headquarters, trying to get information to derail the Democrats' campaign. Nixon was impeached by the House in 1974, on charges of obstruction of justice, abuse of power, and defiance of committee subpoena. He resigned in 1974.

A series of financial scams have taken place more recently. Many of these involve accounting firms. A few of the more notable are Xerox, Enron, Global Crossing, Halliburton, Merck, Quest Communications, AIG, Madoff, and Lehman Brothers. The Enron scandal resulted in criminal charges against Arthur Anderson Company, a leading accounting firm, and caused its demise.

Only a fraction of anomics and their cousins, the psychopaths, are caught and exposed. The great majority are successful, and completely accepted in our society. It is only when there is a fatal flaw (as in Achilles' heel) that they overstep the societal boundaries, and pay the price in ostracism and punishment. Tiger lost his wife and lucrative contracts, Bernie went to prison, and Dick left the White House regarded by half the nation as the reincarnation of Darth Vader. Tiger continues to play in tournaments. Though he is no longer showered with endorsement money by corporations, he has already earned over a billion. Cheney is married to a likeminded woman, and his daughter Liz is following in his ideological footsteps. He had at heart transplant in 2012 which will keep him alive for a while longer. He has no financial worries. Of the triumvirate, only Bernie languishes in jail. Nixon was impeached, Albert Fall was fined and imprisoned, and William Tweed served twelve years in prison. We don't know the fate of anomics who didn't come to public attention, because they were never "caught," so to speak.

A few, like former President Bill Clinton, went through a trial, and came out bloodied but unbowed. He was impeached by the House of Representatives in 1998, and acquitted by the Senate in 1999, largely along party lines. As in Tiger's case, and that of many other public figures, such as Italian Prime Minister Silvio Berlusconi, Eliot Spitzer, John Profumo, Mark Sanford, Wilbur D. Mills, Gary Hart, and Larry E. Craig, sex scandals interrupted their political or other careers. However, Berlusconi and Spitzer have survived these crises, and have to some extent been rehabilitated. Certainly Bill Clinton has prevailed in his new international roles (for example, visiting North Korea to seek the release of two American journalists, and Haiti after the earthquake).

To summarize, the hallmark of the anomic personality is unlimited striving. In the United States it is part and parcel of our social character. It is not a personality disorder, because it is endemic. It is best considered as a "culturally patterned defect." It is widespread in our culture, from the boy who has to win every game or the girl who has to buy more dresses than her peers, to the crooked salesmen of cars and homes, the doctors and patients who cheat on Medicare and Medicaid, to the CEOs who buy our politicians with hidden contributions, and our leaders who start preemptive wars. As I noted before, they seldom suffer the consequences of their striving behavior, nor do they become ostracized by their peers, who are busily engaged in similar behavior.

I selected Tiger, Bernie and Dick because they are familiar figures, exemplifying unlimited sexual behavior, unlimited accumulation of money, and unlimited acquisition of power. The deregulation of behavior in these individuals is mirrored in the deregulation of our financial institutions: the banks, the stock market, and corporations.

This book is an attempt to combine some of the insights of sociology and criminology with the clinical insights of psychology and psychiatry. My career in research has been in the field of social psychiatry. Because of this training, I can say that the anomic personality type in the United States is the result of a multitude of factors. Some of these are: our history of Westward expansion, our political and governmental system, our child-rearing patterns, our Protestant/Calvinist forbears (See Max Weber), and especially our lack of limitation of both individual and corporate behavior.

A balance between excessive freedom and excessive regulation must be maintained in any society for the benefit of its citizens. That balance has been lost, and has created an incessant striving in our zero-sum culture, where you are either a winner or a loser. The great majority, it seems, consider themselves losers, and in fact, they are losers in terms of worldly goods and power.

In a San Francisco fundraiser Obama (then a junior senator from Illinois) made a politically unfortunate but true comment about the people "in small towns in Pennsylvania and…in the Midwest." Their jobs were gone for 25 years, "And it's not surprising then they get bitter, they cling to their guns or religion or antipathy to people who aren't like them or anti-immigrant sentiment or anti-trade sentiment to explain their frustrations." That bitterness and anger is now spreading to the middle class, as the gap between the very rich and the rest of us widens. The bitter Tea Partiers and the Donald Trump lovers of 2016 seem, by voting Republican, to want to empower the very people who have historically exploited them.

CHAPTER THREE

TIGER WOODS

Let's take a look at our anomic triumvirate, Tiger, Bernie, and Dick, to see how well they fit the characteristics of the anomic personality cultural defect discussed in Chapter Two.

Eldrick Tont Woods was born in 1975. Like many anomics, he is an overachiever. His "achievements to date rank him as among the most successful golfers of all time. Formerly the World No. 1, he is the highest-paid professional athlete in the world, having earned an estimated $90.5 million from winnings and endorsements in (one year) 2010."

(Woods, T, Wikipedia) [http//en.wikipedia.org/wiki/Tiger __Woods] In the number of Grand Slams, World Golf Championships, and PGA Tours won, he is clearly a leader. He was world No. 1 golfer in part of 1999-2004 and in part of 2005-2010.

Tiger's troubles began in November, 2009, when news of his infidelity to his wife, Elin Nordegren, broke. Since that time through April, 2011, he had been winless; a total of 17 months. In 2013-2014 he returned to No. 1 ranking. In 2014 he had back surgery, and his ranking since has been as low as #104. He made a remarkable recovery, and has won 18 World Golf Championships.

Tiger was born in Cypress, California. His father was Earl Woods, a retired Lieutenant-Colonel and a Vietnam War veteran. His mother, Kultida, is of mixed Thai, Chinese and Dutch background. His father was a mixture of African American, Chinese, and Native American. Perhaps Tiger is an outstanding example of "hybrid vigor." Barack Obama is another example. As our country becomes more of a genetic melting-pot, we will probably see greater athletes, writers, actors, artists and even greater presidents coming from these interracial marriages. But I digress.

From childhood Tiger was raised as a Buddhist and actively practiced his faith from childhood well into his adult career. He has attributed his deviations and infidelity to his losing track of Buddhism. He said that "Buddhism teaches us to stop following every impulse and to learn restraint. Obviously I lost track of what I was taught." (Wikipedia, op. cit.).His use of the term "learned restraint" suggests the internalization of behavioral norms and rules, based on the internalization of his father's behavior, modeling, and religious prohibitions. What happens to this early internalized regulation and makes it go astray later, is a crucial question. This is not the lack of internalization of controls that is typical of the psychopath; that is, a "lack of conscience."

Tiger's father, a golfer and college basketball player, started him on golf at age two. Between the age of three and eight he won several championships. He beat his father at golf from age eleven on.

The list of his wins and championships is endless. He graduated from Western High School in Anaheim, California at 18. He then got a golf scholarship at Stanford, majoring in economics. His determination, a common feature of the anomic, is shown by his winning even with a severe foot injury. He had also played for almost a year with a torn anterior cruciate ligament in his left knee. The countless hours of training and practice needed to achieve the pinnacle of golf also attests to his perseverance. Woods founded several charitable projects, including golf clinics. He also established Start Something, a program in character development.

In 2004 Tiger married Elin Nordegren. She was a Swedish former model, born to high status parents. Tiger and Elin had homes in Jackson, Wyoming; California, and Sweden. They also bought a $39 million residence on Jupiter Island, Florida, home to many professional golfers. They had a daughter in 2007, and then a son in 2009. They were divorced in 2010.

How did this remarkable individual fall from public (and corporate) grace? On November 25, 2009, *The National Enquirer* ran a story about Tiger having an extramarital affair with a Manhattan nightclub manager, Rachel Uchitel. (In 2011 she is training to be a private investigator!) A little over a day later, Woods smashed up his car, hitting a fire hydrant and a tree. His wife Elin got him out of the car by using a golf club. Within days, a San Diego cocktail waitress, Jaimee Grubbs, said that she had an affair with Tiger for over two years. She claimed a voice message from him said "Hey, it's Tiger, I need you to do me a huge favor. Can you please take your name off your phone? My wife went through my phone…You got to do this for me. Huge. Quickly. Bye."

Tiger then made the first of several public apologies. On December 11th he admitted to infidelity, and announced a hiatus from golf. His lawyers obtained an injunction in the United Kingdom to prevent the publication of any nude photos of him naked or having intercourse. "The following week, one of the women who had undertaken media interviews regarding her relationship with Woods admitted having taken photographs of Woods naked, on the pre-meditated premise that she would sell them if they ever broke up." (Wiki, op. cit.).

The day after Tiger's first statement of infidelity and apology, corporations started to cancel their endorsement arrangements. These included Accenture, Gillette, Tag Heuer, AT&T and Gatorade. *Golf Digest* cancelled its monthly golf instruction articles. "A December 2009 study by Christopher R. Knittel and Victor Stango, economics professors at the University of California at Davis, estimated that the shareholder loss caused by Woods' extramarital affairs to be between $5 billion and $12 billion."(Wiki, op. cit.).

The *National Enquirer* stated that Woods had confessed to his wife about having 120 affairs, in addition to having a one-night-stand with his neighbors' 21-year-old daughter Raychel Coudriet, whom he has known since she was 14. It is little wonder that his wife sued for divorce. Elin Nordegren got a settlement of about $100 million, and joint custody of their two children.

At this point, it might be appropriate to bring up the subject of the seeming lack of judgment involved in much of the behavior of anomics. Surely Tiger must have realized that porn stars and cocktail waitresses are not Mother Teresa in disguise. Woods is highly intelligent, as testified by his organizational ability, his numerous charitable and educational efforts, and his ability to convince profit-minded CEOs to use him for publicity. Hubris certainly helps to explain this paradox of stupid behavior in an intelligent individual.

We can understand the almost incredible stupidity of Eliot Spitzer who paid prostitutes for sex with a credit card, if we take into account the hubris of a very rich boy who never lacked for anything. This feeling of invincibility may also have led him to withdraw sums over $10,000 from his bank account, which is a well-known red flag. His political enemies had no trouble getting the goods on him.

Tiger, in a televised speech, said that "he had been unfaithful to his wife. He said he used to believe he was entitled to do whatever he wanted to do, and that, due to his success, normal rules did not apply to him." (Wiki, op. cit.). While this speech may have been written for him, it does express the hubris that is characteristic of the anomic. It also fits the picture of the careful planner who turns a blind eye to the eventual outcome of his behavior. Madoff knew, at some level of consciousness, that his Ponzi scheme would eventually fail, but he couldn't stop himself.

Hubris in its original sense of defying the gods, is implied in the stories of both Icarus and Niobe. If we can see the gods as projections of parental figures and promoters of the moral codes of society, then hubris can be defined as defying the moral codes of society. Don't fly too high or set yourself above others. Don't think your children are better and more beautiful than the children of others. A review of *The Icarus Syndrome: A History of American Hubris*, by Peter Beinart, was criticized by Geoffrey Wheatcroft (Wheatcroft, G. 2010) [Wheatcroft, Geoffrey, The New York Review of Books, November 11, 2010, Vol. LVII, No. 17, pp. 50-52.]

"He has just spent four hundred pages describing the consequences of "hubris," which is really misplaced optimism." (op. cit., p. 52).

Given the complex origin of the extreme behavior exhibited by those I have called "anomic personalities," this seems reductionist. The fact that our society is extremely optimistic and competitive sets the stage for unlimited striving for success. Our myth is "Anyone can become rich, or president, through hard work." If we look under the hood of the car, so to speak, the narcissistic manipulative striver is often a pessimist who craves attention, due to some early loss or psychic injury. Napoleon is a good example. Spitzer, on the other hand, had always lived in comparative luxury and had no obvious need to climb to the top, His optimism was born of the continuous rewards and good fortune that resulted from his birthright. His overconfidence was bred by opulence and seriatim successes.

But if we temporarily disregard the anomie of capitalism, the motor force of narcissistic injury, the complexities of sibling rivalry, the mythology of the American Dream, and other factors making for the endemic anomic personality, the contribution of the common error of misplaced optimism is worth discussing.

In a discussion of systematic errors in thinking of normal people, Kahneman (Kahneman, D. 2011) [Kahneman, Daniel, *Thinking, Fast and Slow*, Farrar, Straus & Giroux. 2011] gives top billing to "optimistic bias." In his review of the book, Jim Holt (Holt, J. 2011) ["Two Brains Running," The New York Times Book Review, November 27, 2011, pp. 16-17]s says "The planning fallacy is 'only one of the manifestations of a pervasive optimistic bias...which may well be the most significant of the cognitive biases." (p. 17). An example; people overestimate benefits, and underestimate cost, and tend to take on risky projects (call girls, securitized subprime mortgages?) If this optimistic bias is so pervasive, we then have to explain how it is that these anomic outliers seem to be prone to such *extreme* and *blind* optimism. Our sample is biased, for we see only those who have lost their optimism, for they have been "caught" with their hand in the cookie jar, or in *flagrante delicto*. Hubris, a central trait of the anomic personality, is of complex origin, as are many other components such as narcissism, need for admiration, fear of dying and manipulation of others. It is not simply common optimistic bias.

Hubris and a strong sense of entitlement are common among many of the prominent members of our society, and perhaps in all countries. A recent example is the case of Dominique Strauss-Kahn. Here is a prominent French economist, lawyer, and a potential candidate to run against Nicolas Sarkozy for the presidency of France. Instead of carrying the Socialist Party to victory, he was arrested on May 14th, 2011. He was accused of forcing a housekeeper to perform oral sex and to submit to anal sex in his $3000 a night room at the Sofitel Hotel in New York City. It turned out that the accuser, Nafissatou Diallo of Guinea, 32 years old, told her boyfriend, who was in jail in Arizona on drug charges, "Don't worry, this guy has lots of money. I know what I'm doing."

Soon after this revelation, and the discovery of numerous inconsistencies in Diallo's story, Strauss-Kahn was acquitted, but only after being walked in handcuffs before the paparazzi. This so-called "perp walk" (short for perpetrator) is a nasty American custom, in use when VIPs or notorious criminals are arrested. A second case of possible sexual assault by Strauss-Kahn brought by the writer Tristane Banon has been dismissed due to the French statute of limitations.

As in the case of both Tiger and Spitzer, there is no doubt of Strauss-Kahn's high intelligence. As Managing Director of the IMF (International Monetary Fund) he has had to make complicated decisions about funding whole nations during the recent worldwide financial meltdown. He has had to meet with heads of state in many countries. Yet his career has already been marked by several incidents of groping and extra-marital affaires. These were not major assaults, and were overlooked by the French, who have a reputation for protecting an aberrant leader. While supporters suggest that he was set up by his rival, Nicolas Sarkozy, his track record suggests he may be guilty of some of the charges.

Once an ordinary guy becomes prominent; a politician, a boss or CEO, a professor or teacher; anyone who may have power over a subordinate, do they necessarily turn into sexual predators?

"Power is a facilitator…It provides opportunities to men with certain appetites, but seldom changes personality in any fundamental way." (Levant, R.F. 2011) [Ronald F. Levant, psychologist at the University of Akron, and co-editor of *Men and Sex: New Psychological Perspectives,* quoted *in NYT,* Week in Review, 5/22/2011.] Tiger's confession of 120 women bedded during his brief marriage, Strauss-Kahn's history of woman-chasing, and Spitzer's dalliance with call girls, along with many professional athletes' incredible philandering, suggests that at this level of power and fame, marriage vows are honored more in the breach than in the observance. What stands out is the consistency of the behavior. The activity goes on until the Don Juan is caught, or till senescence sets in.

Another factor in the sexual anomic with his (or her) unlimited activity, is the apparent strong need in some individuals for stimulation. They are depressed, or have attention deficit disorder (ADHD) and they feel bored, even if they are very active. They seek thrills which can involve sex, crime, or dangerous activities (like hang-gliding, bungee jumping, mountain climbing, and other counterphobic activities.) Illicit sex is more stimulating for those who are in routine or unsatisfying sexual relationships. The demands for relating intimately with a mate may be more than some people can meet, and this seems particularly true of some high-profile men we have described. If you pay for sex, or forcibly take it, you do not have to consider the needs of your "partner." She is just an object, and the terms "slut," "whore," and "bitch" denote her sub-human status.

The violence involved in some extreme sexual activity partakes of the criminality involved in Factor 2 discussed in Chapter 2. Most of the sexual anomics do not cross over into physical violence and criminal behavior, but the very act of sexual intercourse is to some degree violent. The extreme narcissist, the charismatic manipulator, may be too self-absorbed to even get involved with the other sex (that is, women). Yet there are suggestions that many of the sexual anomics, the high-scoring ladies' men, engage in rough sex. This is seldom written up in the pages of *The New York Times,* but Strauss-Kahn's approach, according to his young French interviewer, is a case in point.

Tiger seems to partake of Factor 2. While he has no record of juvenile delinquency or arrests, he apparently favors some of the more aggressive aspects of his activity off the golf course. Tiger's porn star mistress, Joslyn James, released e-mails from Tiger and from Tiger's associate, Byron Bell. "Rough sex" is probably more suited to the young and to athletes in top physical shape. (The Huffington Post, March 28, 2010)
["http://www.huffingtonpost.com/2010/03/18/tiger-woods-joslyn-james_n_504087.html]

A sampling of e-mails reveals further denigration of his sex objects. By animalization ("bitch") the woman can be mistreated, since she is considered a sub-human.

"The e-mails follow in a string of salacious text messages, allegedly sent to James by Tiger. ("Joslyn James releases e-mails fingering Tiger Woods pal in sex meetings" Haggerty, J. 2010.) [Haggerty, J. 2010.3/24/2010Cultural Oddities Examiner]

Who were some of Tiger's lovers? Did they have any particular characteristics, other than their willingness to have sex for pay and a good set of physical proportions? Scanning the blogs turns up Cori Rist, "blonde bombshell, a 31-year-old Manhattan club-goer," and Jamie Jungers "26, a lingerie model." Add Jaimee Grubbs, "a Las Vegas cocktail waitress." These women do not have professional degrees, but they are probably professionals.

Among the 120 women Tiger claimed to have bedded, a dozen or more came forward soon after his car crash and first confession. Several had been waiting for the time they could sue him for some of that billion he had earned.

While Tiger's claim to 120 liaisons may seem astounding to the reader, particularly those inhabiting the rapidly disappearing middle-class, he doesn't even make it on a list of the top ten sexual athletes. (Alfred Kinsey, the famous sex researcher, was reputed to have quipped that if a boy from the slums had not had intercourse by age twelve, he was either retarded or on his way to college. Levels of sexual activity probably increase as one looks at decreasing levels of social class or socioeconomic status.) This list is obviously based on hearsay and the braggadocio of those listed. At least four of these champions are unknown to me. Four are musicians or singers. Two are star athletes, and two are movie stars (or were stars, in the case of Charlie Sheen).

10. Bill Wyman (Rolling Stones bassist) - 1,000
9. Earvin (Magic) Johnson (basketball star) - 1,000
8. Lemmy Kilmister (Motorhead frontman) - 1,200
7. Jack Nicholson (actor) - 2,000
6. Ilie Nastase (tennis star) - 2,500
5. Engelbert Humperdinck (singer) - 3,000
4. Julio Iglesias (singer) - 3,000
3. Gene Simmons (Kiss frontman) - 4,600
2. Charlie Sheen (actor) - 5,000
1. Umberto Billo (Venetian hotel porter) - 8,000

("Sheen Only No. 2 on 'Living Sex Legends' List," Zap2It.com | May 30, 2006) (http://www.zap2it.com/tv/news/zap-charliesheenmaximlivingsexl egends,0,5057260.story.)

The list was published in *Maxim* magazine, and was surely not peer reviewed. I was upset to find that Wilt ("The Stilt") Chamberlain was not on the list, with 20,000 ladies to his credit. In Wilt's biography he wrote that "At my age that equals out to having sex with one or two women a day every day since I was fifteen years old." Perhaps athletes have more energy than just plain folks, but this would not account for singers and actors, who don't depend on their physical prowess for success.

Can we make any generalizations from the fact that Charlie Sheen is the runner-up on the list? Certainly not. He, in contrast to his fellow Don Juans, has been on a downward path for several years. He is drug-addicted, is an alcoholic, and has often been in violent confrontations with co-workers. He has lost his role as the star of *Two and a Half Men,* a once popular television show. To my knowledge, the other nine sexanomics have all had reasonably successful careers.

The leader of the list is a true "dark horse," an unknown coming up from behind in the race, to win. Surprisingly, the top lothario isn't anyone rich or famous at all, until now. The men's magazine claims that lowly Venetian hotel porter Umberto Billo has charmed 8,000 women to his bed. 'They crossed oceans to see me,' he boasts. While guest satisfaction is the randy Italian's trademark, his work ethic isn't. *Maxim* reports that he has ben fired after getting it on took precedence over his paid duties. 'Sometimes he was too exhausted to carry the guests' luggage,' says his ex-boss." (Sheen, op. cit.)

The list of leading Casanovas suggests a strong factor in the etiology of sexual anomie. The singers, the actors, and the star athletes all had great public exposure. They were seen on television and movie screens. They were heard on radio, CDs, iPhone, and all the other gadgets that carry pop culture to Americans. They have money, and they are in contact with lots of women. The list is a list of celebrities, and we are a nation of celebrity worshipers. This includes quasi-worship of our presidents, such as Franklin Roosevelt, Reagan, and Kennedy. I was struck by the blind quality of this admiration. A recent biography of John Kennedy (*Jack Kennedy, Elusive Hero,* by Chris Matthews, was criticized by Andrew Sullivan on the talk show *Real Time with Bill Maher* on November 12th, 2011. Matthews hosts *Hardball with Chris Matthews* on MSNBC, and Sullivan blogs *The Dish* on

The Daily Beast. The other panel members were visibly upset by Sullivan's attack on Kennedy as a "war-monger," and Maher had to interrupt the argument, which was getting heated.

Attachment theory was first elaborated by John Bowlby, a British psychiatrist. (Bowlby, J. (1973). [Bowlby, J., *Separation, Anxiety and Anger,* Vol. II. New York: Basic Books, 1973] He saw that it was necessary for the child to form a lasting bond or attachment to the mother, and if this bond was not properly formed, it could have serious consequences for later emotional development. The role of "peek-a-boo" in reassuring the child of the mother's return and availability, and of "transitional objects" such as pacifiers or security blankets, were steps toward eventual independence. The attachment, however, had to remain even after independence was established.

The original attachment to mother is not a popular subject in current popular songs, though it was in earlier songs and poetry we may now consider sentimental. However, the attachment ("identification attachment") to a male or female lover or spouse is still very much in evidence, in popular songs, plays, novels, film and television. My familiarity with pop music ends somewhere just before the advent of the Gregorian chant, yet I must admit to some acquaintance with the songs of Rodgers and Hart. These lyrics show the attachment to the face (especially eyes and mouth), voice, and touch, of the love object. Some examples follow:

> "With a song in my heart
> I behold your adorable face
> And at the sound of your voice
> Heaven opens its portals to me"

("With a Song in My Heart" is a show tune from the 1929 Rodgers and Hart musical *Spring is Here.*)

> "Grand to see your face, feel your touch,
> Hear your voice say I'm all your own"

> "I wanted love, and here it wa
> Shining out of your eyes."

("I Didn't Know What Time It Was,"
1939, Rodgers & Hart, "Too Many Girls.")

"I'm wild again, Beguiled again,
A simpering, whimpering child again,
Bewitched, bothered and bewildered am I"
(1940, Rodgers & Hart, "Pal Joey")

In "Bewitched," Hart captured the infantilization that accompanies falling in love. Becoming "a child again" may be a replay of the strong feelings of the imprinting and very first attachment soon after birth.

In thinking about our adult attachment to a wide range of celebrities and public figures, I wondered about the incredible power of these feelings. How was it possible for adult blind devotion to ignore the shortcomings and even the criminality of some of their beloved leaders and "stars?" One would expect a desperate attempt to hold onto a positive image of parents to be widespread in children, because of their utter dependency on their parents for survival. ("Christine Beauchamp, 'in (anon.) *quotation from Morton Prince.)* Christine Beauchamp's story illustrates this "desperate attempt." to maintain the illusion that her mother loves her.)

"Ms. B. was a nervous impressionable child, given to daydreaming and living in her imagination. Her mother exhibited a great dislike to her, and for no reason, excepting that the child resembled her father in looks...her presence having been ignored by her mother except on occasions of reprimand. On the other hand she herself idealized her mother, bestowing upon her an almost morbid affection; and believing that the fault was her own, and that her mother's lack of affection was due to her own imperfections, she gave herself up to introspection, and concluded that if she could only purify herself and make herself worthy, her mother's affection would be given her." (Prince, M. (1906). [Prince, M. *The Dissociation of a Personality* (2nd edition, 1969, is a reprint of original 1906 edition.). Westport, CT: Greenwood Press.]

Similarly in adults, the positive image of leaders, politicians, actors, singers and star athletes is maintained, even wholly constructed, despite public evidence to the contrary. (See *De L'Amour* by Stendhal, 1822) who first revealed the strong role of construction of the beloved by the lover).

It is clearly seen in the fact that about half the nation votes against its own economic interests. The search for an explanation as to why this maladaptive behavior persists is the subject of my book, (anon.). An additional explanation or contributing factor occurred to me recently.

A while ago I read a newspaper article describing the short life-span of our ancestors, the Cro-Magnons, and the Neanderthals, with whom they apparently interbred. They lived on average not much more than 30 years, barely enough time to mature and reproduce. During the last third of their lives, from 20 to 30, they would have been in "old age," and not as capable of defending and nourishing their children. Many of the skeletons show evidence of wounds and broken bones due to the rigors of that Darwinian world. They had to mate at what would be early adolescence for us, and raise and protect their children when they themselves on average were in their teens.

"One of the more interesting things we now think about Neandertal is that they had a relatively short life expectancy. Based on a profile of all the Neanderthals we know about, only 10% were aged 35 or over. That contrasts to a figure of about 50% for modern hunter/gatherers." ("The Neandertal Story" ["The Neandertal Story" www.mesacc.edu/dept/d10/asb/origins/hominid.../neandertal.html]

"The oldest Neanderthals appear to be just over 30." (*Neanderthal Study Guide: A Few Important Facts. archaeology.about.com/od/hominid ancestors/a/neander_2.htm*)

According to archeological estimates, half of all Neanderthals (the archetypal caveman living one hundred thousand to thirty-five thousand years ago) and Upper Paleolithic homo sapiens (beginning forty thousand years ago and including Cro-Magnon man) died by the time they were twenty, with only a few living beyond age fifty...However, like their predecessors, the vast majority of Cro-Magnons continued to die at an average age of eighteen to twenty.
(Butler, R. 2008) ["Dr. Robert Butler '49 Keeps Going", excerpt from *The Longevity Revolution: The Benefits and Challenges of Living a Long Life.* New York: Public Affairs, 2008. http://www.college.columbia.edu/cct/jan_feb09/webexclusive/dr_robert_butler_49_keeps_ going]

The absolute necessity of bonding between mother and child in a world of rival groups and predatory animals was undoubtedly even greater than the need for attachment in modern times. In an article reviewing *Mothers and Others,* by Sarah Blaffer Hrdy, the anthropologist Melvin Konner, in "It Does Take a Village," shows how Bowlby's theory of attachment was influenced by the work of Konrad Lorenz on imprinting. (Konner, M 2008) [Konner, Merlvin. "It Does Take A Village." New York Review of Books," 12/8/2008] To give an example:

When I was in Bali, I saw a boy of about ten holding a long bamboo pole with a square of white cloth attached to its end. Following every movement of the cloth was a group of at least two hundred ducks. They had been exposed to the cloth immediately after hatching, and like chicken hatchlings, were imprinted and bonded to that cloth "mother." If the mother duck had been there when they hatched, the ducklings would have been imprinted and attached to her in the same way.

Konner gives a good description of the survival value of attachment and imprinting:

"For our own ancestors, attachment was evolution's answer to a world of hungry predators—hawks above, leopards and snakes below—who could make a living at the expense of monkey infants much more easily if those infants were alone; thus the relentless press of natural selection urging infants and caregivers to be together. The result was a bond whose absence or interruption could cause suffering and psychological damage, especially for the infant." (Koner, M. 2011) [Konner, M. "It Does Take a Village," *Then New York Review of Books,* 12/8/2011, pp. 37-8]

The importance of strong early attachment for survival of infants in a dangerous world may have left us with that same strong inherited need for attachment in a much less dangerous world. In the additional 30 to 60 years of our modern life span we continue to attach to leaders, movie stars, athletes, singers and musicians.

The role of physical contact between mother and infant has been shown to be crucial for the formation of attachment. Newborns are placed on the mother's stomach soon after birth to start the process. The importance of bodily contact was shown by the experiments of Harry Harlow, who exposed baby rhesus monkeys to soft terry cloth and hard wire surrogate "mothers," each supplying milk. The babies clung to the cloth mothers in preference to the hard wire surrogate mothers when under stress. When not stressed, even if milk was available from the wire but not from the cloth mother, they favored the cloth mother.

Rene Spitz (Spitz et. al. 1946) [Spitz, R. A., & Wolf, K. M. Anaclitic depression: an inquiry into the genesis of psychiatric conditions in early childhood. II. *Psychoanalytic Study of the Child*, (2), 313-342. 1946]. showed that children in an orphanage wasted away from lack of bonding and the absence of the stimulus of physical contact.

In later research, negative brain and physiological changes were found to be associated with a lack of touch and grooming in monkeys. (karger.com) [http://content.karger.com/ProdukteDB/produkte.asp?Aktion=Show Fulltext&ProduktNr=224107&Ausgabe=229365&ArtikelNr=71465]

Moreover, the immune systems of touch-deprived animals were compromised, and their antibody levels were low. (Landenslager, M.L. et al.1993)

[Laudenslager ML, Rasmussen KLR, Berman CM, Suomi SJ, and Berger CB. Specific antibody levels in free-ranging rhesus monkeys: relationships to plasma hormones, cardiac parameters, and early behavior. Developmental Psychology. 1993; 26: 407-420.]

Of broader interest is the persistence of attachment in spite of the lack of reward from authority figures. This is maladaptive behavior, and is seen in the case of the poor and minorities who vote against their own economic, health, and educational interests. Their attachment to demagogic or authoritarian figures is the triumph of emotion over cognition. In the case of the baby monkeys, even the biological need for (or conditioned response to) food (milk) is overridden by the emotional attachment to the cloth mother. In some cases, then, attachment can be lethal, or have a negative survival value.

What happened when the life-span suddenly became 50 years, around the time of the industrial revolution, and then suddenly became 80 years plus with the advent of better medical care and food supply? The attachment to mother may have been laid down for survival value, but its protective function carried over in attachment to figures outside the family after age 15 or 20 must have been diminished.

While hypotheses in evolutionary psychology about the "hard-wiring" of early man's behavior are often speculative of necessity (you can't observe cave men) it seems to me that the prolonged (adult) attachment, (in its most primitive form of uncritical bonding) is often dysfunctional in our society. While successful secure bonding in infancy is probably crucial for sustaining the marital bond, blind attachment to movie stars, athletes, singers, and hero worship of presidents, generals, or even religious figures, does not make for autonomy. In a democracy, the selection of political figures has to be made as much on the basis of issues as possible, not on the basis of physical attractiveness or charisma of candidates. Prolonged attachment, hard-wired if you will, may have made modern man into the perpetual adolescent. He looks to demagogic leaders, is swayed by slogans, and sucks on the television tit for his pacifier. (P.S. I love TV serials, such as *The Affair, Homeland, or The Americans.*)

That a professional golfer can make a billion dollars, 2500 times the annual salary ($400,000) of the president, is incredible. The president gets two terms of four years, for a total of eight years, so he gets $3,200,000 in salary. Tiger gets 312 times that in his brief career. It is a form of idolatry, enhanced by the advertising skills of big business (Gillette, Accenture, General Motors, and Gatorade).

Attachment, which has crucial survival value for the infant, can be lethal for the adult. The attachment to dictators such as Mussolini, Hitler, and Stalin, or more recently to Saddam Hussein (Iraq), Muammar al Gaddafi (Libya), Hosni Mubarak (Egypt), Ali Abdullah Saleh (Yemen), and Bashar al Assad (Syria) in the Middle East, has cost the freedom and death of countless millions. Many dictators oppress their people, such as Kim Jong-Il, (North Korea) who recently died. He is succeeded by his son, Kim Jong-Un, who follows in his father's footsteps, including public executions and sending people to political prison camps. It took World Wat II to break that grip of attachment to Hitler in Germany and to Hirohito in Japan.

What about the attachment of the male college grad to the football team he never made? Football coaches make millions, ($30 million at Penn State) while their student-players get almost nothing, and the teachers get tiny salaries by comparison. The adult male attachment to beloved alma mater and her team is perverting our basic values. Well, it does raise funds and adds to the college endowment.

What are some of the factors that enable a Tiger Woods, other great athletes, singers, actors and some politicians to become so extremely sexually active? Certainly, public exposure on stage, screen or TV is involved. Also important is the role of money. This makes them attractive to women. Physical fitness and attractiveness has helped propel various types of "stars" to fame, and these are top considerations in women's mate selection, along with the ability to provide financial security for raising children. A culture that emphasizes success and competition contributes to the development of "stars;" a zero sum culture where few "make it" and the 99%, as the recent Occupy Wall Street slogan goes, are failures. The male with power is also attractive to women, and that doesn't necessarily mean physical power. Henry Kissinger was not exactly an Adonis or a Hercules, yet women flocked to him. He once said "Power is an aphrodisiac."

.In keeping with my thesis, a crucial factor in women's widespread attachment to star males, which enables the activity of male sexual athletes, is the state of sexual anomie in our society and in many similar European countries. (This does not mean to exclude men's similar attachment to stars and authority figures, which I suggest is hard-wired. Women's attachments are also hard wired, but these other factors act along with attachment to make star males attractive to them.)

A review of a recent Broadway play seems to indicate a growing awareness of the role of sexual anomie in producing sexual outliers or addicts. The central figure of the play "Shame" is Brandon, whose compulsive sexual activity includes pick-ups, prostitutes, Internet chats, and masturbation during work hours, depending on what is available. His sister cuts herself and sounds like a borderline. The reviewer says:

> "The New York they find themselves in is a melancholy and seductive place, where easy money and relaxed sexual mores combine to produce an atmosphere of general anomie brightened by a few glimmers of comic possibility." (Scott, A.O., 2011) ["Only One Thing On His Mind," A.O. Scott, *The New York Times*, December 2, 2011, pp C1 & C18.]

I think Emile Durkheim would be pleased to see that after more than one hundred years a well-known reviewer has used his term, anomie, to describe the deregulation of sexual activity ("relaxed sexual mores")

(Durkheim, E. 1897) [Durkheim, E. *Le Suicide*. Paris: Alcan, 1897.] Durkheim's discovery that unmarried men had much higher rates of suicide than married men led him to posit that marriage held men's appetites in check. Sexual anomie was a state of society which allowed for the pursuit of limitless goals. Bedding an infinite number of women would not produce happiness, but instead eventual frustration. (How interesting that Freud and Hobbes also viewed mankind as having sexual and aggressive drives that society needed to control. All three had an essentially "dark view.")

The response of Joe Six-Pack might be, "Well, if bedding all those women is frustration, then the heck with happiness!" Remember, not all the sexual anomics get in trouble. Many of them are happy campers, working their way through bevies of women. A Charlie Sheen may suffer from drugs and narcissistic rages, and his peccadilloes don't seem to make him happy. Tiger, on the other hand, was presumably happy and functioning well until his extra-marital philandering came out and he lost his sponsors and his wife. Spitzer would have had a great political career, but lost it due to carelessness in his sexual contacts. He didn't seem unhappy in pursuing his limitless sexual goals, until he got caught out (probably by his political enemies, with the help of "dirty trickster" Roger Stone.

Yet so much misery is associated with sexual hyperactivity, especially for the married male, (not to mention his spouse). Herman Cain (CEO of Godfather's Pizza!) lost his place among the Republican presidential candidates for the 2012 election, due to his various dalliances, gropings, and a thirteen year affair. Bill Clinton was impeached for his liaison with Monica Lewinsky (one of a long string of women) and he didn't seem unhappy until his political enemies (Andrew Mellon Scaife and his hired legal hatchet men) attacked him. Gary Hart had to drop out of a presidential race, because of the outing of his affair. CEOs have been fired for extramarital affairs. Harry Stonecipher, the CEO of the Boeing Corporation, had to step down because he was having an affair with a fifty-eight-year-old woman, an executive in "Accounts Receivable." For shame! You've got to be kidding!

Durkheim's explanation of the feeling state accompanying sexual anomie is similar to the frustration of Tantalus reaching for his ever-receding grapes. More about this later. (How smart the Greeks were, until they started paying with euros.) The goal is ever out of reach. Today this seems to be only one of the possible emotions accompanying sexual hyperactivity. The frustration and depression for most of the cases that get great publicity is because the Lothario loses his job, his wife, his children, or his money because he is sued by a call girl and her politically-backed lawyer. And yet, even over one hundred years after Durkheim found that French unmarried males had higher suicide rates than married males, their modern American counterparts show a similar disparity.

While we are on the topic of sexual anomics, why does it seem so difficult to find a list of hypersexual women? We seldom hear about a female Don Juan, although Elizabeth Taylor's eight marriages (and seven husbands) seem to set a record for Hollywood actresses. But she was adhering to societal norms, even marrying Richard Burton twice. A website, (Gabriel, Philo, 2011) ["Top Ten Most Promiscuous Women," is a product of Yahoo Voices. (Philo Gabriel, contributor, February 26, 2011)] I am so out of the sexual loop that I don't even recognize Pamela Anderson (star of *Baywatch*), and Naomi Campbell (British supermodel), I am familiar with others on the list; starting chronologically with Cleopatra, Catherine the Great, Clara Bow, (the "It" girl), Joan Crawford (dubbed "Crone Jawford" by a dear departed friend of mine), Marilyn Monroe, Paris Hilton, and Madonna. The only figures given are between twenty to thirty lovers. If true, then the ten most promiscuous women of all time don't begin to measure up to the Lothario list. Note that no Asians, Africans, or Latinas are mentioned. The research is unreliable. It seems as if women are less apt to boast about their triumphs, unlike the boys in the locker rooms.

Modern women are less likely to profit psychologically from marriage. Over 100 years ago, Durkheim's married males (Durkheim, E. op. cit.) profited by their marriages (by having lower suicide rates than unmarried males) while his French females did not show a lowering of suicide rates because of marriage. Similarly, in rates of mental disorder, unmarried males by age 45 were at high risk, while women, (never married, single, divorced, and married) showed no difference in risk of mental disorder by marital status. (anon.), (anon.) Except for the greater opprobrium attached to female than male dalliance, women might well be marrying less and dallying more.

We have digressed from Tiger and his anomic (deregulated) *sexual* behavior (peccadilloes), to speculations about the role of life-span and attachment in hero worship (athletes, actors, singers, and political leaders), and men's and women's leading sexual outliers. We must use the next chapter to explore the world of deregulated *financial* behavior. That world is the home of Bernie and Dick, so we should examine it before focusing specifically on their lives.

CHAPTER FOUR

CAPITALISM GONE WILD:
1% VERSUS 99%
SOCIAL AND PERSONAL DEREGULATION
THE DARK TRIAD
THE GRAPES OF TANTALUS

Social and Personal Deregulation

Donald, Tiger, Bernie and Dick are the members of our quadumvirate (a. We looked at a brief history of Tiger's accomplishments in the world of sports and at his group of four powerful people) representing the Anomic Personality. Donald came first, because he's the worst exploits in the sexual sphere. While he may stand as a symbol of sexual anomie (sexual deregulation) in our society, the deregulation of the economy puts us in a much greater danger of collapse as a nation. (In France, the peccadilloes of national leaders don't seem to throw the nation into a tizzy.) The collapse of our financial institutions, our banks, our stock and commodity markets, and our corporations can very well cause a national crisis.

So before taking a look at Bernie Madoff's and Dick Cheney's life stories and why they are anomic avatars (in Chapters Five and Six), I want to discuss in detail the deregulation of our behavior in the economic sphere. How has it produced the *excessive striving and rampant competition* that are the hallmarks of our formerly center-right capitalist society, now become alt-right? Bernie and Dick partake more directly in the financial and economic world than Tiger. Though Tiger was sponsored by corporate millions, he was never a CEO. Bernie, on the other hand, was directly involved in the stock market. Madoff Securities developed a computer program to give stock quotes. That became the National Association Securities Dealers Automated Quotations, or NASDAQ, and after some time Madoff became president of the board of directors for the NASDAQ stock exchange. Bernie banked $400 million in a personal account at the Chase Bank. In addition, he banked the funds he stole from his clients who thought they were investing in the market. "A series of Madoff accounts were linked under the umbrella of a centralized "concentration account" known as the "703 Account" that received the overwhelming majority of funds that Madoff's victims invested with Madoff Securities. The account at its peak in August 2008 held about $5.6 billion, the U.S. said." (Hurtado, P., et al.,2014) ["JPMorgan to Pay $2.6 Billion Over Madoff Scheme Lapses." Patricia Hurtado, Greg Farrell and Hugh Son. 6/8/2014] The bank turned a "blind eye" to the source of his illegal millions.

Dick was the CEO of Halliburton Corporation, a company that made tremendous profits by providing oil drilling equipment installed in Iraq after our invasion. As Vice President, he greatly increased the power of the G.O.P. and the wealthy 1% through an "Imperial Presidency."

In this chapter we can see how our "culturally patterned defect," The Anomic Personality, easily morphs into "wrongdoing," antisocial behavior, and major crime (that which is punishable *by law*.) We'll look at the Mafia and juvenile delinquent gangs as examples of "strain" a condition arising when those social groups and classes that are blocked from upward mobility turn to means of achieving success goals that *presumably* are not legitimate in our society. We ask why, despite being "blocked" from upward mobility, and being well aware of the economic and other inequalities they suffer, their poll responses show them to be strongly conservative. This raises the question I have asked before (anon,) 2009) *Why* do the majority (or almost the majority) of our public vote against their own best interests?

We'll also consider White Collar Crime. That's where Bernie and Dick fit in. They were not blocked by the social class structure from achieving success, the American Dream. Tiger might have been blocked, since he rose from non-White minority status, but he overcame this great disadvantage. The effect of wealthy donors on our political and economic system will be discussed. How did we get to the 1% versus the 99% level of wealth and income inequality? Bernie and Dick were both involved in the world of finance when the banks became stockbrokers and thus helped trigger the 2008 recession. Their criminal behavior is clear: the Ponzi scheme and the widely presumed motivation for the Iraq invasion, to bolster the oil-drilling profits of the Halliburton Corporation. More wrongdoing on the part of Dick could be cited, such as the promotion of torture, (waterboarding) or his false claim on August 26, 2002 that Saddam Hussein had "weapons of mass destruction." The outing of Valerie Plame, whose husband refuted the WMD false intelligence, was arranged by "Scooter" Libby, Dick's factotum. Revealing the identity of a Federal Agent is a crime, and Libby was the fall guy for his boss. He served 30 months, and was fined $250,000. Bernie and Dick operated at a time of widespread fraud and crime by the banks, by hedge fund directors. This financial Armageddon," "a war of all against all," is still with us.

We must ask, how do Tiger, Bernie and Dick fit into the "Dark Triad" of narcissism, Machiavellianism and psychopathy? How does the Anomic personality develop? How do our parental practices, our competitive high-schools and colleges, and our winner-take-all society help to create and foster the Anomic Personality? Is wrongdoing and antisocial behavior, often morphing into punishable crime, now the new norm (the tacitly approved model of behavior)?

Other questions we will try to cover include: How does anomie (deregulation, especially in the financial world) help to create anomic personalities? Are anomic personalities in fact a *good* adaptation to our *bad* state of financial anomie (limitless striving for financial gain)? Why is "tantalizing" a good description of the primary emotion or feeling state of the anomic personality? How are the idée fixe and grandiosity connected to the anomic personality? Are "irrational exuberance" or "bright-sidedness" common human cognitive errors?

I chose Donald, Tiger, Bernie and Dick because they are anomic outliers. They are the avatars, the exemplars, the archetypes that I think best represent the goals and motor force of the American male (and to a lesser extent, the goals of American women).Those overriding goals are sex, money and power. Since their sexual, financial or political behavior was so extreme, they made good examples of what societal deregulation can look like when it affects individuals.

While their behavior may seem unfortunate, illegal, or immoral, the rest of the country is not far behind them in similar activities.

The end result of capitalism gone wild, without the constraints needed to give all our citizens their fair share and equal opportunity, is a constant striving for gain, success, and keeping up with (or even ahead of) the Joneses. As I said before, Max Weber claimed that this all started with the Protestant Ethic; a desire to achieve a state of grace by showing God that you worked hard and had many cows and worldly goods. This hard work he called "worldly asceticism."

Along came Thorstein Veblen (Veblen, T. 1934, 1899) [Veblen, T. *The Theory of the Leisure Class,* 1899, 1934 ed. New York: The Modern Library] his concept of "conspicuous consumption," an extension of the display of worldly goods, and consumerism. Today everyone has to have the latest iPod, TV set, headphones, computer, clothing, car, home, and so forth, but not everyone has the money to purchase these items. They fall behind their neighbors, (or see minorities rise) and many are downwardly mobile. They see the income disparity between the 1% and the 99%. As Obama said in 2008:

"You go into some of these small towns in Pennsylvania, and like a lot of small towns in the Midwest, the jobs have been gone now for 25 years and nothing's replaced them. . . And it's not surprising, then they get bitter, they cling to guns or religion or antipathy to people who aren't like them or anti-immigrant sentiment or anti-trade sentiment as a way to explain their frustrations." (Obama, B. 2008) [Obama, Barack. Remarks to wealthy California backers at a San Francisco fund-raiser, April 6th, 2008]

He might have been talking about a large portion of the nation, and in 2015, even about the middle class.

Since 1987, the Pew Research Center has found that around three quarters of the public think that the rich are getting richer and the poor are getting poorer. While income disparity has accelerated in the last few decades after World War II, this widening gap doesn't always seem to translate into public opinion. Andrew Kohut says "People don't necessarily want to take money from the wealthy; they just want a better chance to get rich themselves."(Kohut, A. 2012) [Kohut, A. "Don't Mind the Gap." *The New York Times,* January 26, 2012] Anger was focused on the bailout of the auto industry, even though the same people said they wanted to protect the "job creators." Just over half said that the bank bailouts were wrong. These opinions do not seem to mobilize the public to take political action to improve their lot. One explanation is that they believe they will one day become millionaires, and at that future date they will not want to be heavily taxed. This phenomenon of "irrational exuberance" (coined by Alan Greenspan, former Chairman of the Federal Reserve Bank, economic guru, and an early disciple of Ayn Rand!) is a general tendency of human cognition, discussed previously. In earlier times, people used to call it "hope."

A closer look at the answers to the poll questions suggests that increased depression, a shift from internal to external locus of control, and increased political alienation may all be at work.("For the public, it's not about class warfare, but fairness." 3/12/2012, (http://www.people-press. org/2012/03/02/for-the-public-its-not-about-class-warfare-but-fairness/)

First let's look at some responses that have remained fairly constant from 1994 to 2012 of the "helpless-hopeless" variety, pointing to depression, and external locus of control. These people see no future, and feel controlled by outside forces, rather than by their own inner goals and judgments. For example, "Success in life is pretty much determined by forces outside of our control." In 1994 18% agreed, and in 2012 19% agreed. There is no change here, despite the worst depression since the 1930s. Similarly, there is little change in response to "Everyone has it in their own power to succeed." (79% to 75%, only a slight drop.) However, 10% changes in agreement with two statements seem more in touch with current economic realities. "Most people who want to get ahead can make it if they're willing to work hard." (a drop from 68% to 58% agreement). "Hard work and determination are no guarantee of success for most people." (A rise in agreement from 30% to 40%).

The Pew reports (2009 and 2011) found high agreement with statements about economic unfairness and inequality of income and power. "Too much power is in the hands of a few rich people and large corporations" (71% agree). "The rich just keep getting richer, the poor get poorer." (71%) The country's economic system unfairly favors the wealthy." (61%). This high level of agreement with fairly radical statements would seem to support Andrew Kohut's feeling that there is a gap between opinion (and feelings?) and political action.

But Andrew Kohut could be wrong in his interpretation of the survey responses; namely that the anger expressed doesn't result in political action.

There has been a recent surge of political action and anger directed at the banks, at Wall Street, at Congress, at Obama and his administration, at gays, immigrants, and at women (evidenced by a tidal wave of anti-abortion and anti-contraception legislation and proposals. The Occupy Wall Street movement in major cities can hardly be discounted as a minor protest. Its lack of central leadership, its ill-defined goals, and the advent of the 2012 elections virtually wiped out its media coverage since December, 2011.

Whence this groundswell of protest on both the left and right? A lot of it seems to be about money. The Tea Partiers rail against "elites" but their support comes from the Koch brothers, and Rupert Murdoch, three of the richest (elite) men in the world. The presidential campaign brought out the worst evidence of our nation's "pay to play" politics. The Supreme Court's decision in "Citizens United" has opened the floodgates of money into PACS (political action committees).The rich can now write unlimited checks to these PACS, without having to hide their donations' purpose by giving to single issue organizations. Millions are just chicken feed for these very wealthy donors. Sheldon Adelson and his wife each gave five million to Newt Gingrich on top of other money for the 2012 presidential campaign. He is the CEO of the Las Vegas Sands Corp. His money comes from the hotel, night club, and gambling.

Foster Friess, the wealthy benefactor of the Rick Santorum-supporting super PAC, is a born–again Christian. His self-made fortune, acquired through careful market investments, is estimated at half a billion. His comment on contraception embarrassed even Rick Santorum, the major recipient of Friess' largess at that time, who called it "a bad off-color joke\."

"And this contraceptive thing, my gosh, it's so–it's such–inexpensive, you know, back in my days, they used Bayer Aspirin for contraception. The gals put it between their knees and it wasn't that costly." (Lucy Madison, 2012) [Lucy Madison, CBS News 2/17/2012]

The Koch family fortune was founded on a new method of cracking oil to make gasoline. David and Charles Koch are the two brothers out of four still with the Koch Industries. The annual corporate profits are estimated to be a hundred billion dollars. Since the 1980's the Koch's have given 100 million to such conservative or libertarian organizations as the Cato Institute, the Heritage Foundation, Americans for Prosperity and Freedom Works. They have been the major support of the Tea Party.

The Citizens United decision has made it easy for the Koch brothers to come out of hiding, and make their right wing political donations openly.

The Koch agenda is crystal clear. It is faith-based, opposing abortion and contraception, and supports the denial of climate change by attacking scientists who work in that field. Of course, those whose billions come from oil want to deny that fossil fuel is creating massive changes in our atmosphere, our biodiversity, and eventually in our land mass due to the rise of the oceans in mid-century by an estimated three feet or more.

There are many other wealthy GOP donors. All told, the group, Restore Our Future, raised about $43 million from just 470 individuals and organizations in 2011 and the first quarter of 2012. Bob Perry (CEO of Perry Homes) gave three million. Seven others gave one million each, including Robert Mercer (Renaissance Technologies), John Paulson (George W. Bush's former economic advisor), and Paul Singer. The donors are typically CEOs or hedge fund managers. Mitt Romney's former colleagues at Bain Capital contributed a total of $750,000; William Koch, the brother of Charles and David, gave $1 million personally or through Oxbow Carbon, his energy company. (Donors, 2012) [Donors to Restore Our Future, 2012, http://www.opensecrets.org/outsidespending/contrib. php?cmte=C00490045&type=A]

There were wealthy Democratic contributors, though two of the usually most active, George Soros and Peter Singer, did not contribute as much in 2012 compared to their largesse in 2004. Priorities USA Action, a super PAC supporting the president's re-election, reported $2 million in February donations, group officials said, including $1 million from the television host Bill Maher." That is far from the $6.6 million the pro-Mitt Romney super PAC raised in January 2012. (super-pacs-donors) [http://www.huffingtonpost.com/2012/03/14/super-pacs-donors-500000-dollars_n_1339169.html]

The composition of the large donors to political campaigns seems to have changed between the 2012 and the 2016 campaigns. There is a growing concentration of extremely wealthy donors, and they gave predominantly to the GOP candidates. There were 158 families that gave $250,000 or more through June 30th, 2015. Of these, 138 (87%) gave to Republican candidates, compared to only 13% giving to Democrat candidates. If the 200 families who gave more than $100,000 are added to the 158, these

358 families gave more than half of the money contributed early in the 2016 presidential election campaign. (Confessore, N. 2015) [Confessore, N. et al., "The Families Funding the 2016 Presidential Election." *The New York Times,* 10/10/2015).]

Of great interest is the distribution of wealthy donors among various industries. Of the 158 highest donors, 64 (40%) came from finance (hedge funds, private equity or venture capital), 17 from natural resources (oil & gas), and 15 from real estate and construction. (Confessore, N., *supra.*) This mirrors a shift from "old money" to the new money of self-made men. They make their money not through developing industry, but through market manipulation and smart investment. Hedge fund managers are not the "job creators" the GOP is so fond of. Money makes money, but not if it goes to buy more money. It has to be invested in corporations that use people, not machines, as workers.

It is clear that income inequality, the huge conservative contributions to the PACS, the Supreme Court Citizens United decision, the bailout of the banks but not of those millions whose mortgages are "under water," and the unemployment and underemployment of millions, has tilted the balance of well-being greatly in favor of the wealthy and powerful. Thomas Friedman questions how a democracy can survive without correcting this imbalance.

"When the private sector overwhelms the public, you get the 2008 subprime crisis. When the public overwhelms the private, you get choking regulations. You need a balance, which is why we have to get past this cartoonish argument that the choice is either all government or all the market,' argues Rothkopf (in *Power. Inc.*). The lesson of history, he adds, is that capitalism thrives best when you have this balance, and 'when you lose that balance, you get in trouble.'" (Friedman, T.L., 2012) [Friedman, Thomas L., *Capitalism, Version 2012, The New York Times,* 3/14/2012, Op-Ed, p A27]

Is the 71% agreement with the statement that "The rich just keep getting richer, the poor get poorer." based on fact? In January 2014 Paul Krugman gives us the bad news.

"The reality of rising American inequality is stark. Since the late 1970s real wages for the bottom half of the work force have *stagnated or fallen*, while the incomes of the top 1 percent have *nearly quadrupled*, (and the incomes of the top 0.1 percent have risen even more)". (Krugman, P., 2014) [Krugman, P. The Undeserving Rich,"? The NY Times 1/19/2014]

Is this disparity in wages and the consequent disparity in life chances a trigger for anger at the very rich? Surprisingly, the Koch Brothers, Rupert Murdoch and similar super-rich are not the direct targets of anger, They make their contributions quietly through PACS (political action committees). They are not the *conspicuous* spenders that heighten the public's craving for more and more. It is the wealthy movie stars, leading athletes, the Saudis, and other visiting potentates who create envy and are subconscious role models for the public. They are in the news, and have public relations teams behind them.

An example of the extreme consumption that makes income disparity tangible and jarring is the rise of opulent hotel suites in New York and many major cities.

"In New York the race to capture the highest end of the market continues. In November, the Mandarin Oriental, New York, opened a 3300 square-foot suite that includes floor-to-ceiling windows and a dining room that seats ten; its rate is $28,000 a night." (White, M.C, 2014) [White, Martha C. Hotels Race to Attract Superrich, The New York Times, 1/21/2014, p. B4]

The article goes on to say that this super-suite trend started in Singapore, London and major Middle Eastern cities. Las Vegas, Miami and Dallas supersuites are not far behind New York in price. "…It makes it special that you're in a room no one else in the hotel has." The New York Palace manager, David Chase, said "This hotel already had a fantastic flow of high-net-worth people using our suites…Saudi diplomats and royalty, as well Hollywood and sports stars, as regular guests. They also indirectly attract an aspirational middle-class traveler….. It is the attention— the halo effect—doing a suite like this brings…..some travelers want to brush elbows with that level of wealth." (,White, M.C., op cit).

In Chapter 2 I make the point that the homeostasis of the human body, which is maintained by an elaborate system of automatic checks and balances, is not available in a democratic political system. Despite the "separation of powers" into the executive, judicial and legislative branches of government, the balance between the two main parties, between the rich and the poor, and among the many special interest groups, is difficult to achieve.

There has always been a struggle between the haves and the have-nots. For long periods in history, there has been the grumbling of the masses, the *ressentiment*, that doesn't erupt in violence. From time to time, especially when there is a great scarcity of food or shelter, the violence flares up. The extreme language of the Tea Partiers, and even some of the GOP presidential candidates in 2011-2012 and 2015-2016, along with the attack mode of many right wing commentators, has poured fuel on the fire of division. In March, 2012, Rush Limbaugh, for example, excoriated Sandra Fluke, 30, an activist Georgetown University law student, for testifying before the congressional committee on birth control. She told of the great expense of her own birth control. For this he labeled her a slut and a prostitute. After an outburst of criticism, he apologized.

The composition of the Occupy Wall Street movement, that is the political opposite of the Tea Partiers, is rather heterogeneous. It involved a wide range of socioeconomic status, but the overnight tent-dwellers have been primarily the poor and unemployed. The Tea Partiers, in contrast, were somewhat more homogeneous. They tended to be older, and almost exclusively white. They are covetous of their own government benefits but eager to deny those same safety nets to minorities and immigrants. At one time their cry was "Keep your hands off my Medicare." Yet they were united against what they disparage as "Obamacare," which seeks to extend those same benefits to others.

In a review of *The Age of Austerity,* by Thomas Byrne Edsall (Doubleday) Mark Schmitt sums up the dynamics of the Tea Party and right wing.

"In a climate of austerity and limits, struggling older voters cling all the more desperately to what they have, and are all the more willing to see that same thing denied to those who are not them or don't look like them."(Schmitt, M. 2012) [Schmitt, M. *Within Limits,* The New York Times Book Review, 1/22/2012, p.16,]

It is interesting that Schmitt uses the words "*cling* all the more desperately to what they have." It echoes Obama's famous but insightful 2008 gaffe I quoted earlier in this chapter about those who "*cling* to guns or religion or antipathy to people who aren't like them." The word "cling" does call to mind the image of a child clinging to a father or mother with the "blind attachment" that seems to underlie the motivation of the Trump's base.

The central thesis of this book is that deregulation of the economy and a widespread personal deregulation result in a culturally patterned defect that can be called "the anomic personality." This personality type, so pervasive in our culture, had its roots in the Protestant Ethic of "secular asceticism." However, showing God that you might be eligible for salvation because of your hard work (asceticism), meant acquisition of worldly goods—cows, chickens, and barns. Then clothing and other possessions became a sign of eligibility for salvation. Soon "conspicuous consumption" took over from asceticism (hard work). The shift in our economic production from manufacturing (especially steel and heavy industry) to a service economy, and the consumption of outsourced products (electronics such as TVs and cell phones) cut back the number of semi-skilled and unskilled jobs, and increased the demand for possessions which many could not afford. The shift from heavy industry to a consumer and service economy, and the shift from exports to imports, abetted by mass marketing, gave birth to a new type of capitalism. Its dominant industry was the financial world; the buying and selling of money or financial instruments representing money. Subprime loans were first "bundled" and securitized around 1990. They were sold to investors in "tranches" which concealed the low value of the mortgages involved. Stocks, bonds, and commodities were not enough; securitization ran rampant. A few of the types, many of them inscrutable, were collateralized mortgage obligations (CMOs, such as auto loans, credit card debt), mortgage backed securities (MBS) and asset back securities (ABS). The securitization of commercial loans produced collateralized debt obligations, or CDOs. The banks' former primary role was to underwrite the manufacturers and small businesses. Now the banks could buy and sell the old and new securities, and even invest for themselves. They became brokers, and they and the hedge funds triggered the "recession" of 2008, which continues with a very slow recovery.

The income disparity, the concentration of power in corporations and the wealthy, and the widespread corruption or bias in Congress, the Senate, and even the Supreme Court, have led to a general lack of trust.

Approximately half the country didn't trust our President. They thought he was a Muslim; (52% in Mississippi, and 45% in Alabama). In a 2010 poll, 41% of Republicans thought Obama was foreign born; that is, not a citizen, and 27% of the public believed it too. www.politico.com/news/stories/0810/40644.html

Our democracy is heavily based on trust; in our institutions, our government, and our leaders. Many banks have the word "Trust" in their titles. Our coins say "In God We Trust." God is still a stand-in for all authority. (Americans have always had some reservations about authority and each other; vide "In God we trust, all others pay cash," and "Trust in God, but keep your powder dry.") Bankers Trust had misled customers like Procter & Gamble with complex "interest rate swaps." Speaking among themselves, bankers used the term 'R.O.F.' It stood for "rip-off factor," the amount the bank could take from unsuspecting clients."(Norris, F., 2012) [Norris, F. "Paving path to fraud on Wall Street." The New York Times, 3/16/2012, p B1.] Similar thievery turned up at Goldman-Sachs and other large banks that bet against the investments they made for their clients. The ideal of fiduciary duty, where the bank or financial advisor takes responsibility for helping the less informed advisee, is apparently becoming a thing of the past.

It is hard not to share the anger of both left and right at banks, Wall Street, and the "elite". The liberals were surprised when Obama chose Larry Summers and Timothy Geithner as his economic advisors. Both men were heavily entrenched in Wall Street and banking. Geithner had worked as head of the Federal Bank of New York. He became Obama's Secretary of the Treasury. Lawrence Summers was Geithner's mentor at the National Economic Council. As President of Harvard, Summers claimed that "innate differences" between men and women, along with 80 hour work weeks and discrimination, may account for the lack of top-level female professionals in science and engineering, This created a hue and cry, and Summers made a public retraction. It did exemplify his penchant for a blunt approach.

There is a tendency for people to think like those around them, (the core of the "differential association" theory of criminality). Robert Rubin and Alan Greenspan have been presidential economic advisors, and deeply entrenched in Wall Street and its philosophy. Rubin, Secretary of the Treasury to Clinton, spent 26 years at Goldman Sachs, eventually serving as co-chairman. Greenspan served as Chairman of the Federal Reserve of the United States from 1987 to 2006. The entire financial world hung on his every word, or rather on his often inscrutable pronouncements about the economy. Interestingly, he was one of the founding members of the Objectivist Movement in the 1950s, a cult centered on their guru, Ayn Rand, whose novel, *Atlas Shrugged*, has become a conservative bible. Greenspan said "Talking to Ayn Rand was like starting a game of chess thinking I was good, and suddenly finding myself in checkmate." (Objectivist Movement, Wikipedia) [Objectivist Movement, Wikipedia, http://en.wikipedia.org/wiki/Objectivist_movement#The_Collective]

Paul Krugman wrote in the New York Times that Greenspan, "By repeatedly shilling for whatever the Bush administration wants, he has betrayed the trust placed in Fed chairmen, and deserves to be treated as just another partisan hack." (Krugman, P.., 2005, "Three Card Maestro") [Krugman, P. "Three Card Maestro," The New York Times, Op Ed, February 18, 2005] Three Card Maestro is a reference to Three Card Monte, a shell game used by con men, in which the mark must find the "money card."

The con man and his buddy, the cooler, are the perfect metaphor for the super-rich and powerful who use the political, legal, and public relations skills of their employees to delude the public, (the mark).The coolers are the conservative radio and TV hosts, and even the psychiatrists, psychologists, and social workers who too often focus on early trauma and the family, instead of the social stresses of job loss or the pressure of competition. A nation on street drugs or on tranquilizers by prescription will not have much energy left for effecting positive social change. A good portion of that nation is "cooled out."

A brilliant and classic article, "On Cooling the Mark Out" by Erving Goffman (Goffman, E., 1952) [Goffman, E, *Journal of Interpersonal Relations*, 1952., also at (http://www.tau.ac.il/~algazi/mat/Goffman--Cooling.htm,] describes how scam artist criminals go about ensuring that the people whose money they have stolen don't come back and pursue them or call the police. It is called "cooling." The confidence game, the "con," is performed by the operator. His confederate, the "steerer" or "roper," (male or female) builds up a friendship and trust with the carefully selected "mark." Being greedy, the mark falls for a gambling scheme supposedly fixed in his favor. He gets to win some money, and this makes him salivate for more. (Think of Bernie Madoff's Ponzi scheme, where you win at first, but the pyramid finally collapses.) Then the operator departs with all the money the mark paid out.

After his money is stolen, the mark is rightfully angry. He may pursue the gang, or go to the police. One of the operators, or the roper, may stay behind, and attempt to console the mark. He will also point out that the scheme was illegal, so the mark can't really go to the police. This person is known as the "cooler," and he "cools the mark out." The coolers abound in our society. Among them are the politicians and their wordsmiths who mislead the public, the advertising agencies, the psychiatrists, psychologists and social workers who (unwittingly?) treat situational or structural problems and depression with individual therapy, and the drug and tranquilizer dealers on the street and in doctor's offices. (If the government fails to help, most people need some kind of cooler.)

Our zero-sum, winner take all, 1% versus 99% kleptocracy has grown very lopsided with income disparity, (now morphing into "income inequality"). The promise of good jobs, good education, affordable health care, and equal opportunity, once seen as realizable, now threatens to evaporate under the threat of prolonged unemployment, the housing collapse, and the national debt. The 2012 Republican presidential candidates, including Mitt Romney, vied with one another to promise the most draconian cuts in health, education, unemployment insurance and all safety net programs. The military and the Social Security benefits were to be financed, but all those discretionary areas were to be cut by our fiscal conservatives. The 2016 GOP presidential candidates promise to make even more draconian cuts than their predecessors. When House Speaker John Boehner is forced to retire by the hardline GOP conservatives, Paul Krugman thinks it is evidence that "madness has consumed the GOP." (September, 2015).

Yet the Republicans promised to reduce unemployment by cutting the taxes of "job-creators." They promised to get out of Iraq and Afghanistan, but were already beating the drums to attack Iran. Thus the "military-industrial complex" Ike Eisenhower warned us against will continue to profit. The No Child Left Behind program under George Bush promised better public education. Schools are now staggering under drastic cutbacks, and some teachers, if not laid off, are reported spending their own money to buy toilet paper for inner city schools.

The 99% see the 1% as calling all the shots. Their powerlessness creates political alienation. (Some theorists who stress alienation, (Marxists,?) hold anomie theory in disfavor. But alienation in the U.S. does not produce grumbling masses.and does not necessarily stop people from striving for more, and for "success.") Knowing that almost everyone at the top cheats—sexually, financially, or steals power— creates a lack of trust or faith in the system; in democracy. Bernie stole money, while Dick stole power. Cheney played Svengali to Bush's hypnotized Trilby until the last year of the second term. He created what was called the "Imperial Presidency." In the name of "executive privilege," he overrode laws and treaties enacted by Congress. He enabled the use of torture, "extraordinary rendition," and warrantless surveillance in the name of national security. (Huq A., 2008) [Huq, A. "Dismantling the Imperial Presidency," Cross posted from *The Nation*,.12/23/2008http://www.brennancenter.org/content/resource/dismantling_the_imperial_presidency1.]

The founding fathers (not just those in the U.S., but in many countries) had the wisdom to create a separation of powers, by dividing the government into several branches. Our government is divided into the executive (the President), legislative (Congress), and judiciary (Supreme Court). A system of "checks and balances" is supposed to keep any one branch from acquiring too much power. Under Cheney as V.P., the power shifted to the "Imperial Presidency."

Now the grab for power has shifted to the Supreme Court. The 2010 "Citizens United" decision is a flagrant example of the political power of five conservative justices. With the 2016 presidential elections coming up, the ability of the new president to appoint Supreme Court justices who are more likely to decide cases in line with his or her political leanings may have greater impact on the future of the country than who gets to win the House or the Senate.

The Court made "liberal" decisions in 2015 on gay marriage and Obamacare, but most cases coming up before the death of Justice Scalia in February 2016 suggested a return to the dominance of the five conservative justices.

For a while after Scalia's death the justices were tied, four liberals to four conservatives, making for a deadlocked court on major issues. The justices get to choose what cases they will hear, so before Scalia's death, the 5-4 majority *got to select cases that favor conservative interests.* For example, restrict the ability of labor unions to collect dues from employees, (aimed to overthrow Abood versus Detroit Board of Education, 1977, and weaken unions). (Examples are from Roberts, D. "U.S. supreme court: conservatives set to take reins after year of liberal wins." *The Guardian*, 9/29/2015.) Example: Affirmative action at universities, Fisher vs University of Texas. Example: Limit the ability of consumers and employees to bring class action suits against corporations. Tyson Foods will try to overturn a judgment of $5.8 million against it, for skipping overtime pay at an Iowa meat processing plant.

The age distribution of the Supreme Court poses a serious threat to our democracy, since most of the conservative justices are relatively young, and the justices have life tenure. Scalia (76 as of 4/28/2012), died on 2/13/2016. Kennedy (75,) was the "swing voter" who voted heavily conservative. He retired in 2018, leaving room for Trump to try appointing Brett Kavanaugh, who has been accused of sexual assault by Prof. Christine Blasey Ford, when both were in their teens. The other three conservatives average age 60, (Roberts 57, Alito 62, and Thomas 63. On average they can live 30 years more. (The liberals are split on age, with Ginsburg (79) and Breyer (73) older, and Kagan (57) and Sotomayor (57) younger.

If Hillary Clinton became president, she could have replaced Ginsburg, Breyer and Kennedy, making for a young liberal majority. She might have appointed Judge Merrick Garland who was chosen by Obama to replace Scalia but was blocked by the GOP. Once Trump was elected, he replaced Scalia with Gorsuch, a conservbative, and is trying to replace Kennedy with Kavanaugh, making a young conservative 6-3 majority. (*Trump did replace Scalia with Neil Gorsuch, a confirmed conservative, Gorsuch will probably serve 30 years. His appointment by Trump may do more damage to our democracy than all the other Trump attacks on liberalism combined.*) Since Kennedy is the swing justice, replacing him will in itself push the court to the right. Trump has chosen Brett Kavanaugh to replace Kennedy. The democrats (September, 2018) are raising an outcry, for not only will this put *two* conservative Trump judges on the Court, *but put in place a judge, Kavanaugh, who specifically wrote an opinion that a sitting president cannot be indicted. Again, Trump is self-serving, and not concerned with the balance of the court.*

Most interesting is the previous religious background of the justices. All of the conservatives are Roman Catholic. Three of the liberals are Jewish, and the fourth, Sonia Sotomayor, is a Catholic but Hispanic minority member born in the Bronx. (Except for Clarence Thomas, the other conservatives are all majority whites.) This does seem to question the assumption that social background has nothing to do with judicial opinions!

"If the Roberts' court continues on the course suggested by its first five years, it is likely to allow a greater role for religion in public life, to permit more participation by unions and corporations in elections and to elaborate further on the scope of the Second Amendment's right to bear arms. Abortion rights are likely to be curtailed, as are affirmative action and protections for people accused of crimes." (Aziz Huq, supra.)

If you can't trust the president; either George Bush or Barack Obama, as many people feel (Obama is labeled a Muslim, a foreigner, or even the antichrist) then whom can you trust? If you can't trust the members of the Supreme Court, whose wisdom and erudition supposedly exceeds that of almost all Americans then whom indeed can you trust?

If you can't trust the banks, many of whom call themselves "Trusts," then whom can you trust? If Goldman Sachs (a full service global investment banking and securities firm") bets against its stock recommendations to its own powerful corporate customers, then how can the man in the street trust his bank?

If JPMorgan Chase Bank, our biggest bank, was fined $1.7 billion in 2014 for not exerting "due diligence" in handling the accounts of Bernie Madoff, then whom can we trust?

With this spreading failure of trust, and the flexible morality of the country's highest authorities as models, the 99% can't help but indulge their own criminal proclivities, (social learning theory and behavior modeling). We all have a predisposition to cut corners, to deceive, to bend the rules. (Some would deny the dark side of our nature, but I strongly believe that our nature is not composed only of "better angels." The "fallen angels" are exemplified by Lucifer, the Devil himself. When bending or reinterpreting the supposed rules or norms we claim to live by become endemic, outright breaking of these rules spreads. What we have, in due course, is a pandemic of mild to severe psychopathy, looking more like the Factor One described in Chapter Two. I repeat its components here, for clarity.

Factor 1: Aggressive Narcissism

Glibness, superficial charm

Grandiose sense of self-worth
Pathological lying
Cunning/manipulative
Lack of remorse or guilt
Emotionally shallow
Callous/lack of empathy
Failure to accept responsibility for own actions

This personality factor overlaps with Factor 2, "Socially Deviant Lifestyle." which is clearly criminal behavior. We see the overlap in Bernie, who for years is the aggressive narcissist, liar and manipulator, and when outed, morphs into the master criminal (Factor 1 and 2).

The Dark Triad

Daniel Goleman, in his book *Social Intelligence,* (see reference *infra*) posited a "Dark Triad" that divides the continuum of antisocial behavior. Further research transformed the Triad into a Tetrad, with the addition of Sadism. (Theories about narcissism differ widely. This overview is bound to do injustice to some of the approaches. Primary narcissism, with its central grandiosity, develops in the infant. It becomes normal self-regard or self-esteem, as the child identifies with (or introjects) the parents. If there is a lack of attachment and identification with a parental figure due to trauma (rejection, abuse, lack of mirroring) the child suffers a narcissistic injury, and the primitive narcissism remains. Primary narcissism is not part of the triad. The primitive narcissist who has suffered an "injury" is the one we will be focusing on.)

In increasing antisocial and aggressive behavior Goleman ranks the narcissist, the Machiavellian (or "Mach"), and last of all the psychopath. The narcissist has all the features of Factor 1, Aggressive Narcissism (above) but may be less aggressive. The Machs feel that "my ends justify the means." Goleman says:

"The Mach shares many traits with the other two branches of the Dark Triad, such as a disagreeable nature and selfishness. But far more than the narcissist or the psychopath, the Mach remains realistic about himself and others, neither making inflated claims nor striving to impress. The Mach prefers to see things clearly in order to exploit them." (Goleman, D, p. 126) [Goleman, D. Social Intelligence, Bantam Dell, New York, N.Y., paperback, 8, 2007.]

Goleman suggests the "kiss-up-kick-down" manager as the prototype of the Mach. Though often successful, their bad relations with others may result in their downfall. Their history will be "littered with resentful ex-friends, ex-lovers, and ex-business associates" (Think Donald Trump, Steve Jobs).

The psychopath is at the high end of the Triad. He was also known as the sociopath, and today is diagnosed as the antisocial personality disorder. (The DSM Manual tends to see the antisocial personality almost always as clearly criminal. As I have noted elsewhere, this is because it is more difficult and time-consuming to elicit psychopathic ideation, while an arrest or incarceration offers an easily achieved statistical reliability and high concordance of paired diagnosticians.) While the narcissist and Mach lack empathy, the psychopath has none.

". . . Unlike Machs and narcissists, psychopaths feel virtually no anxiety" or fear. Because of this, they are "virtually oblivious to the threat of punishment." (Goleman, supra, p. 128.) Thus they end up as convicted criminals much more often than the Machs and narcissists, who are capable of the fear of punishment.

"Successful psychopaths" have committed crimes, but have never been caught or arrested. This is because they "react more anxiously to anticipated threats," which "leads to a bit of caution." (supra, p. 129)

How might Tiger, Bernie and Dick fit into the Dark Triad? My guess would be that Tiger is the narcissist. He has sexually exploited many women, and shown a callous disregard for his wife and children. His superficial charm endeared him to millions of fans. While he gave a great deal of money to charity, this hardly disqualifies him as self-centered. He betrayed the religious concepts which guided him in his youth. He lied consistently, until he was outed by his publicity-seeking call girls. Except for his incredible athletic skill and the excessive risk-taking involved in his numerous peccadilloes, he is very much like the average American male narcissist; cheating on his marriage and self-possessed.

What about Dick? He fits the Machiavellian, or Mach, quite well. While the Mach is selfish and disagreeable (Cheney was dubbed "Darth Vader") he also is clear about his goals, and unlikely to be physically violent. He is very close to the manipulative royalty that Machiavelli was teaching in his book, *The Prince* (1532). An example: "Men are so simple and so much inclined to obey immediate needs that a deceiver will never lack victims for his deceptions." The Mach uses others to do his dirty work. When it looked as if Saddam Hussein did *not* buy yellowcake uranium ore to make Weapons of Mass Destruction, Cheney, Karl Rove, Richard Armitage, I. "Scooter" Libby, Donald Rumsfeld, Richard Perle, Paul Wolfowitz, Irving Kristol and others in Washington who wanted to invade Iraq were furious. Ambassador Joseph C. Wilson IV wrote an Op Ed piece in the New York Times, refuting the yellowcake story. In retaliation, Libby and others outed Wilson's wife, Valerie Plame, who was working for the CIA on nuclear proliferation. Since revealing the identity of a CIA officer is a crime, Libby went to jail. He took the fall for Cheney. George W. Bush, who so badly wanted to have WMDs ("Weapons of Mass Destruction") as an excuse for war, commuted Libby's jail sentence of 30 months.

The employment of retaliation and the use of underlings to "take the fall" is typically Machiavellian. This episode and other incidents that support Dick's membership in the Mach clan are treated in our extended discussion of Cheney. That he is anomic is supported by his incredible rise to power, and his role as the first Vice President to actually run the country and to create an "imperial presidency." The limitlessness of his ambition and his excessive need for power is the very "deregulation" *in an individual* that Durkheim saw in a *state of society*, or anomie.

How does Bernie fit into the Dark Triad? He has a lot in common with the psychopath. The hallmark of the psychopath is a total lack of empathy. During a prison interview by Barbara Walters, he downplayed the impact of his thievery. "The average person thinks I robbed widows and orphans, but I made wealthier people wealthier." (Smith, A., 2011) [Smith, A. CNN Money, 10/27/2011, quoting Barbara Walters] This was clearly a lie and a rationalization of his crimes by a man who had lied for many years to his family, his temple congregation, and to thousands of investors. The proof of his real feelings about his victims came from a fellow inmate.

"But that evening an inmate badgered Madoff about the victims of his $65 billion scheme, and kept at it. According to K.C. White, a bank robber and prison artist who escorted a sick friend that evening (to the evening pill line) Madoff stopped smiling and got angry. 'Fuck my victims,' he said, loud enough for other inmates to hear. 'I carried them for twenty years, and now I'm doing 150 years.'" (Fishman, S., 2010) [Fishman, S., "Bernie Madoff, Free at Last." New York Magazine, 6/6/2010.]

Bernie claimed that he lived for twenty years in fear of being arrested, and that it was a relief to be rid of that fear once he was jailed. Most psychopaths are "virtually oblivious to the threat of punishment" (Goleman, *supra*).Bernie's fear lessens his odds of being a psychopath, and puts him somewhere in between Machiavellian and a Psychopath. *I would call him a sub-clinical-level Mach with psychopathic features.* Despite his fear of being caught, he continued to steal from 16,000 people, taking life savings from many. His fear wasn't strong enough to stop him, as occurs in "successful psychopaths" who never get arrested. His remorse, if any, seems to be for the suicide of his son, Mark. He was reported despondent for many days, when he did not report for the prison meals.

After the brief review of political, financial, judicial, executive, legal and even presidential skullduggery and deception, there can be little doubt that there is aggressive narcissism, Machiavellianism and psychopathy (and sadism) from the top to the bottom of our social pyramid. But how widespread is this behavior and social character, which I have dubbed the "Anomic Personality," and how far back does it go?

We all know that "An honest politician is one who when he's bought stays bought." (Attributed to Simon Cameron, 1799-1889). Even further back in time, lawyers were suspect, and now are still the butt of numerous slurs and jokes. "What is the difference between a lawyer and a rooster?" Answer: "A rooster clucks defiance." In *Utopia*, (1516) Thomas More wrote "They have no lawyers among them, for they consider them as a sort of people whose profession it is to disguise matters." There's no need to document at length the history of dishonesty or criminality at the very top of society (The Supreme Court, and many presidents). For example, Nixon ("I am not a crook" denial of Watergate involvement) and George H.W. Bush, ("Read my lips, no new taxes," a promise soon broken.). Bill

Clinton's behavior with Monica Lewinsky was not criminal. But lying under oath was. "I did not have sexual relations with that woman.").

Lawyers comprise around 37% of the House and 60% of the Senate. A large number of them become lobbyists for corporations and alternate between "serving the people" in their role as congressmen, and serving the same corporations for whose interests they voted previously. The scandals surrounding lobbyist Jack Abramoff involved Representatives Tom Delay (R-Texas) and Bob Ney (R-Ohio). Ney resigned after pleading guilty to conspiracy and other charges. Delay, the former House Majority Leader, pleaded guilty to charges of money laundering and conspiracy in a later scandal, and was sentenced to three years in prison.

How widespread is Aggressive Narcissism? It seems a large portion of the 99% partake of it, but not to the extreme of the outliers I have called the Anomic Personalities. Not many people have the brains, the brass, or the sheer ambition of Tiger, Bernie and Dick. Not many have the opportunity to harm as many people as Bernie and Dick, or to disappoint as many as Tiger. But I think you will agree with me, after you read the following examples, that cheating, lying, stealing, callous manipulation of others, grandiosity, and a low level of guilt or empathy are endemic in our country. Surely there are some who are candidates for sainthood, but they are, as in most cultures, far and few between.

The development of the Anomic Personality doesn't start in adulthood, through the emulation of the leading aggressive narcissists. Modeling and imitation of bad adult models are not enough. The Anomic Personality (the narcissist and the Mach, but perhaps excluding the outright psychopath) needs the special anxiety and depression of our competitive and demanding childhood and adolescence as a foundation. (Goleman mentions possible organic brain damage in psychopaths, in the amygdala and prefrontal cortex, supra p.128) Narcissism is believed by some clinicians to be a defense against a wounding, or "narcissistic injury." There is much evidence for this view, especially in patient case histories. In general, a lack of love from parents who are cold, punitive, and unpredictable (or "labile") as shown in my longitudinal research, is responsible for a wide range of emotional disorder in children and teens. (anon.), op. cit.) Rejection by the peer group is also a large factor. The connection between this early environment and "vulture capitalism" (used in a broader sense than that applied to Mitt

Romney by his Democratic and Republican critics) is made by David Denby in a review of the movie, "The Hunger Games,"

The plot, briefly, revolves around a teen girl, Katniss Everdeen, who must hunt down and kill teens representing other districts, so that food and glory will accrue to her own district. This film, based on an extremely popular trilogy, depicts "a Hobbesian war of all against all." Denby likens it to "*Lord of the Flies*, to *Survivor* TV shows, and to Donald Trump's TV show *The Apprentice*. Denby shows how commentators have tried to explain the "extraordinary popularity" of the trilogy and now the movies.

"Perhaps it's that the books" (on which the movie is based) "offer a hyper-charged version of high school, an everyday place with incessant anxieties: constant judgment by adults; hazing, bullying and cliques; and, finally, college-entry traumas. If you stretch the metaphor a bit, the books could be seen as a menacing fable of capitalism, in which an ethos of capitalism increasingly yields winner-take-all victors." (Denby, D., 2012) [David Denby, "Kids At Risk," *The New Yorker,* 4/2/2012, pp 68-70]

Modeling and imitation of adults outside the family certainly play a major role in this societal breakdown, on top of exposure to narcissistic parents. If you see cheating and lying at the top, and if you are still only in the 99%, you may say to yourself, "If they cheat, why can't I? I'll only do it on a smaller scale. If Tim Cook, the CEO of Apple, makes one million a day, which I'll never make in a lifetime, then why not bend the rules a little? Maybe cheat on my income tax? Hire an illegal immigrant at $6 per hour or less? If my contract calls for drywall, I'll save money by buying the Chinese drywall that emits sulfur fumes. So what if it causes sleep apnea and corrodes electric fixtures and plumbing?

Modeling and imitation are terms for learned behavior. This learning can be that of the child taking cues or even verbal statements of values from the parents, or it can be the adult learning of corporate behavior or gang behavior by "differential association." That is, you learn to behave by the social subgroup (gang, trading floor, medical school) in which you find yourself (or to which you are attracted by your personality).

The question I am posing here is; given the widespread disobedience to the law, can we say that it is 'deviant behavior?' If the norms (not the statistical norms, but the rules by which people are supposed to behave)

have been bent so far out of shape that they have drastically changed, then what used to be deviant behavior has become "normative."

Norms change. Homosexuality used to be considered a psychiatric illness that needed to be "cured" by therapy. As late as 1952 Alan Turing, often called "the father of theoretical computer science and artificial intelligence," (Wikipedia) was prosecuted for homosexuality, a crime in Britain at that time. He was chemically castrated in lieu of prison. He died two years later, a suicide by cyanide. A war hero for breaking the German "Enigma" codes, he was pardoned in 2013, sixty-one years later! Homosexuality is no longer considered a mental illness in the DSM V (Diagnostic and Statistical Manual of Mental Disorders). In 1973 it was removed from the DSM by a vote of the American Psychiatric Association, but in 1980 it was redefined as "ego-dystonic homosexuality." (Definition: "A psychosexual disorder in which an individual has persistent distress associated with same-sex preference...") No wonder being gay could be dystonic in a period when gay-bashing was still popular among thugs and politicians. Finally, in 1986 it was removed from the DSM.

In 1920 women in all the United States finally got to vote. Many countries and individual states allowed women to vote well before 1920. The norms of dating and sexual behavior have changed radically. "Sexting" on a cell phone, "hooking up" and "friends with benefits" are among the many innovations.

I think there is enough evidence for saying that the norms governing a wide swath of interpersonal, social, sexual, political, religious, military, educational, and all major institutional behavior have been changing rapidly. This rapid change has various roots, but I am convinced that the major thrust comes from the Protestant Ethic, the rise of conspicuous consumption, the Industrial Revolution, the decline of the family farm, and the fiercely competitive nature of globalized capitalism that outsources our disappearing factories and jobs. It leaves us with an ethic of all against all, of "I'm all right, Jack—I've got mine." This fierce competition and unlimited striving *is* the state of anomie, and our personalities have become anomic because of the tantalizing grapes of success. Out of reach, but never out of mind.

In his well-known article, "Social Structure and Anomie," Robert K. Merton, (Merton, R.K., 1938) [*Merton, R.K. American Sociological Review*, Vol. 3, No. 5. (Oct., 1938), pp. 672-682.and 1957] University Professor in the graduate Department of Sociology at Columbia University, took another approach to Durkheim's concept of anomie. He drew up a fourfold table which looked at acceptance of societal goals and acceptance of the approved means of attaining those goals. The disparity or "mismatch" between acceptance (internalization) of goals and the means of attaining them he called "strain."

This was actually a radical departure from Durkheim's underlying assumption about the motor force driving anomie. Merton stated his departure from Durkheim in the first sentence of "Social Structure and Anomie." "There persists a notable tendency in sociological theory to attribute the malfunctioning of social structure to those of man's imperial biological drives which are not adequately restrained by social control." He says this viewpoint "provides no basis for determining the nonbiological conditions which induce deviations from prescribed patterns of conduct" (Merton, supra).

Here we have the gist of Merton's parting with not only Durkheim, but with Freud and even Hobbes. He focused on a particular nonbiological condition, that of "strain," which he saw as a disparity between behavior in conformity to accepted goals, and behavior in keeping with accepted means of achieving those goals. Anomie and strain have been conflated.

"Anomie refers to a state of social organization. (social disorganization, deregulation, and rapid social change) whereas strain is a mechanism (disparity between goals and means) that induces deviant behavior." (Deflem, M, Anomie) [Mathieu Deflem, Anomie, http://www.cas.sc.edeu/ spcy/faculty/deflem/zanomienency.pdf]

It was Durkheim's singular contribution to show that the lack of societal regulation was associated with higher rates of suicide. Married men's sexual drives were more regulated than those of unmarried men, and thus the suicide rates of the relatively unregulated unmarried men were much higher than those of their married peers. Similarly, Catholics in several countries had lower rates of suicide than their Protestant fellow-countrymen. Catholics, he pointed out, were more regulated by church condemnation of suicide. Catholic doctrine considers it a mortal sin. The Protestant church did not see suicide as so sinful that one would suffer eternal damnation.

Here are two examples; the biological sex drive, and aggression turned in upon the self, that Durkheim used as the driving forces in his study of suicide (although he was not explicit about the role of self-aggression in men, Protestant or Catholic.)

Durkheim's view was that society's rules, norms, and restrictions that comprise regulation were necessary to curb what he felt were strong human drives. He didn't use the word "drive" or "instinct", but called anomie a "derangement," and "an insatiable will."

Freud famously and more darkly said:

"Men are not gentle creatures, who want to be loved, who at the most can defend themselves if they are attacked; they are, on the contrary, creatures among whose instinctual endowments is to be reckoned a powerful share of aggressiveness. As a result, their neighbor is for them not only a potential helper or sexual object, but also someone who tempts them to satisfy their aggressiveness on him, to exploit his capacity for work without compensation, to use him sexually without his consent, to seize his possessions, to humiliate him, to cause him pain, to torture and to kill him. *Homo homine lupus.* [man is wolf to man"] (Freud, S., 1929) [Freud, S., 1929. "Civilisation and Its Discontents." (In *Civilisation, War and Death) London,* The Hogarth Press. Translated by Joan Riviere (written 1929, revised ed. 1953).]

Given his view of man as wolf, he saw social control as the primary function of society.

"Civilization has to use its utmost efforts in order to set limits to man's aggressive instincts and to hold the manifestations of them in check by psychical reaction-formations. Hence, therefore, the use of methods intended to incite people into identifications and aim-inhibited relations of love, hence the restriction upon sexual life, and hence too the ideal's commandment to love one's neighbor as oneself" (Civilisation and Its Discontents, supra)

Another great thinker, Thomas Hobbes, also emphasized the importance of social control, or regulation, with the implication that aggression to the point of war is a biological given, and has to be held in check by force. "During the time men live without a common power to keep them all in awe, they are in that condition which is called war, and such a war, as is of every man, against every man." (*Leviathan, I, 13)*

Now as a sociologist, Merton tries to look at societal conditions or "states" that shape human behavior, much as Durkheim did. But he consciously focuses on a mechanism, the disparity between goals and means that has (in my view) the unfortunate consequence of stripping the biological and psychological from his discourse. He carefully avoids the use of the terms "instinct," "drive," or "need" for explaining "deviant behavior." But it may be necessary to cross several "explanatory levels" to understand a social phenomenon, and human behavior in general. Hence fields like social psychology, neuropsychology, and evolutionary psychology keep growing in number and kind.

Let's take a look at Merton's "fourfold table" (in a slightly simplified version). Here the move is away from deregulation or anomie, and toward the examination of the relationship between societally approved goals and the socially acceptable means of achieving those goals. "Strain," Merton's term for the disparity between acceptance (or internalization) of socially approved goals and acceptance of the legitimate means of achieving those goals, is not an emotional state, such as frustration, anger, or alienation. It is basically an abstract disparity, a mechanism. Filling in the various emotional states engendered by this disparity, and the specific behaviors that follow from those emotions, is the job of the social psychologist.

INTERNALIZATION OF SOCIETALLY APPROVED GOALS

	YES +	NO -
INTERNALIZATION OF SOCIETALLY APPROVED MEANS OF ACHIEVING THOSE GOALS YES +		
NO -		

+ + = Conformist

+ - = Innovation

- + = Ritualism

- - = Retreatism

In Merton's fourfold table, those who accept our societally approved goals and the approved means to those goals are the Conformists. (++). These are presumably the average Joe or Jill? Those who accept the goals but not the approved means of attaining them are the Innovators (+-), exemplified by the Mafia. Those who have internalized the means, but seem to have forgotten what the goals were (-+) are represented by the Ritualists (bureaucrats, obsessive compulsives).Those who have internalized neither the acceptable goals nor the means of attaining them are the Retreatists (- -) represented by addicts, vagrants and schizophrenics.

Durkheim's original contribution of lack of limitation, lack of regulation, and the focus on the tremendous power of biological drives and the feeling states or emotions associated with their decontrol, is purposely missing in Merton's revision. He wants to talk about the role of *goals/means disparity* in promoting antisocial behavior, not about the role of *emotions*. Yet for me, Durkheim made a special contribution within the sociological concept of a *societal state* that he called anomie. He described the *feeling state(s)* that accompany it. That is purposely missing in Merton's approach.

The Grapes of Tantalus

In my view, the metaphor that best describes this contribution of anomie is in the Greek myth, "The Grapes of Tantalus." Punished by the gods for infanticide and cannibalism, King Tantalus could not reach the receding grapes overhead, nor drink the receding water in which he stood. It is "tantalizing" to live in a culture where the grapes are always out of reach, no matter how hard you try or how high you jump. That tantalizing results in anxiety, depression, antisocial behavior, aggressive narcissism, or withdrawal, dependimg on the personality structure of the frustrated individual and his position in our society. It wasn't enough for Tiger to be the top-earning golfer and perhaps the highest-earning athlete of all time, for Bernie to be a highly successful stock broker, nor for Dick to be the most powerful vice president in U.S. history. They were "tantalized." They needed more of sex, money and power.

"The Fox and the Grapes," one of the best-known fables of La Fontaine, offers another reaction to a tantalizing situation, the coping mechanism of "sour grapes." In this case, the unattainable goals are disparaged. Withdrawal results. If you can't achieve your goals, then disparaging them is a way of reducing your anger. This is seen in the "pointed-headed intellectuals" remark made by former vice-president Spiro Agnew. He was deriding the Eastern "elite" who were Nixon's enemies. This denigration of intellect and higher education was meant to appeal to the frustration of those who were not well-educated. Given our public school system, which ranks 25th in math and 21st in science internationally, there are plenty of educationally-frustrated citizens. (*broadeducation*.org/about/crisis_stats. html.) The "elite" are often painted as "intelligent but without wisdom." This is another form of "sour grapes." What I can't have is not worth having."

The crucial cell in Merton's typology is the +-(plus minus) cell, which he labels "Innovation." This adaptation involves acceptance (or internalization) of the societally approved goals of "success," usually meaning in our culture sex, money and power, *but <u>not</u> the internalization of the societally approved **means** of attaining those goals, namely hard work, patience, self-control, planning, and executive functions in general* (Executive functions are the self-regulation and cognitive skills involved in planning, focusing, and remembering They are located primarily in the prefrontal regions of the frontal lobe of the brain.) The entries for (inhabitants of) this cell were the Mafia, delinquents, and common criminals. But what if we put Edwin Sutherland's White-Collar Criminal into this cell? (Sutherland, E.H., 1940 and 1949.) [Sutherland, Edwin H., 1940. The White-collar criminal. *American Sociological Review* 5:1-12, and 1949. White Collar Crime, New York: Dryden.]

Sutherland defined white collar crime "approximately as a crime committed by a person of respectability and high social status in the course of his occupation." In his 1940 book, *White Collar Crime*, he named many of the corporate thieves of his generation. The CEOs got together and sued the publisher. They managed to delete all references to corporate criminal individuals and their corporations. The unexpurgated edition of his book was not published until 1983 by Yale University Press!

For the White Collar individual, the means used in achieving success goals are much less likely to have been blocked than the means of achieving upward mobility for the lower social levels. Thus little or no "strain" in the Mertonian sense can exist for those who start out in life higher up in the social class system than the average person. Bernie and Dick pursued the same success goals. They became wealthy white collar individuals, helped in part by their middle-class origins, but they ignored the "societally-approved means" for achieving that success by scamming and by grabbing too much power.

Tiger fits strain theory better than Bernie, Dick. or Donald. He came up "the hard way" as a minority group member. Yet his father's dedication to training him as a star athlete gave him a leg up that few children from minority group families receive. Sports are a path to the American Dream of success for minority children. Athletes (boxers, basketball, football, baseball, golf and tennis players) don't need a good education to get ahead. However, the competition for the very limited top spots in sports is intense. In this way, strain is present in the blocking of educational pathways to jobs that require training in modern technology.

What happens when so many "innovators" *at all social levels* become successful by lying, cheating, and stealing from others that it becomes the norm? It is not only the "innovators" who have been blocked from achieving success in the approved manner, such as the Mafia, gang members and common criminals, who are bypassing the once acceptable means of achieving success. It has been the (relatively unblocked) White Collar segment of our society that has become criminal in droves. When you see your neighbors, or even your country's leaders, "getting away with it", you think, "Maybe I'll try to bend or break those rules in order to get ahead." This becomes a vicious circle. The more people cheat with impunity, the more others will follow. Thus the former "deviant" solution becomes normative, in the true sense of the word. (Norms describe how you *ought* to behave). Then the innovators have actually become conformists. *My sad conclusion is that antisocial behavior, to varying degrees, has become the norm, from the top to the bottom of our society. Corruption is no longer deviant. It is not a deviation from the new norm. It is the new norm. Trump has lowered the bar not only on presidential speech and behavior, but on speech and behavior in general.*

Let's look again at the inhabitants of Merton's four cells. He called those who accepted both the goals and the societally approved means of attaining them "Conformists" (the ++ cell). They are usually assumed to be in the majority. But if the majority of the population is conforming to new norms of what was formerly unacceptable or even criminal behavior, then the +-cell of "Innovators", (those who accept goals but not the approved means of achieving them) has actually moved and is continuing to move into the Conformist cell.

If indeed the vast majority of Americans are conforming to the new norms of success at any price; "get it while you can," "everybody does it, so why not I?" then the question arises, "What is deviant behavior?" Is it behavior that deviates from norms that have largely been abandoned? Not likely. Is it conformity to new sets of norms, formed by social subgroups such as the Mafia, delinquent gangs, *and* the corporate board rooms? If so, then "social learning" theories of crime apply, and "deviance" seems irrelevant. Kick out the poor or elderly to jack up the rent? Raise the insurance rates? Cut funds for schools? Raise the age for Social Security payments? Pay less than the minimum wage? Jack up the price of prescription drugs? Hey, everybody does it. It's the norm! Since 2007, Mylan Corp. has raised the price of an EpiPen by 400%. It now costs about $500. Epinephrine is used in cases of potentially fatal allergy attacks. Some EMS workers claim that they can't afford to keep the pens in their ambulances. Perhaps even more egregious is the case of Martin Shkrell, former head of Turing Pharmaceuticals. In 2015 he raised the price of Daraprim (used to treat toxoplasmosis) 5556%, from, $13.50 to $750 per tablet. He calls it "underpriced." He has been arrested and charged with securities fraud, but he and other drug CEOs are free under U.S. law to charge exorbitant (eye-popping) prices for drugs.

Merton also felt that the "Ritualists," who focus on the means, (hard work, attention to detail) but have abandoned or forgotten the success goal, might really be "superconformists." The bureaucrat is the prime example. Kenneth Burke famously described the bureaucrat as being "unfitted by being fit in an unfit fitness." (Burke, K., 1954) [Burke, <u>Kenneth.</u> *Permanence and Change.* Hermes Publications: Los Altos, CA, 1954.] *So in our advanced form of "vulture" capitalism, the only cell populated by other than conformists may be the - - (minus-minus) cell, or Retreatism.* This cell is populated by drunks, drug addicts, psychotics and vagrants. They have neither internalized the goals of our society, nor the "proper" means of attaining them.

Wall Street exemplifies the normative quality of our anti-social behavior, for what the CEO banker or the floor trader does is verging on criminal behavior, and is widespread. These activities are "normal:" stock manipulation, insider trading, promotion of subprime (relatively worthless) mortgages, undercapitalization (lack of sufficient reserve funds by banks), high speed trading, "dark pools" of trading not open to the public, financial support of shoddy products, and buying politicians with campaign money, among many others.

Actually, insider trading *is* legally a crime, and was recently prosecuted in the case of Raj Rajaratnam. He is serving eleven years in prison, and has paid a fine of ten million dollars (chump change?). Lip service is given to stopping or curbing these practices, but they are part of our system. Only recently have there been prosecutions or fines that give promise of regulation, the bête noir of the right wing.

The theory of "differential association" (Sutherland, *White Collar Crime*, supra) would be more applicable to white collar crime as well as to the Mafia and delinquent gangs than strain theory. If you meet at the country club, the board room, the professional organization, or the local Italian restaurant, you are associating with your own kind, and reinforcing (and creating or shaping) the values and behavior of your subculture. Durkheim's (and Freud's and Hobbes') emphasis is on "social control" theory (controlling irrepressible instincts or drives). Merton introduced "strain theory", focusing on the disparity between goals and means of attaining them. When we look at white collar criminals, we see the advantages of "learned behavior" approaches; differential association, and subcultural theory. Albert Cohen's book, *Delinquent Boys*, (Cohen, A. 1955) [Albert K. Cohen, *Delinquent Boys*, Glencoe, Ill.: The Free Press, 1955] and William Whyte's study, *Street Corner Society*, (Whyte, W.F. 1943) were both based on participant observation of delinquent gangs, and examined the elaborate rules for stealing and bowling. [William F. Whyte, *Street Corner Society, University of Chicago Press, 1943, 4th edition 1993]* (anon.)

It is easy to think of some of our many subcultures and settings, where antisocial behavior may develop and be learned: the high-school clique, the college fraternity or sorority, the board room, the trade floor, the bank, the drug scene, male and female prostitution, the country club, the sports team and coach, Broadway, and Hollywood. Each has its own rules. While those rules specify the means of achieving success in America (by trading, selling your body, golfing, basketball, selling drugs, using the casting couch, the goal is the same; sex, money and power, usually in some combination.

Strain theory suggests crime develops when there is a disparity between approved success goals and means of achieving those goals; blockages, constraints, barriers. These may be poor education, poor health, racial discrimination, or lack of the new skills needed in a service economy rather than the physical labor of farming or factory work. But corruption (cheating, stealing, even violence) does not necessarily occur only when pathways to upward mobility are blocked. Depending on personality structure, depression, anxiety, or withdrawal may be the reaction. In the delinquent, underlying depression and the antisocial are often linked.

Corruption occurs when pathways are not only open, but are actually greased. The majority of CEOs, professionals and politicians of the first half of the 20st century have not "come up the hard way." (Lately a majority of billionaires have made fortunes through finance and high-end technology, a modified version of the "hard way") Their pathways to riches and power were lubricated by previous wealth, access to higher education, and "start-up" money. George W. Bush, for example, got money from his family and other connections to invest in an oil company, and later in a baseball team. Just over a third, (36%) of Congress (the House and Senate) is made up of lawyers, many of them extremely wealthy. Our recent presidents tend to come from "old money" families; (the Roosevelts, the Bushes) or had wealthy "self-made" fathers; (John Kennedy, liquor dealer, Jimmy Carter, peanut farmer). Few have come up from real poverty, except Lincoln. It takes money to become a president, either your own or the donations of wealthy backers, to whom you are then beholden.

What would have happened if Merton had tried to place Sutherland's "white collar criminals" in his four-fold table? Are the corporate CEOs deviant in the same way as the Mafia or juvenile gangs? Have they internalized success goals but been blocked from realizing those goals by prejudice, poor education, lack of starting capital? Hardly. Remember that Trump got a startup of perhaps $15 million from his real-estate millionaire father.

A large proportion of corporate officers have been well educated. Many have come from wealthy families, and have had the help of "legacy" when entering college. With few exceptions they seem to follow a similar career, maximizing profits rather than products, gobbling up corporations, downsizing them or shutting them down, without regard for the former employees. These are the "job creators," the same people the GOP claims must not have their taxes raised, or they won't invest. Mitt Romney (a Harvard MBA whose father was CEO of American Motors Corporation) was pilloried by a fellow Republican, Rick Perry, for being a "vulture capitalist" rather than a "venture capitalist," because of the history of Bain Capital. Since private equity firms are very private, not much evidence of this accusation has become public. Nevertheless, the routine is often "buy, downsize, and close down." The term "corporate raider" is widely used, and paints an ugly picture.

White collar crime is not confined to the CEOs and bankers. There is plenty of crime in the middle and upper classes, and much of that behavior has become endemic and normative. For example, cheating on income taxes, fixing traffic tickets, buying their children into top schools and colleges through gift giving, and paying lawyers to cover up their peccadilloes. The hiring of illegal immigrants as servants appears to be a specialty of politicians, but that may seem so because they are apt to be outed by the opposing party. Lying under oath about sexual transgressions is the politician's nightmare, and frequently leads to the end of their careers. Bill Clinton survived his denial, but he had to fight the combined efforts of Monica Lewinsky, Linda Tripp, and a team of conservative lawyers hired by Richard Mellon Scaife, heir to the Mellon fortune. (Incidentally, Scaife funded the "Swiftboating" campaign against John Kerry, which led to the continued presidency of George W. Bush.) This smearing of a decorated war hero is another glaring example of white collar crime that has enormous consequences for our country, among them the continuation of the war in Iraq and a recession/depression. Is defamation of character always acceptable (non-criminal) behavior when directed at a politician or public figure? It seems sitting presidents are no longer exempt. Is Obama really a Muslim, foreign born, or the anti-Christ? If so, he must have multiple personalities. For years, even after Obama produced his U.S. birth certificate, Donald Trump continued his "birther" attack.

Are the conservative Supreme Court judges conforming to the new antisocial norms? One might say so, for their Citizens United decision, that corporations are individuals, and thus have unlimited rights to free speech (that is, speech in the form of money from corporations, wealthy donors, and unions) is an outright gift to the Republican Party. The Mafia Dons and the conservative Supreme Court justices are not that far apart in the acceptance of the new norms of antisocial behavior. The damage of that court decision will probably outweigh any damage the Mafia can inflict on the U.S., and it will last for years, as long as there is a 5/4 or even a 6/3conservative majority. The ruling will be hard to overturn without an amendment to the Constitution, which is always a difficult task. If Hillary Clinton had became president, you can be sure there would have been a liberal majority in the Supreme Court, and Citizens United might have been overturned.

Bernie is a psychopath, a convicted criminal, much like the lower class con man, but instead of the dropped purse scam, the "pigeon drop," (described previously) he used the Ponzi scheme and modern technology. The "pigeon drop" scam doesn't inflict the widespread damage of the Ponzi scheme. They are nevertheless both scams, though they operate at very different social levels. The pigeon drop steals from the elderly and poor. Bernie's Ponzi scheme stole from the wealthy and the very rich, such as Elie Wiesel (a Nobel Laureate), Kevin Bacon, Henry Kissinger, Larry King, John Malkovich, and Zsa Zsa Gabor, as well as members of his own synagogue, and thousands of others.

Of the anomic triumvirate, (now a "quadumvirate") only Bernie is a convicted criminal. He was not born dirt poor, nor were Tiger, Dick or Donald. As I mentioned, a majority of CEOs and politicians born approximately between 1900 and 2015, like Mitt Romney (1947, the son of a CEO) were "born with a silver spoon in their mouths." This is a crucial point that is often overlooked in discussions of wrongdoing. (*The term "wrongdoing" seems applicable to crime which is punishable by law, and also to behavior which, though harmful to others and society in general, is not covered by law. An example would be financial support of lobbying for deregulation of high-powered automatic weapons.*)

Let's look at a couple of anomic wrongdoers, who have skirted the edge of criminality but whose deeds, or at least the deeds of others under their command, could be considered criminal.

Jamie Dimon is chairman and chief executive of JPMorgan Chase. His pay in 2011 was $23.1 million, the highest pay for a chief executive at a large U.S. bank.

The rules of monetary compensation seem reversed in the case of Dimon and others in the top 1% or 0.1%. Ordinarily, if someone makes costly mistakes on the job, they may be fired, and certainly do not receive a pay increase the following year. After a $6 billion dollar loss due to a trading blunder on Dimon's watch, his total pay for 2012 was "cut" by the Board of Directors to $11.5 million, a $10 million bonus and $1.5 million salary. This $24 million total was just one million *higher* than his pay in 2011!

But in addition to the $6 billion dollar fine for the trading blowup, Chase was fined $13 billion because it sold bundled mortgages which they knew were not worth much, and even bet against (hedged) their recommendations to their own investment customers. As said previously, in addition they paid a fine of $2 billion because they turned a "blind eye" to the obvious signs of Bernie Madoff's scam. Note that the government brought *criminal* charges against Chase, but Dimon was apparently able to make a deal with the Attorney General (Eric Holder, a Democrat!) to drop the criminal charges in exchange for the fines. The bigger the theft, the less the penalty? Stealing a TV would get you jail. Topsy-turvy. *The banks are not only "too big to fail," but also what I would call "too big to jail."* (Greenberg, J & Craig, S. 2014) [Jessica Silver-Greenberg and Suzanne Craig, JPMorgan Chase Will Give Dimon a Raise, The New York Times, 1/23/14]

Given these huge fines, you would think that Chase would cut Dimon's total pay for 2013, or at least keep it at $11.5 million. Instead the Board announced in January that it will keep his salary constant at $1.5 million, but give him $18.5 million in stock as his 2013 bonus. Chase has shown a large profit for 2013, which is the only consideration on Wall Street. No wonder there is so much resentment against the banks. Billions have finally become chump change.

It is facts like these that illustrate a huge shift in American morality. The rewards go to the high level predators and criminals, while the relatively innocent are punished. Is life today any different from the Biblical maxim, "For to everyone that has shall be given, and he shall have abundance: but from him that has not shall be taken away even that which he has?" (Matthew 13:12) The Chase reward to Dimon, and similar rewards to the undeserving by any code other than that of Wall Street, again support my contention that Merton's "Innovation", or criminality as it is usually called, is not deviant behavior in the U.S., but is *conforming* behavior from the top down to the lowest jaywalker, the butcher with his finger on the scale, or the speeder on the highway. Every day "innovators" are breaking into corporate websites to steal credit card information. Millions have suffered identity theft in the recent Target Company hacking. That some states are cutting the length of unemployment payments (2014) when the country is only slowly recovering from the Bush-induced depression is just as criminal, in my eyes, as a common theft. *We are in an age of topsy-turvy morality.*

This loss of morality is hard to measure. Aside from police reports which are biased by race and social class, one clue is the general degree of trust, and the professions that are most mistrusted. A 2012 Gallup Poll asked the following question. "Please tell me how you would rate the honesty and ethical standards of people in these different fields very high, high, average, low or very low. How about?"— (professions are read off to respondents in random order.)

The following professions had the highest percentages of Low and Very Low ratings: members of Congress, 54%; car salesmen, 49; senators, 45; stockbrokers, 39; lawyers, 38; insurance salespeople, 36; state governors, 31; advertising practitioners, 30; journalists, 30; HMO managers, 27; business executives, 27; and bankers, 24.

Note that politicians are least trusted, and bankers are distrusted more than you might expect. Of course, the public doesn't come in contact with high bank officers, but rather the tellers, who do not make bank policy. With the exception of car salesmen and insurance salesmen, the other professions are made up mostly of middle and upper class members. So the public is well aware and wary of white collar crime.

If morality and trust are at a low ebb, are we "going down the tubes" that George Carlin said have never been found? Is this the cry of Chicken Little, who is hit on the head by an acorn, and tells Henny Penny "The sky is falling," who in turn tells Ducky Lucky. They tell Foxey Loxey, who takes them to his den and "they never come out again."? Surely Chicken Little is a false prophet of doom with little but an acorn to back up her prophesy. Cassandra, on the other hand, was able to predict future events accurately. Apollo put a curse on her because she refused his advances.

Thus no one would listen to or believe her predictions. This predicament is standard fare in movies. The hero or heroine knows something terrible, but no one, especially the police, will listen.

Both Chicken Little and Cassandra look on the dark side, and I remind you that Hobbes, Freud, Nietzsche, Voltaire, Sartre and many other great thinkers had a dim view of human nature and the future. With a balance between regulation and laissez faire, between left and right, between Republicans and Democrats, with constraints on rampant capitalism, our nation will probably survive. But will it and the rest of the world survive global warming? Al Gore and James Hansen are seen by many on the right as the Chicken Littles of our time, raising a hue and cry over an acorn. Global Warming is no acorn. Two winters ago my wife and I were exposed to what she calls the "bipolar vortex" weakening, which allows cold arctic air to descend onto the Northern Hemisphere. We were experiencing Fahrenheit temperatures between zero and 10 degrees for several weeks.

Those who deny global warming are putting present financial gain (in oil and coal) ahead of the long term health of the planet and its inhabitants. This is grandiosity of global proportions.

The slap on the wrist received by JPMorgan Chase and Dimon for deceiving the public, the government, and even its own private investors, must have reinforced the grandiosity of Chase's bank officers and that of many other U.S. bank CEOs. We already saw the delusions of grandeur in the 2009 statement by Lloyd Blankfein, CEO of Goldman Sachs defending the exorbitant bonuses of his officers, that the banks are "doing God's work." Another famous pronouncement we cited that was indicative of extreme grandiosity was reported by Ron Suskind in 2004, attributed to an unnamed aide to Bush, widely believed to be Karl Rove: "We're an empire now, and when we act, we create our own reality." (Danner, M., 2007) [Danner, Mark. "Words in a Time of War," tomdspatch.com, May 31, 2007.]

Along with, and part of grandiosity is an important characteristic of many high level anomic personalities. This is the idée fixe. It's also called an obsession, and sometimes a "dream" that is a driving force in the individual's life. This obsession can be for the good of society, or it can be destructive. The anomic is usually convinced that it is beneficial to all, ("God's work," Jamie Dimon) though it is often beneficial only to that individual.

We saw that grandiosity is a common trait in the anomic, and this grandiosity impels the anomic outliers, such as Tiger, Bernie, Dick, and Donald to do "great deeds." Tiger had a dream of being the top golfer and highest paid athlete, and he only did harm to his wife and children, to his numerous lovers, and to the millions who admired him. Bernie had a dream of being rich and of having a lifestyle of yachts, travel, and multiple homes. His obsession with more and more money destroyed the lives of thousands, including his own family. His idée fixe was so strong that he continued the scam even when he knew that it would eventually collapse. Dick had an obsession with power, and an idée fixe of an "imperial presidency" which he actually controlled until "W" (George W. Bush) woke up toward the end of his second term as president, and let him go. Donald Trump fulfilled his dream of becoming president, even if it meant borrowing from Russian banks, playing toady to Putin, and paying off prostitutes to avoid scandal just before the 2016 election. These moves will eventually cost him the presidency he prized.

Donald Rumsfeld had an idée fixe. He was a skilled CEO with an excellent managerial record. He was Secretary of Defense under President "W." Iraq was invaded on March 20th, 2003, an invasion justified by "Weapons of Mass Destruction" (WMDs) purportedly found in Iraq but which were never found. On May 1, 2003, the invasion was over, and victory was apparent. Time to cut back the troops! But by 2004 Iraq was in a state of open warfare. Suicide bombings and improvised explosive devices were killing civilians and U.S. soldiers. The Sunnis who were deposed by the American invasion and the death of Saddam Hussein were fighting the Shiites. The invasion had purposely been made by a minimal force of 150,000, highly mobile and computerized in keeping with Rumsfeld's obsession; a total revision of the military, based on efficiency. Six months after the invasion, the troop strength had been cut down to under 30,000. Rumsfeld had no plans for an occupation of Iraq! His idea of efficiency might work in the corporate world, but in Iraq there was a need for "boots on the ground." Mark Danner, commenting on Rumsfeld's habit of denying reality, says:

"It bespeaks a man who, having begun by believing that he could change the world by the force of his own power and will, came to assume that the world must be as he wills it to be." (Danner, M., 2014) [Mark Danner, Rumsfeld: "Why We Live in His Ruins, The New York Review of Books, 2/6/14, p. 36.] Danner feels that the legacy of Rumsfeld is the current internecine chaos in Iraq, in Afghanistan with a Taliban resurgence, and in Syria with Iraqi jihadists, including ISIS, joining the rebellion against Assad.

Grandiosity paired with an obsession also comes with an almost childlike attitude of invulnerability. In Rumsfeld's case he was sure we couldn't lose, despite his drastic troop cuts after the supposed "victory" in Iraq.

We know that teens are often reckless drivers, and their high insurance rates reflect their high accident rate. Their accident rates also reflect their unwarranted confidence that nothing can happen to them. I spoke of lawyer Eliot Spitzer's extreme risk-taking by paying call girls with his credit card. Any lawyer would know better. Raised in opulence, he had always been protected by his family's real estate fortune.

"Mr. Spitzer cast himself, self-consciously......long predawn runs, fierce basketball games.......as the alpha male. . . He was viewed as *reckless* (my emphasis) by both friends and enemies." (Greenberg, B.A., 2014) [Brad A. Greenberg, Spitzer's Folly, Jewish Journal, 3/10/2008. Posted 1/24/14/] Recklessness, acting as if there were no tomorrow, tends to be a teen male folly. Of course, when Alan Greenspan suggested that "irrational exuberance has unduly inflated asset values," he was speaking of the irrational exuberance of *adult* stock brokers and investors, not teenagers.

We know that an idée fixe, an obsession, or a dream can result in great benefits to society. The dreams of Martin Luther King and Mohandas Gandhi, of Darwin, or Einstein, have changed the way we think and live. It is clear that you have to be virtually obsessed to fight for change in politics or science and to make those ideas be accepted and those dreams come true.

In our society the goals of sex, money and power, or as Karen Horney put it, prestige, power and possession, are endemic. These goals are generally achieved at the expense of others and the larger society. The means of achieving these goals, once considered deviant, criminal, or harmful to others, have become generally accepted at all levels of society. They are no longer "deviant." from an established norm of "good" behavior.

The problem of establishing control after behavior, both individual and corporate has become decontrolled, is that extreme controls would make us prisoners, slaves, or captives in a dictatorship. This was a concern of Durkheim over 100 years ago. Strangely, today's more extreme Republicans want to control women's *sexual* activity but want to *de*control corporations and assault rifles. Concern with preserving life ostensibly leads the right wing to fight abortion. Yet the same "right to lifers" tend to support the death penalty. Birth control pills, now more easily available than ever, are still being fought tooth and nail by some legislators. Birth control was achieved with aspirin in the old days, according to Foster Friess, the Wyoming born-again billionaire mutual fund manager. (Maybe the "Wolf of Wall Street" has a rival in Wyoming.) "Back in my day they used Bayer aspirin for contraceptives. The gals put it between their knees and it wasn't costly." (Baker, M., 2014) [Marge Baker, Aspirin as the New Birth Control, Huffington Post, Politics, 1/28/2014.] Friess has funded the usual conservative causes. He opposes health reform, funds "school choice" (charter schools), and was a main contributor to Republican Rick Santorum's 2012 Super Pac as a presidential candidate. What is scary is the ability of some super-wealthy anomics with such extreme views to pour money into right-wing political action committees (PACs). The goal clearly seems to be social control of others and decontrol of business.

Women, youth and minorities are weaker, and make good targets for control. Freedom is more likely to be seen as freedom *to* make profits by conservatives, and more likely to be interpreted as freedom *from* poverty and oppression and freedom *of* expression by liberals.

SUMMARY

This chapter has defined the anomic personality, using as a model the traits of the Aggressive Narcissist, and the model of Daniel Goleman and Delroy Paulhus that they call the "Dark Triad/Tetrad." The triad of narcissist, Machiavellian and psychopath constitutes, in my model, the more extreme end of a culturally patterned defect, in Erich Fromm's sense. That defect is the "anomic personality of our time" (to mirror Karen

Horney's title, op.cit.). Examples of individuals showing these anomic personality traits (which closely follow those of the aggressive narcissist) were given. In Chapter One we listed the traits that are found in the Anomic Personality. These are: 1. Relentless pursuit of goals. 2. Limitless goals. 3. Treat people as objects. 4. Cunning, smooth talkers. 5. Usually charismatic. 6. Sexual addiction. 7. Strong drive for power.

The disastrous effects of inequality caused by the rise of the Anomic Personalities in our culture were discussed. The extent of this personality type and its behavior was shown, from politicians and CEOs to bank presidents and members of the Supreme Court down to the Mafia, the common con man, the income tax cheater and even the jaywalker.

The question of whether crime and even reprehensible and misbehavior (wrongdoing) are "deviant", in that they ignore common accepted norms of behavior, was addressed. Robert Merton, in "Social Structure and Anomie", presented a fourfold table. There are the "Innovators" who accept success goals but not the means of achieving them (because Merton thinks they are blocked from the usual paths to success, hence "Strain theory"). There are the "Conformists" who accept both goals and approved means of achieving them. When White Collar criminals are added to the mix, it looks as if our population lies on a continuum from mild misbehavior (gossiping, snubbing, jaywalking) through delinquency, high-school pranks, college hazing, to white collar non-violent crime (securitization, insider trading, bribing politicians and "pay for play," ending with assault, battery, rape, murder, and perhaps initiating wars. Crime that's punishable by law is only a small part of that continuum of mild wrongdoing to destructive behavior.

As a result of including White Collar criminality, the innovators and conformists merge into a huge group of conformists who conform to increasingly accepted norms concerning success and what you can do to achieve it. Lip service is still given to the old norms and rules that go by the name of old fashioned morality. The loss of this morality is much bemoaned, especially on the right. The "Ritualists" or bureaucrats, focus on the means, not the goals, and exhibit compulsivity. They too can do damage, by blocking others from mobility or action by rigidly sticking to the rules. The "Retreatists" (addicts, schizophrenics) have given up on both the goals and the means of achieving them. They are not under the "strain" of blocked pathways to success. They are also not around in great numbers, compared to the new conformists to new norms of allowable behavior.

(However, recent mortality statistics, we'll show later, indicate that the White Retreatists are increasing in number, only to die in midlife.) It is only when the 1% come to wield such power that the scope of rotten behavior from the bottom to the very top of our society comes into focus. Cries of "Inequality!" are heard throughout the land, and around the world.

How does this state of economic deregulation and personal deregulation known as anomie affect the individual's emotions? One of the many great contributions of Durkheim is the recognition that the *feeling state* accompanying capitalism (and the financial world) and its usual societal state of anomie is tantalizing. One reaches for the grapes, which are always out of reach and receding upward. One needs more and more. He called it a "derangement" and "an insatiable will." The goal is limitless. We see this recently in the progression from millionaires to billionaires. Individuals in the financial world (hedge fund managers) can make a billion in a day!

The concept of an "insatiable will" is hard to understand. Is it the same for the sex addict, who may need more and more stimulation and multiple partners for satisfaction, and the striving CEO?? The concept of extinction may be applicable here. When you have been in a horse stable for 15 minutes, the original strong odor has been greatly reduced. Similarly, the 24 hour bouts of honeymoon intercourse dim in later years, due to this same extinction of a stimulus. Is it extinction of the stimulus that is forcing the sexual anomic to turn to multiple partners, or an exorbitant and overwhelming sex drive and capacity? There may be a mix of motivations, including the locker-room kudos given to the sexual athlete. The sexual conquests can be akin to the scalps garnered by the Comanche and the Cheyenne in the custom of "counting coup." For each coup or conquest, you can stick an eagle feather in your coup stick. This might be painful for sex addicts.

The sex drive has to be of interest to sociologists as well as psychiatrists and psychologists, since its presence is felt everywhere; in our movies, novels, the porn industry, prostitution, teen dating, and the procession of outed politicians and famous people who have strayed from the marital bed. I doubt that marriage has as much power nowadays to limit male suicide, as it did in Durkheim's day a century ago. Nevertheless, unmarried males still have much higher rates of suicide than married males in the U.S.

The rate of suicide in the world of finance is high, as Durkheim said. I use the U.S. White rate as a very rough measure of suicide in the financial sector, since rates are not available by sector. Generally, Whites have high rates of death by suicide (14.2 per 100,000 in 2013) and low rates of death by homicide (2.5 per 100,000). African Americans have low rates of suicide (5.4 per 100,000 in 2013) *but the highest rate of death by homicide of any subgroup in the U.S. and in almost all countries of the world (19.4 per 100,000 in 2013).*

A recent sharp increase in the mortality rate of lower class Whites seems to fly in the face of expectations and past experience. While mortality rates for virtually all groups (by country, by age, sex, ethnic background, socioeconomic status, etc.) *have gone down* due to worldwide better nutrition, better medical care and innovation, mortality rates for middle-age U.S. Whites (45 to 54) with "no more than a high school education" have "*increased* by 134 deaths per 100,000 from 1999 to 2014." (Kolata, G., 2015) [Kolata, G. "Rise in Deaths for U.S. Whites in Middle Age." *The New York Times,* 11/3/2015.]

When the Princeton economists, Dr. Angus Deaton (2015 Nobel Prize in Economics) and Anne Case discovered this shocking reversal of expectations in their mortality data, "they concluded that taken together, *suicides, drugs and alcohol* explained the overall increase in deaths." (My emphasis.) In the high-school or less-educated group, death rates *rose* by 22%, while they *fell* for the college educated. (Kolata, G. op. cit.) I will discuss the acquisition of survival skills needed in an anomic competitive system in Chapter Eight. Many of these are gained through college education. In part they are language facility and glibness, social skills that include manipulation of others, feelings of superiority (grandiosity), a lack of empathy (the rich tend to be less empathic toward those below) and a feeling of continued invulnerability due to the cushioning of wealth. The anomic personality is clearly an adaptation to a winner-take-all society.

But education level is closely linked to income. "In the period examined by Dr. Deaton and Dr. Case, the inflation-adjusted income for households headed by a high-school graduate fell by 19 percent." (Kolata, G., supra). Economic deprivation (being poor) is a powerful depressant.

In addition, Whites with no college suffer from *relative deprivation*, because Whites are somehow expected to go to college and graduate. The statistical results showing a surge in mortality of 22% in this group of less-educated Whites, with increased reports of pain, poor health and distress, suffering a 19% loss of income, and with the mortality rising in the specific areas of suicides, drugs and alcohol, seems to me a slam dunk argument for *situational or reactive depression*. Poor and less educated Whites are suffering from a quadruple whammy; lack of anomic survival skills learned in college, recent sharp loss of income, poor health, and relative deprivation by comparison with their reference group, rich Whites. I can't help but think once again of my favorite quote shown in full early in this chapter. As Obama said "You go into some of these small towns in Pennsylvania, and …..the Midwest, the jobs have been gone now for 25 years and nothing's replaced them. . . And it's not surprising, then they get bitter, they cling to guns or religion or antipathy to people who aren't like them…. as a way to explain their frustrations." (Obama, B. supra) *And they take drugs and alcohol and commit suicide to ease the pain.*

CHAPTER FIVE

BERNARD L. "BERNIE" MADOFF

Over one hundred years ago, Durkheim wrote that the financial world was in a state of perpetual anomie, or deregulation. Today we see a continuation of this societal state, evidenced by the Enron and WorldCom scandals, ("creative accounting"'), the dot-com (Internet) bubble, the Savings and Loan crisis, the subprime loan and housing bubble, and the subsequent recessions and depressions. At the same time these scandals, scams and bursting financial bubbles were begging for governmental (*societal*) regulation, the people involved in these activities were *individually* deregulated. It takes individuals to make up an anomic (or any) society, and my claim is that these individuals in our society have an anomic personality that partakes of the "dark tetrad" or *spectrum* of psychopathy, the manipulative, narcissistic Factor 1, the Manichaean, the Sadism, and often the criminality Factor 2 discussed previously.

We remember a few of these financial anomics because they are household names. They are etched in memory due to the extremes of greed and hubris they exhibited. Among them are Charles Ponzi, Senator Albert Fall of the Teapot Dome scandal, Boss Tweed of Tammany Hall, Jeffrey Skilling (former CEO of Enron Corporation), and Bernard Ebbers (former CEO of WorldCom Corporation).

Among all of these financial anomics, Bernie Madoff still stands out today. He dwarfs even his famous predecessor, Charles Ponzi, because of the enormity of his stealing. Bernie's Ponzi scheme is hailed as the largest financial scam in U.S. history. The estimates of the money he stole have varied from 50 billion to 175 billion and the exact amount may never be known, but recent estimates put it closer to $20 billion. While Tiger Woods may have been king below the belt, Bernie is currently still king of thieves. He represents the manipulative interpersonal skills, the cold-blooded disregard for other people (including his own family), and the cunning required to keep a Ponzi pyramid of investors in the dark for many years.

Before we look at Bernie M.'s history, and try to understand his personality, let it be said that he, like Tiger Woods and Dick Cheney, was at the top of his profession. He was one of the founders of the NASDAQ stock exchange, and its chairman for several terms. He helped to introduce innovative computer information technology that make stock quotes available, which led to the formation of NASDAQ. He managed to outfox some of the smartest people in the financial industry, and fooled government investigators for many years before his Ponzi scheme inevitably broke down. What a pity that his skills were not turned to some activity that would have helped the world.

In this chapter I will give short shrift to the details of Bernie's financial history and eventual downfall which is common knowledge by now, and place more emphasis on what little I can find that speaks to his personality. Finding just how he fits the criteria for psychopathy other than his gigantic robbery of thousands of people poses a particular problem, since what most observers were shown before his arrest was a façade, a deliberate persona put on for the public. That public, which he so cleverly misled, consisted of thousands of investors, government investigators and regulators, the members of his synagogue, and even his close family members. Because he played his cards so close to the chest, it was only in especially rare and stressful moments that his true character came out. Even after his arrest, his controlled demeanor seldom showed the explosive force and disdain for others that he contained.

Bernie M., as we shall call him, was born in 1938 in Queens. New York His parents, Ralph and Sylvia Madoff, (née Muntner) married during the Depression of the 1930s. Ralph was of Polish-Jewish background, and Sylvia was of Romanian-Austrian Jewish extraction. Ralph worked for years as a plumber. It was only in the 1950s that the couple became involved in finance, and became more secure. The SEC (Securities and

Exchange Commission) closed Sylvia Madoff's brokerage-dealer business for lack of reporting its financial condition.

His mother's history of illegal financial behavior could have foreshadowed Bernie's tussles with the S.E.C. His parents probably acted as models for his adult scheming. Both parents were broker-dealers, and may well have been involved in crooked financial activities other than the mother's failure to report income.

Bernie was on the swimming team at Far Rockaway High School, and the coach got him a job as a lifeguard in a club at Atlantic Beach. He saved the $5000 he made there, and along with some money he earned installing lawn sprinklers, used it to start his investment company. His behavior early on shows excellent long range planning functions. These are the "executive functions" of the frontal cortex. But some plans have a built-in bad end; the Ponzi scheme for example, which inevitably blows up when the investors at the bottom of the pyramid get too numerous, and start to demand their money.

Bernie graduated from high school in 1956, and from Hofstra in 1960. In 1959 he married Ruth Alpern, his sweetheart since high school. She studied finance at Queens College, and earned her BA there. Her father was a retired C.P.A., and helped the young couple start Bernard L. Madoff Investment Securities, LLC. The firm grew rapidly because of reported returns of 10% or more, and as we all know, many famous people, including actors and athletes, invested much or all of their life savings with Madoff.

Madoff Securities developed a computer program to give stock quotes. That became the National Association Securities Dealers Automated Quotations, or NASDAQ, and after some time Madoff became president of the board of directors for the NASDAQ stock exchange.

Bernie brought family members into the firm, not an unusual move, but a wise one since they could be controlled, and would be loath to testify against him. His brother Peter, his sons Andrew and Mark, and Peter's son Roger and daughter Shana, held various positions. Bernie's cousin, Charles Weiner, ran the trading section of Madoff Securities, where Andrew and Mark worked.

On December 10th, 2008, Bernie told his sons the truth of his lies: that all their wealth had come from the Ponzi scheme. He had not bought stock for most of the investors who were his clients. Instead, he deposited the money in his own Chase Bank account, and used it to pay off the early investors. The sons reported their father to federal agents, and Bernie was arrested the next day. He was charged with various counts of fraud, money laundering, perjury and theft.

On December 11th, 2010, Mark was found hanged in his apartment, a suicide the day before, exactly two years after his father's arrest. He and Andrew each received millions from their father's Chase accounts, and deposited relatively tiny sums of their own. They must have known that something was amiss, but they worked in the trading section and were not allowed into the locked upper floor offices, where all the falsification of stock sales documents went on. The compartmentalization of the firm into the legitimate trading and criminal Ponzi operation attests to Bernie's genius. It also supports the idea that his compulsivity facilitated the juggling act he had to perform. He had to keep two separate businesses going, and had to lead two separate lives; the publicly acclaimed investor-philanthropist and the computer-savvy con man. His trading office downstairs was immaculate, and decorated in conservative grey. Any dust, dirt, or spills had to be cleaned up immediately, accompanied by a severe reprimand. His Ponzi office was on the floor above, always locked, with access granted to only three people. It was the complete opposite of the trading office, never cleaned, because the cleaning personnel might catch on to the illegal goings-on. Leading such a complex double-life took great skill, and a commensurate compulsive personality. While it may seem that compulsivity and psychopathy are incompatible, the psychopath often engages in elaborate planning and develops a sophisticated *modus operandi*. (Madoff B. 2014) [Bernard L Madoff, 2014. The Biography.com website. http://www.biography.com/people/bernard-madoff-46636 6.].

Psychopaths vary in the degree of violence they exhibit. Let's look at one of the more violent examples.

Ted Bundy, the killer of at least thirty young women, lured many of them into his Volkswagen car by pretending to have a broken arm in a sling or a cast on his leg, which he fashioned. He would ask the woman victim to help him put his luggage or books into the back of his wagon, and when she obliged out of pity for this apparently helpless injured man, he would push her into the wagon and bludgeon her into unconsciousness. His killings were elaborately planned, so that no incriminating evidence, such as guns or bullets. would be found. Obsessive-compulsive behavior, seemingly incompatible with murder or theft, is often found in psychopaths.

A whole series of lawsuits followed Bernie's conviction and sentencing to 150 years in federal prison. These lawsuits can be followed on line and in the references for this chapter. A trustee, Irving Picard, was appointed to go after the money and property that Bernie, his relatives and his associates stole.

Some of the more prominent victims will be mentioned later. One victim is worth mentioning in some detail, for it gives us a true picture of Bernie's lack of empathy, a hallmark of the psychopath. "Twelve days after Bernard Madoff admitted to the FBI that he had cheated thousands of people out of billions of dollars, one of his victims committed suicide. Rene-Thierry Magon de la Villehuchet, a sixty-five-year-old French aristocrat who lived and worked in New York as an investment adviser for Access International Advisors, was found dead in his office in Manhattan on December 23. He had taken sleeping pills and then slit his wrists. Madoff was at the kitchen table of his penthouse apartment, under luxurious house arrest, when he learned of the suicide. He sneered. 'That guy couldn't pick a stock if his life depended on it." (Ross, b. 2009) [Ross, B. *The Madoff Chronicles.* New York: Hyperion/HarperCollins, 2009, back jacket copy].

The façade that Bernie presented to the public was at odds with what he said and felt in private. During the trial, he apologized to his victims.

"I have left a legacy of shame, as some of my victims have pointed out, to my family and my grandchildren. This is something I will live in for the rest of my life. I'm sorry. I know that doesn't help you." (Wikipedia, Madoff)

Note that he is really saying that he's sorry about his legacy of shame, but doesn't say he is sorry that he stole the victim's money. His real feelings for the victims come out when he is in prison.

"…that evening an inmate badgered Madoff about the victims of his $65 billion scheme, and kept at it. According to K.C. White, a bank robber and prison artist who escorted a sick friend that evening, Madoff stopped smiling and got angry. 'Fuck my victims,' he said. Loud enough for other inmates to hear. 'I carried them for twenty years, and now I'm doing 150 years.'"(Fishman, S., 2010) [Fishman, S. "Bernie Madoff, Free at Last," *New York Magazine*, June 6, 2010 published online at NYMag.com.]

. This seeming acceptance or at least tolerance of the ability to turn lies into truths is part of the topsy-turvy world we live in. "Creating our own reality" at the highest levels of government is truly frightening. Madoff injured thousands. Rumsfeld, Cheney and Scooter Libby injured millions by invading Iraq, thus aligning it with Iran, a nuclear loose-cannon, after Iraq became Shiite-led. Saddam Hussein was a Sunni and a very bad guy, but look at the carnage still going on in Iraq today between the angry dethroned Sunnis (most notoriously the ISIS with their repeated beheading of Americans) and the dominant Shiites. After repeating their own lies, like finding Weapons of Mass Destruction, our leaders begin to believe them. No leader of the G.W. Bush eight years has publicly shown remorse for American lives lost because of Iraq, Afghanistan, or Vietnam. As shown by his quotes and tweets, Trump has shown no remorse. He scores high in Psychopathy, as well as in the other three symptom clusters in the Dark Tetrasd.

Bernie is not alone among financial thieves. He has the company of 183 well-known Americans convicted of similar large-scale fraud. Here are just fourteen of them, as a reminder of the popularity of this "road to success." These are the famous crooks: Ivan Boesky, John Gotti, Rajat Gupta, Leona Helmsley, Jimmy Hoffa, L. Ron Hubbard, Clifford Irving, Charles Keating, Lyndon La Rouche, Jeb Stuart Magruder, John McNamara, Raj Rajaratnam, Kenneth Starr, and Michael Milken. The not so famous, and the ones never caught or convicted, are countless.

Ivan Boesky, convicted of insider trading, was fined $100 million, served two years of a 3.5 year sentence and was permanently barred from working in securities. Speaking to the Berkeley, California, School of Business commencement ceremony in 1986, he famously said "I think greed is healthy. You can be greedy and still feel good about yourself." That seems to sum up the new morality of the anomic personality. Driven to succeed by any and all means in a competitive and cut-throat society, these terrifying yet pitiable figures dominate in most, or perhaps in all fields of endeavor. We see the Icaruses that have flown too near the sun and crashed into the sea. We don't see the millions whose wing wax has not melted, are still flying, and have not been caught.

Who were some of the more well-known injured parties that Bernie bilked? This is a partial list, more complete than mentioned before. Some of these clients were billionaire investors; Steven Spielberg (Hollywood mogul), David Gottesman (First Manhattan Company), Norman Braman (art collector), Elie Wiesel (his nonprofit Foundation for Humanity lost $15 million), and Mort Zuckerman (real estate), Other celebrities but not necessarily billionaires were Sandy Koufax (baseball star), Fred Wilpon (N.Y. Mets owner), actors Kevin Bacon and wife Kyra Sedgwick, and Zsa Zsa Gabor. The 2009 list of clients covers 162 pages, and includes charitable foundations and pension funds of towns that hoped to increase their support of the needy. Thousands of individual investors who invested in three feeder funds are not even listed. Most of the clients lost all or a large part of their money.

Let's take a more detailed look at some of Bernie's behavior that would lead us to believe that he is a pre-clinical psychopath. The nomenclature commonly used to describe a person with Bernie's personality is confusing. The terms psychopath and sociopath are often used interchangeably. In addition, the Diagnostic and Statistical Manual (DSM V) has pared down the personality disorders to six. They are Antisocial, Narcissistic, Obsessive-Compulsive, Borderline, Avoidant, and Schizotypal. I have put them in the order which I think is closest to their dominance in Bernie's makeup. He is clearly *antisocial*, since he is a convicted criminal. However, he is also strikingly *narcissistic*, due to his grandiosity, lack of empathy or remorse, and extreme manipulation of others. In addition, he has a secondary set of behaviors which make him a likely candidate for *obsessive-compulsive personality disorder*. Obviously, the symptoms and traits defining an individual's diagnosis tend to overlap considerably, and the end label hopefully depends upon the dominant or "primary" set of symptoms.

I chose to use the symptom list of Factor 1, because it is based on a factor analysis of traits found in a sample of subjects given the Hare Psychopathy Checklist and a structured interview.

The characteristics of the "aggressive narcissist" or Factor 1 come closest to defining the psychopath, without even including Factor 2, (overtly criminal behavior). I have made the distinction between the "aggressive narcissist" who shares many traits with the psychopath, and the "everyday narcissist," who is primarily egocentric and grandiose, but not very "nasty." Here are some of the Factor 1 traits, as they appear in Bernie:

Glibness, superficial charm: Bernie was able to handle his relations with his wealthy clients with great ease. He built up an aura of respectability around himself by attracting rich and well-known people up front, who could spread the word about his unbelievable 10% to 15% returns. He was at ease with all social levels, including the somewhat shady characters he later brought into the scam who were not relatives. When asked by the FBI and SEC investigators, he gave glib answers, and concocted elaborate explanations to explain why he, alone, was getting such high returns. He charmed older female investors in particular. If they asked too many questions, he would threaten to drop them as investors. Since he could make up any stock sale report after the fact, he would show suspicious investors the fake sales reports he made up for such individuals. Under his façade of charm as the respectable investment advisor was a seething resentment of the very rich whom he claimed to "carry for twenty years."

Grandiose sense of self-worth: Bernie's decision to start a Ponzi scheme is the best evidence for his grandiosity. Ponzi scams have a built-in failure, stemming from the fact that although early investors can be paid back their money, the later investors at the bottom of the pyramid inevitably grow so fast that there is no more money to pay them. Their demands for payment lead to the eventual arrest of the criminal. Even the average financier knows this. Bernie's grandiosity led him to ignore this fact. He thought he could beat the odds, even when at some level of consciousness he knew it was impossible.

Bernie's grandiosity clearly shows in his excessively extravagant life style. He aspired to live like the richest men in the U.S., if not the world. The family yacht, *Bull,* was worth $7 million, and was moored at Cap d'Antibes on the French Riviera. His penthouse in New York was worth $7.5 million. "They traveled the world together in two private luxury jets co-owned by Madoff with family and friends. Bernie and Ruth adopted a life style and demeanor that belied their outer-borough upbringing. They sought the 'old money' look, even though their money was freshly stolen." (Ross, *supra.* p. 88.)

A few weeks before his arrest, he spent $1299 for a blue Polo shirt and $2000 for a pair of light grey cashmere slacks at Trillion, a men's store in

Palm Beach. He had four houses; Manhattan, Montauk, Palm Beach and the French Riviera. (Ross, p. 89) In addition to frequent visits to their houses, Bernie and Ruth made the rounds of Cabo San Lucas, Mexico, and went skiing in St. Moritz, Vail and Aspen. (Ross, p. 90)

Everything had to be on a grand scale for Bernie. He had 13 gold watches. He owned 20 pairs of sueded loafers. (This was no match for Imelda Marcos, who owned thousands of shoes.) His grandiosity may have stemmed in part from the attempt of an arriviste to appear as part of American aristocracy, but it failed by virtue of its excess.

Pathological lying: Bernie's Ponzi scam was one enormous lie that lasted for at least thirty years, depending on when he started to cheat his clients. But he apparently was already adept at lying as a sophomore in high school. His classmate and friend, Jay Portnoy, remembered an incident that shows him as a glib liar. "He hadn't read a book and he was called on in English class to give a book report. So Bernie got up there and just made it up while he went along. After Bernie's presentation, the teacher looked a little suspicious. She asked Bernie to show the class the book, but Bernie said he had already returned it to the public library." (Ross, p 26.)

Brazen adult lies were common. He lied to his wife, his sons, and all of his employees who were not directly involved in the scam, but were in the trading portion of his empire. He lied to numerous government investigators. He lied in small ways, but always cunningly. For example, he posted his profile on the company website. It said Madoff "founded the firm soon after leaving law school." That was true, but it did not say that he *dropped out* of law school after one year. (Ross, p.63.) How often have we heard of public officials eventually being caught after having falsified service in the armed forces, or graduation from college? Bernie the lying dropout is in good company. The anomic personality is legion and ubiquitous.

In retrospect it is a miracle that Bernie wasn't caught sooner, for even this master liar often had no good answers to queries about his operation. "Madoff was known to become irritated if someone asked too many questions, and he refused to answer standard industry questions about the percentages held in cash, the amount of borrowed money....Of course the reason for this was that he had no good answers. The entire operation was a fabrication. No stocks were traded. No options were purchased…"

(Ross, p 74.) Each day after the stock market closed, Madoff and his right hand man, DiPascali, would pick the stocks that did well and create fake trading records that could be shown to the clients. The money his clients gave him went directly into Bernie's Chase account! (Ross, p. 52.)

Cunning/manipulative: Eleanor Squillari, Madoff's faithful secretary, turned on him after his arrest. She had fared very well financially during the scam years, but apparently did not know what the upper floor was doing. "I told the FBI, if he's trying to convince anybody that he's losing it, come and talk to me because I know he was calm as a cucumber up until the day of his arrest...He is so good, we now know, at manipulating everybody. In the entire world." (Ross, p. 52.) Brad Garrett, a former FBI agent, pointed out the cunning technique Bernie used to control his employees. "If you surround yourself with people who are beholden to you and you've elevated them to a position they would have probably never reached on their own, then you control them." (Ross, p. 78.) Madoff's cheating wasn't limited to his Ponzi scheme. In addition to swindling his investors, investigators say there is evidence he stole from some of them outright by looting the estates of clients who had named him the executor. An executor has a fiduciary duty to perform; he must look after his clients' best interests. Bernie looked after his own interests first, by hook and crook.

Emotionally shallow: In his relations with his clients he obviously was duplicitous, and the façade of the trusted and caring investment counselor he presented was totally false. His relationships with office personnel, and even with his own brother, Peter, were dictatorial, alternating with cruelty. "Madoff could be a difficult boss, whose needling, crude jokes and insulting comments were unrelenting. He would come out of the men's room with his zipper down, and when Eleanor (his long-time secretary) rolled her eyes, he would say "Oh, come on, you know you want it" (Ross, p. 129.)

Lack of remorse or guilt: Nick Casale's firm was hired to provide security for Madoff. Nick, a former New York City policemen, said "He was almost blank, he didn't show emotion. A serial killer type....He did not seem like the most contrite person I ever met." (Ross, p. 52, 53) Bernie's lack of remorse is caught with crystalline clarity in his angry exclamation, "Fuck the clients" quoted above. He is the opposite of remorseful. He sees himself as the victim, not those he injured. This is typical of the psychopath. His public apology is interesting, because he says (quoted above) that "I have left a legacy of shame ...to my family and grandchildren." He doesn't apologize to his victims, *but to his family for bringing shame on them!* For that he is "sorry." His remorse is limited to self and family.

Callous, lack of empathy: Stealing from strangers certainly shows a lack of consideration for others. But planning the financial ruination of a close friend and his family seems an especially callous act. Marty Joel shared an office with Bernie early in their careers. "Madoff delivered the eulogy at Joel's funeral, and he hired Joel's daughter, Amy, to work for him. The Joel family thought it had more than $20 million invested with Madoff, and was wiped out when their loyal friend and Amy's boss was revealed to be a crook." (Ross, p. 62.)

Failure to take responsibility for own actions: When he was to go to trial, Bernie made a half-hearted apology for his crime. His true feelings were revealed in jail, when he blurted out that he had "carried" his victims for twenty years. It is true that a few early investors came out ahead and unscathed. But the vast majority lost their money, and many were wiped out financially. The psychopath's excuse when caught, is that his victims were greedy, "so it's their own fault they lost their money, not mine."

There are several important traits that Bernie exhibited which do not fall directly under the rubric of Aggressive Narcissism or Psychopathy. One is suspiciousness. Another is obsessive-compulsive behavior.

Suspiciousness: When involved in a major criminal undertaking, such as a Ponzi scheme, the possibility of discovery and arrest is constantly on the con man's mind. A state of heightened vigilance is necessary to avoid any error or any clue that might tip off the authorities. With such a large operation, even one disloyal employee can become an informer. "Despite nurturing a familial atmosphere in his offices, he installed two cameras on the small trading floor of the firm's London operations so he could monitor the unit remotely from New York."
((Creswell, J & Thomas, L. 2009) [Creswell, J & Thomas, L. "The Talented Mr. Madoff," The New York Times, January 24, 2009.]

Obsessive-Compulsive Behavior; One usually thinks of the Obsessive-Compulsive individual as a neurotic, possibly concerned with germs and given to frequent hand-washing. Bernie's obsessive-compulsive behavior was undoubtedly part of his defense against being caught, because attention to minute detail and micro-management was a way to control damage and discovery. But that doesn't mean that OCD wasn't always part of his makeup. The Ponzi scheme dominated his life, and compulsivity was needed to monitor this complex operation.

His compulsivity spilled over into everyday activities. For example, "He was .....an avid collector of vintage watches and took time each morning to match his wedding ring—he owned at least two—to the platinum or gold watch band he was wearing on that day." (Creswell, 2009)

Frequently his obsession with control, order and cleanliness resulted in bizarre behavior at work. "Mr. Madoff scouted the office for potential filth. Once, when he spotted an employee eating a pear at his desk in New York, this person (a former employee) said, Mr. Madoff spied some juice dripping onto the grey carpet. 'What are you doing?' this person recalls Mr. Madoff demanding. 'Eating a pear,' the employee replied. Mr. Madoff ripped the soiled carpet from the floor, then rushed to a closet to retrieve a similar swatch to replace it." (Creswell, supra). Others reported that for Madoff, "everything had to be perfect," and that he was a "micromanager." Bernie said after his arrest that he was in constant fear of being caught, and that being in prison was a kind of relief from the complicated charade he had been carrying on for many years.

The color schemes of the New York and London office were tightly controlled by Bernie. "He imposed a sleek black and gray color scheme on the office décor. Employees were allowed to have only one or two personal photographs on their desks, and they had to be in a Madoff-approved silver or black picture frame. (Ross, p. 66.)

That Bernie fits the profile of the "aggressive narcissist" should be clear. He is also a close fit to the DSM IV definition of "antisocial personality disorder," or ASPD. It has been pointed out that the psychopath (a close fit to the aggressive narcissist) differs from the ASPD in that the ASPD diagnosis focuses on behavior in an attempt to get more reliability. The psychopath is identified not only by behavior, but also by affective (emotional) factors and interpersonal behavior. The thoughts and feelings of the psychopath and his relationships with others are much harder to elicit than his record of bad behavior from police or court records. Thoughts and feelings are much more subject to distortion, since they are based on self-reports. Thus the DSM sacrifices the symptoms of grandiosity, glibness, lack of empathy and remorse, etc., in return for greater reliability. A diagnosis of Antisocial Personality leaves us with only a bare bones description of these complex members of the dark triad Each individual has to be placed in a diagnostic category for purposes of third party payments, so DSM I through V are necessary constructions. In describing the members of the dark triad/tetrad, however, we need finer categories such as narcissist, Machiavellian, and psychopath as described by Daniel Goleman D. (*supra*).and Paulhus, D.L. et al. *supra*) All three are ASPD (Antisocial Personality Disorder). That no individual fits perfectly into any diagnostic category is confirmed once again by the example of Bernie, whose obsessive-compulsive behavior is extreme, and whose suspicion of others (paranoid?) is rampant. Obsessive behavior seems out of keeping with a psychopath, but Bernie has to be on his toes constantly, making sure that his false stock sales are properly based on the day's market highs to impress his clients. Is he suspicious? Yes. His staff may rat on him at any time. The Feds may discover his scam. No wonder he controls the color scheme of his office, and everything else about his work. His immaculate clothing and matching watch and ring are just part of his presentation of self. He must impress his old money clients, who might suspect that a Jewish boy, born on the Lower East Side who grew up in a lower-middle-class neighborhood in Queens, was not only an arriviste, but also a crook.

What makes Bernie an anomic personality? The anomic shares the behavior and emotions of the dark triad/tetrad ranging from the everyday driven, grandiose, and shallow, (usually male) who is deregulated in the area of sex, money or power, to the convicted criminal. Tiger came from a social background that would be considered minority. Bernie, though of middle class background, is still an "outsider" because of being Jewish. The prejudice against Jews is internalized, or "introjected" by many Jews as they adopt the attitudes of the American majority. Bernie's excessive striving for the trappings of the "old money" wealth; the yacht, multiple homes and expensive clothes, reveals his feelings of inferiority and even self-hatred. The stigma of minority status in America is still great.

The American Dream is to climb out of poverty or low status and become a "success." Both Tiger and Bernie had supportive childhoods. Tiger's father trained him as a golfer early on, and probably instilled a competitive spirit, as the parents of professional athletes often do. Bernie's parents were negative role models, having been involved with the Feds. They were certainly striving, and his mother had her own brokerage until she failed to report the financial condition of her company. However, they seemed supportive of their son. Dick's ruthless philosophy; "If you want to be loved, you know, go be a movie star," suggests a much stricter upbringing, combined with a push for success. (Madison, L., 2013) [Madison, Lucy. *The World According to Dick Cheney, a documentary film by R.J. Cutler.* Lucy Madison for CBS News, "Cheney: Politics not for those who "'want to be loved.'" 3/15/2013.]

The choice of the behavior that is to become excessive is not clear, and it would take an intimate knowledge of parenting and early experience to make even a good guess. Possibly Tiger was repressed due to his strict Buddhist upbringing with its emphasis on control. Growing up in the larger U.S. community which was sexually permissive may have been a problem. His excellent physical condition may have involved higher levels of testosterone that would enable him to perform sexually with such frequency. Many of the sexual anomics are professional athletes.

In Chapter Two I defined the Anomic Personality, and of course it overlaps with the Aggressive Narcissist, the Dark Triad (narcissist, Machiavellian, and psychopath), and DSM IV and V Antisocial Personality Disorder. Here is a brief recap of the Anomic Personality.

Anomic Personality:

1. Pursue goals relentlessly
2. Goals are limitless
3. Grandiose
4. Treat people as objects
5. Cunning, especially in use of language to manipulate or justify aggressive or acquisitive behavior
6. Pathological lying
7. Usually charismatic. Leadership, if any, tends toward coercion, dominance, and manipulation
8. Often show lack of empathy
9. Often exhibit sexual hyperactivity
10. Often overachievers

Bernie fits the Anomic profile, His charisma is shown by his ability to convince thousands of presumably intelligent people and charitable organizations to invest their life savings with him. His leadership at work was harsh and domineering. But remember that a milder version of this anomic profile fits a large portion of our nation, particularly males. I have described many well-known men in our society as anomics, such as Rumsfeld, Blankfein, Spitzer, G.W. Bush, and Bill Clinton. There are many others like these men who are *not convicted criminals.* They are primarily narcissists and Machiavellians. There is also a list (supra).of some of the many criminal anomics *convicted of fraud,* most of them in banking or brokerage houses Because of their convictions, we label them psychopaths. Like Tiger, Bernie and Dick, they help us to define the social character of our nation, since they are the outliers and avatars.

CHAPTER SIX

DICK CHENEY

Richard Bruce "Dick" Cheney was the most powerful Vice President in the history of the United States. He openly stated that he would not be the usual weak V.P. in a job that was, in the words of former Vice President "Cactus Jack" Garner "not worth a bucket of warm spit." Dick, as he was most commonly called, had a meteoric career, in both the corporate world and in politics. In the previous chapter I called him a Machiavellian. That position in the "Dark Triad" is a quantum leap into psychopathology from the everyday subclinical American Narcissist (Tiger?) but *seemingly* not as destructive to self and others as the Psychopath, when the criterion for psychopathy is based on arrests and convictions alone. I intend to show that the "Mach" or Machiavellian, (by definition not arrested or convicted, as is the Psychopath), especially when in a position of high power, can be much more destructive than the Psychopath. He fits the profile of the aggressive narcissist, so the line between the Mach and the Psychopath is really very thin. *Anomic Personality*:

Overachiever
Pursues goals relentlessly
Goals are limitless, grandiose
Cunning, especially in use of language to manipulate
Pathological lying
Often charismatic
Leadership, if any, tends toward coercion, dominance, and manipulation.

First we can look at Dick's childhood and young adult life, for any clues to the origins of the very strong drive for success, and perhaps for domination of others, that appear to be the motor forces in his remarkable climb to power. Then we can review some events which give us a better picture of his dark side. After that we can review, trait by trait, how he fits the profile of the Machiavellian. Last of all, it is fitting to tackle the question of why so many leaders in power have gotten away with behavior on a personal or political level that broke the law, but were not seen as psychopaths because of their position. This behavior of the Machiavellian can result in poor health or starvation of millions through budget cuts and various legislation. The "Mach" can lead his country into a war that costs millions of civilian and military lives and trillions of dollars.

Cheney was born in Lincoln, Nebraska on January 30th, 1941, but raised in Sumner, Nebraska and Casper, Wyoming. His mother, Marjorie Lorraine Cheney.

had been a softball star in the 1930's. His father, Richard Herbert Che ney, was a soil conservation agent for the U.S. Department of Agriculture. His biography in Wikipedia notes that both of his parents were Democrats! Dick had two siblings. He finished high school in Casper.

He was popular in high school, and was among the top ten best students in his class. He was captain of the football team. It was there that he met his future wife, Lynne Vincent, who was the Homecoming Queen. This successful beginning was soon clouded by his experience at Yale, where he had a scholarship. He didn't make the football team at Yale, and his grades went downhill. Perhaps he had the experience of so many high school successes who are big fish in the little pond, but become very small fish in the more competitive big pond of college. For whatever the underlying reasons, he flunked out of Yale twice due to poor grades. He lost his scholarship. (Cheney's life events are based on his biography in Wikipedia and other referenced sources.)

After this, he went back to Wyoming and worked as a lineman at $2 per hour. In 1962, at age 21, he was arrested for DWI, and again in 1963. The heavy drinking was probably associated with his failure at and rejection by Yale. Shortly after this, in 1964, he married his high-school sweetheart, Lynne. Then he enrolled in the University of Wyoming, where he received a B.A. and M.A. in Political Science. He started studying for the doctorate at the University of Wisconsin, but did not finish. So far this seems like a rather spotty performance for someone who would become one of his country's most powerful leaders.

Then things started turning around. Lynne had gotten her doctorate in 19th century British literature from the University of Wisconsin, while Dick never finished his Ph.D. Perhaps her diligence and success moved him to knuckle down to business. He became an intern for Congressman William A. Steiger, a Wisconsin Republican.

Some of the important posts he held in his long career were: (Dick Cheney Timeline) [Dick Cheney Timeline, http://trib.com/ne3ws/ state -and-regional/dick-cheney-timeline/art5icle]\

1968 Wins congressional scholarship with William Steiger in D.C..

1969 Joins Nixon administration in number of positions.

1975 White House Chief of Staff under President Gerald Ford.

1978 Elected to House of Representatives for Wyoming.

1980-1988 Re-elected to House.

1989 Secretary of Defense, directs U.S. invasion of Panama and Operation Desert Storm (rescue of Kuwait from invasion by Saddam Hussein).

1995 CEO of Halliburton Energy Company with subsidiary involved in drilling for oil in Iraq.

2000 Bush announces Cheney as V.P. choice, after Cheney leads V.P. search team. Bush-Cheney win election.

2001 Terrorist attack on New York City and Pentagon. Cheney takes charge.

2003 U.S. forces invade Iraq.

2004 Bush-Cheney win second term.

2005 Valerie Plame outing leads to perjury charge, resignation, and finally jail time for Lewis "Scooter" Libby, Cheney's Chief of Staff.

2006 Accidentally shoots hunting companion Harry Whittington, a 78 year old Texas attorney, during a quail hunt in Texas, causing a nonfatal heart attack and atrial fibrillation. Former CIA agent, Valerie Plame, sues over the leak of her identity.

2007 Attempt to kill Cheney by a suicide bomber in Afghanistan.

2014 Criticizes Obama for the current internecine warfare in Iran.

This list hardly does justice to all the events in Dick's career, but I have included enough detail to convince any reader that Dick has been one of the most powerful leaders of our country, including presidents and vice presidents. He seized that power in the name of the "Imperial Presidency," which he touted even while he was a Representative. After a trial presidential run which failed to raise enough money to continue, his only path to real power was through a drastic revision of the vice presidential role.

The light side

Organization and dedication

There are two sides to almost any person. Before looking at Dick's dark side, a few comments are necessary for some balance. On the light side, Dick's organizational skills and his dedication to the job at hand are self-evident. Whatever one may feel about his politics, he came through the 9/11 crisis as a take-charge leader. While Bush was reading a book to school-children, Dick was calling for air strikes against the terrorists who had commandeered our planes (necessary, even though they contained U.S. passengers).

Gay marriage

His public stance on gay marriage was in direct opposition to the one taken by the Bush administration, of which he was a prominent part. "Freedom means freedom for everyone," he said. "People should be free to enter into any kind of relationship they want to enter into." Dick and Lynne's daughter, Mary, is a lesbian. Standing up for his daughter's rights seems like a ray of light amidst his dark record. Cheney's solution; however, is to leave gay rights up to the states. In other words, he would condone the denial of gay rights in any state that passed such laws.

Loyalty

His loyalty to his immediate co-worker is to be commended. Despite Bush's continued refusal, he tried to get a full pardon for Scooter Libby, his right hand man, who was sentenced to two and a half years in prison for "outing" CIA agent Valerie Plame. This was in retaliation for the New York Times Op-Ed piece by Plame's husband, former Ambassador Joseph Wilson, denying that there had been any sale of yellowcake uranium from Niger to Iraq, thus undermining the WMD (Weapons of Mass Destruction) argument for the invasion of Iraq. Bush finally commuted Libby's jail sentence, but a fine of $250,000 still remained.

Turnabout

His turnabout, from college flunk-out and drunk driving arrests to a long successful career in public service, is to be admired. This is the classic American tale of youthful hopes dashed, a downhill slide, a narrow escape from catastrophe, and finally success.

The Dark Side

It is harder for me to find examples of the light side than of the dark side when it comes to Dick. Here are only a few of his myriad dark events and policies (in my opinion and that of many others of a politically liberal or even centrist persuasion).

The Outing of Valerie Plame

This scandal revealed the cunning and manipulation involved in protecting the rationale for invading Iraq. While Libby took the fall for the federal crime of outing of a CIA officer (i.e., a spy) his immediate boss, Cheney, had to be aware of every move. Bush's primary rationale for the invasion of Iraq and the overthrow of Saddam Hussein was that the Iraqis had bought yellowcake uranium from Niger, and that it would be used to make "weapons of mass destruction,", or WMD's.

Joseph Wilson was married to Valerie Plame, am extremely attractive undercover CIA agent. When the story about the uranium broke, Plame, who was monitoring nuclear weapons, may have suggested to the CIA that her husband go to Niger to confirm the purchase. Upon his return he wrote an Op-Ed article for the New York Times, categorically denying that there had been any such purchase. He said the intelligence report was false. It later turned out that the intelligence report was based on a forgery by an unreliable Italian informant! The revelation that the very excuse for the invasion, the existence of WMDs, was false must have been very threatening to Cheney and Scooter Libby.

"Libby was outraged and apparently believed that by claiming that Wilson's wife, Valerie Plame, a CIA agent involved in monitoring the proliferation of such weapons, had been involved in sending her husband to Niger, the trip would be perceived as some kind of boondoggle. In fact, she was not involved in the CIA decision to ask her husband to make the trip, but Libby leaked her covert identity to members of the news media anyway." (Dean, J., 2006. pp. 80-89) [Dean, J. *Conservatives Without Conscience*. New York: Viking Press, 2006.]

Whether by direct order from Cheney, or simply because he knew he had to somehow control the negative impact of the Op-Ed piece, Libby contacted Robert Novak, a conservative columnist, who "outed" or "blew the cover" on Valerie Plame. He identified her as a CIA agent specializing in tracking WMDs. Outing an undercover agent is a federal crime, and often endangers a number of agents working in the same region.

A special prosecutor, Patrick Fitzgerald, was appointed to investigate the leak. Both Karl Rove and Scooter Libby were called to testify. Testimony from the investigation suggests that Cheney got Plame's name from George Tenet, former head of the CIA. As noted before, Libby took the fall for the higher-ups, who may have included not only his immediate boss, but Karl Rove and Bush himself. Character assassination is a common form of retaliation and control in Washington, The impeachment of Bill Clinton, with the aid of a team of lawyers paid for by Richard Scaife, is a prime example of planned assassination.

"Terror Management" studies (Landau, M.J. et al. 2004) [Landau, M.J. et al., "Deliver Us From Evil: The Effects of Mortality Salience and Reminders of 9/11 on Support for President George W. Bush." *Personality and Social Psychology Bulletin,* 30:1136-1150, September, 2004.] have suggested that people with greater fear of dying are more likely to be politically conservative. The Bush/Cheney/Rove program of building on the fear engendered by the 9/11 attack through continual colored alerts and warnings about WMDs may have been responsible for the Bush re-election by some of the very people who least benefited from his policies, the poor and elderly. Dick was in large part responsible for the sharp conservative turn of the administration, and the drumming up of WMD fear.

Taking the job of Vice President when he was supposed to vet others for the job.

In April of 2000, George W. Bush announced that Dick Cheney would be in charge of the search for a vice-presidential candidate to be his running mate. On November 7th, 2000, the election was held, but the outcome was not known until the Supreme Court's decision was announced on December 12th, 2000. The decision stopped the recount of Florida's contested votes, Florida's votes went to Bush, handing him the presidency, even though he did not have a plurality of the popular vote. Thus the almost eight years of Bush/Cheney began under a dark cloud.

Cheney was asked to vet several candidates for the vice-presidency. Some of the potential candidates were Lamar Alexander, Frank Keating, Chuck Hagel, Tom Ridge, John Kasich, William "Bill" Frist, George Pataki and John Engler. All of them were well known politicians, and reasonable candidates for the vice presidential job. Dick assigned the job of gathering information on the possible candidates to David Addington. Long questionnaires had to be filled out. Typically, vetting questions focus heavily on personal information that might be detrimental to the presidential candidate, such as any arrests, any extra-marital dalliances, any treatment for mental disorder, or any activity that might lead to criminal prosecution, such as taking bribes or gifts.

With all this work going into the vetting process, it is hard to understand why George W. Bush did not interview any of his potential running mates.

"The hardest thing to explain was that Bush—who put so much stock in his instinct for people, that knack for decoding a handshake or the quality of a gaze—did not interview a single candidate before he settled on Cheney." (Gellman, B. 2008, p. 20.) [Gellman, B. *Angler: The Cheney Vice Presidency*. New York: The Penguin Press.] Gellman's detective work shows conclusively that actual interviews were scheduled only *after* July 3rd, when Bush asked Cheney to be his running mate.

While each of the other candidates for V.P. had to fill out long questionnaires, Dick did not fill one out. "No one had access to Cheney's tax or corporate records, and no one but his own doctor read a word of his medical files." (Gellman, B., op. cit., p.23.)

Character assassination

In addition to the smokescreen of vetting candidates other than himself while his own appointment as Bush's V.P. running mate was already in the bag, there is evidence that the confidential information gathered was leaked in a least one case, that of Oklahoma Governor Frank Keating. Keating made a wisecrack that suggested Cheney had parlayed his V.P. selection committee chairmanship into the actual Vice Presidency. The leak contained information about cash gifts totaling $250,000 that Keating had received from a fundraiser. While legal, public revelation of such gifts can ruin a career. The only source of this information was in Keating's vetting questionnaire. That this was payback for the wisecrack about Cheney is made clear by Keating, and a fellow governor, John Engler, was in agreement. (Gellman, B. 2008, ibid, pp 30-31.

This release of confidential information against a fellow politician is another example of Cheney's use of character assassination. The outing of Valerie Plame, described above, who was doing secret work as a CIA officer, was an attempt to smear her husband, Ambassador Joseph Wilson, as payback for denying that the purchase of yellowcake uranium by Saddam Hussein ever took place This character assassination attempt backfired, and resulted in Scooter Libby's conviction.

Behavior and ideation that give us clues to Dick's character.

Dick never seemed to be an easy-going fellow, but he appeared to have pretty good control over his emotions. Underneath the façade there may have been great anger left over from the trauma of early failure at college in grades and inability to make the athletic teams in which he excelled in high school. His turnabout and rapid climb to power took a supreme effort. This career survived five heart attacks, starting at age 37, a struggle that ended with a heart transplant in 2012. One particular incident suggests that Dick was a "Type A," while his whole history, including his early onset heart attacks, supports this hunch.

"According to congressional aides, [Sen. Patrick] Leahy said hello to Cheney following the taking of the Senate group photo on the floor of the chamber. Cheney, who is president of the Senate, then ripped into Leahy for the Democratic senator's criticism this week of alleged war profiteering in Iraq by Halliburton, the oil services company that Cheney once ran. During their exchange, Leahy noted that Republicans had accused Democrats of being anti-Catholic because they are opposed to some of President Bush's anti-abortion judges, the aide said. That's when Cheney unloaded with the 'F-bomb,' aides said." (Drum, K., 2004) [Kevin Drum, Political Animal, June 24, 2004.]

That "F-bomb" Cheney to Leahy, was "Go fuck yourself." This is hardly the proper language to use with a Senate colleague. It caused a furor, and made headlines internationally. Was Dick remorseful? Did he eventually regret having fired that shot at Leahy? Quite the contrary. "That's sort of the best thing I ever did," said Dick, reflecting on telling Leahy to "go fuck yourself." (Cheney, R., 2010) [Dick Cheney Interview with Dennis Miller, April 22, 2010 "Dick Cheney Could Not Be Prouder….." www.vanityfair. com/.../2010/dick-cheney]

In the 1950's, cardiologists Friedman and Rosenman studied men between 35 and 59, and found that those they labeled Type A had double the risk of coronary heart disease, when compared with Type B. A second study by this team (1986) suggested that Type A counseling with group cardiac counseling was more effective in preventing a recurrence of myocardial infarction than group cardiac counseling alone (recurrence 28% in the controls, 13% in the Type A counseling treatment group).

Later research suggests that only the *hostility* in Type A individuals is a significant cardiac risk factor. (Wikipedia, A & B Personality Theory) [Type A and Type B Personality Theory. Wikipedia.]

Despite flaws in these studies, the list of personality characteristics associated with Type A fits Dick like a glove.

"The theory describes 'Type A' individuals as ambitious, rigidly organized, highly status conscious, sensitive, impatient, take on more than they can handle, want other people to get to the point, anxious, proactive, and concerned with time management.

"In his 2006 book, *Type A Behavior, Its Diagnosis and Treatment,* Friedman suggests that Type A behavior is expressed in three major symptoms: (1) free-floating hostility, which can be triggered by even minor incidents ; (2) time-urgency and impatience, which causes irritation and exasperation usually described as being 'short-fused;" and (3) a competitive drive, which causes stress and an achievement-driven mentality. The first of these symptoms is believed to be covert and therefore less observable, while the other two are more overt." [Type A and Type B Personality Theory. Wikipedia, op. cit.]

Although free-floating hostility may be more covert, it "can be triggered by even minor incidents," such as Leahy's criticism of war-profiteering by Halliburton (the company formerly headed by Dick.) This covert hostility is seen again in the character assassination of Valerie Plame and her husband, and again in the "leaking" of confidential information about Frank Keating which ruined Keating's career.

The shooting of Harry Whittington, mentioned previously in the Cheney time-line, can be seen as merely an unfortunate accident. However, to my mind, the idea of releasing quail so that wealthy gentlemen may shoot them down is revolting. In ordinary hunting, the animals have more of a chance, since they are not confined and released right in front of the hunters. The carelessness involved in shooting a member of your sports party does not speak well for Dick. Whittington was not a close friend of Dick's, as first reported. He was 78, and a Texas attorney.

"Whittington suffered a minor heart attack and atrial fibrillation due to the shot pellets lodged in or near his heart." (Wikipedia, Dick Cheney hunting incident.) Doctors had to leave the 200 pieces of birdshot in his body. What matters most to us is not the accident or the injuries, but the fact that Dick has never apologized for this serious injury to Whittington! The members of the Dark Triad/Tetrad are not known for their empathy and graciousness. Whittington himself apologized, as some put it, "for being in the way"! He said "My family and I are deeply sorry for all that Vice President and his family have had to go through this past week."

Of course, the Type A personality is part and parcel of *most* ambitious and successful Americans, particularly males. The status-conscious, driven, ambitious, competitive, covertly hostile, short-fused picture heavily overlaps the description of the *anomic personality* and the *aggressive narcissist*. The free-floating hostility was evident in Bernie, who was a martinet with his employees, and scoffed at the tragic losses of his victims. The "rigid organization" and concern with "time management" was seen in Bernie as well. While this suggests an obsessive-compulsive component, these concerns are a necessary part of the individual who is running a complex organization (the United States!) or a gigantic investment scam.

The hostility component is not as clear in the case of Tiger, but his relations with his women probably had a larger-than-usual component of violence, as shown by his emails to them. His Type A performance; driven, years of training and practice, highest-earning athlete of all time, complex charitable donations, suggest a narcissist, the kindliest of the dark triad, without the free-floating hostility of Bernie the Mach-Psychopath, and Dick, the Machiavellian.

But remember, Tiger, Bernie and Dick are only the avatars of the Anomic Personality. They are the embodiment of the American way of life. They are the exemplars of the excessive striving and individual stress created by the American Dream. This dream has become a myth, and threatens to destroy the more balanced capitalism which we had in former years. Rampant inequality has grown, and threatens our democracy. The links between the Anomic Personality and inequality will be explored in a later chapter.

The curious consequence of linking the diagnosis of Psychopath to those individuals who are convicted felons, is that they appear, on first glance, to be more damaging to society than the Machiavellians. But the Machs are, by and large, smarter than the convicted felons, are richer and more powerful; often by virtue of their manipulative skills. They are seldom caught. If caught they can hire the best lawyers, and they can often find a fall-guy to take the rap for following their orders (such as Scooter Libby and the outing of Valerie Plame).

Let's compare the damage done by a psychopath serial killer, who kills five people, with the damage made by the decision to invade Iraq, a decision nominally made by George W. Bush. It was Cheney and Donald Rumsfeld who convinced Bush to go to war. American deaths since the war began (3/19/2003) are 4,489. (4,486 according to Wikipedia.) American wounded (official) are 32,031, but an estimate for civilians wounded is as high as 100,000. (Antiwar.com)

Through 12/31/2010, there have been 16,623 Iraqi military and police killed. From 2003 till late 2011, about 26,405 insurgents were killed. There were 318 deaths of Coalition forces as of 2/24/2009. WikiLeaks reported 99,163 civilian injuries thru December 2009. The Iraqi government reported 239,133 injuries from 2004 to 2011.

Although there are great discrepancies between the body counts and injuries stated by different sources (U.S. vs. Iraqi, for example) yet there were probably 120,000-134,000 civilian deaths due to the war through 12/12/2012. ([UNICEF and Reuters) All deaths on both sides were estimated at 189,000. UNICEF estimated that between 800,000 and a million Iraqi children under 18 lost one or both parents.

This litany of destruction could go on forever. The Iraq war cost the U.S. over $2 trillion. (Trotta, D., 2013) [Daniel Trotta, Reuters, 3/14/2013] Benefits to Iraq war veterans could mount to $6 trillion over the next four decades. The GOP had a reputation for fiscal conservatism, and the Democrats were continuously labeled as "tax and spend" liberals. The decision to go to war has economic consequences for the U.S. over many decades. It has been pointed out that the military over-extension of the Dutch, the Spanish, and the British, caused those countries to become "second-class powers." Has a Mach put us closer to this same fate by his determination to start war in Iraq, to stop the supposed threat of the Weapons of Mass Destruction, or for the many other reasons, such as control of oil or the profits of Halliburton, which had almost exclusive contracts for drilling equipment?

Bush, Cheney and Rumsfeld sold the American public a fairy tale of an inexpensive and brief war in Iraq, whereas it was actually catastrophically expensive and very drawn out. I discussed Rumsfeld's "idée fixe" that consisted of highly mobile units and fewer boots on the ground. The public was told that they wouldn't have to pay for this war, and it wouldn't affect their taxes. How was this sleight of hand performed? Then answer is given by Michael Boyle (Boyle, M., 2013) [Boyle, M. "How the U.S. public was defrauded by the hidden cost of the Iraq war," the guardian.com, 3/1/2013]

"The most striking fact about the cost of the war in Iraq has been the extent to which it has been kept 'off the books' of the government's ledgers and hidden from the American people. The dirty little secret of the Iraq war—one that both Bush and the war hawks in the Democratic party knew, but would never admit—was that the American people would only support a war to get rid of Saddam Hussein if they could be assured that they would pay almost nothing for it."

The most obvious way in which the true cost of the war was kept hidden was with the use of supplemental appropriations to fund the occupation. By one estimate, 70% of the costs of wars in Iraq and Afghanistan between 2003 and 2008 were funded with supplemental or emergency appropriations approved outside the Pentagon's annual budget." (This allowed the war expenses) "to escape the scrutiny that Congress gives to its normal annual regular appropriations…..the Republicans followed the advice of Vice-President Dick Cheney that 'deficits don't matter' and spent freely on domestic programs throughout the Bush years." (Boyle, M., supra.)

Private companies were employed militarily and in non-combat functions such as housing, food, transportation and reconstruction. This too kept the public from knowing the true cost of the war.

The "costs" of the Iraq War and of the policies that Dick created, promoted, or convinced Bush to follow had consequences much more far-reaching than the loss of trillions of dollars and hundreds of thousands of lives. A few of these costs might be worth reviewing at this point. They are part of the dark side.

The invasion of Iraq and the killing of Saddam Hussein (tyrant though he was) essentially handed over Iraq to the Shiites, and took most of the Sunnis' power away. In so doing, it drew Iraq into a closer relationship with Iran, its Shiite neighbor. The wars between Iraq and Iran had kept a lid on Shiite power in the region. After the killing of Saddam Hussein and the takeover of the government by the Shiites, Iran became more of a threat to the U.S., because it had strong ties to Iraq, in addition to its nuclear weapon development. U.S. foreign policy has historically tried to maintain a balance of power in the Middle East, and the invasion of Iraq ignored that history. "He may be a son-of-a-bitch, but he's *our* son-of-a-bitch." This remark was "attributed to President Franklin Roosevelt when he was asked about the wisdom of supporting the Nicaraguan dictator Somoza." (Brandt, B., 2013) [Brandt, Bill. The Lexicans. 4/30/2013] Our foreign policy has supported dictators whenever it seemed to be in our national interest.

The invasion of Iraq created an expansion of Al Qaeda and new offshoots. Terrorists came from foreign countries to join the fight against the U.S. and its "coalition." ISIS, based in Syria, has beheaded American photojournalist James Foley and journalist Steven Sotloff in videos directly challenging President Obama. In 2015 alone, there have been about 20 attacks on civilians linked to or inspired by ISIS, *outside* of Iraq (where they have taken much territory) and Syria. To my mind, the worst of these attacks have been Charlie Hebdo (Paris, 12 dead, worst because of its direct assault on free speech), Yemen Mosque (130 dead), Russian plane downed in Egypt (224 dead), and the Paris attacks in November, 2015 (129 dead, 352 wounded). (Yourish, K., 2016) [Yourish, K. et al. *The New York Times.* "Recent Attacks Demonstrate Islamic State's Ability to Both Inspire and Coordinate Terror" Updated 1/14/2016.]

Despite his determination and promise to avoid sending more combat troops into the Middle East, Obama sent 50 combat troops into Syria to combat ISIS in 2015. He had to deal with the consequences of the military decisions of G.W. Bush, Cheney, and Rumsfeld.

The imposition of secrecy on the executive branch, the invasion of privacy of U.S. citizens, the "rendition" of enemy combatants (flown to countries where they could be tortured without any political fallout), and the creation of legal justification for the use of torture (such as waterboarding) are just a few of the Cheney creations which have had a lasting effect on our democracy. Many of these policies, at first justified by the 9/11 attack, have been difficult to reverse, and still threaten our citizens, even in the time of Obama. John Dean sees these policies as Dick's "bad judgment." (John Dean himself showed bad judgement, when he worked as White House Counsel for Nixon.)

"Bad judgment is Dick Cheney's trademark. It was not George Bush who came up with the idea of imposing blanket secrecy on the executive branch when he and Cheney took over. It was not George Bush who conceived of the horrible—and in some cases actually evil—policies that typify the authoritarian presidency, such as detaining 'enemy combatants' with no due process and contrary to international law. It was not George Bush who had the idea of using torture during interrogations and removing restraints on the National Security Agency from collecting intelligence on Americans. These were policies developed by Cheney and his staff, and sold to the president, and then imposed on many who subsequently objected to this authoritarian lawlessness." (Dean, J., op.cit., p. 160) [Dean, J., *Conservatives Without Conscience*. New York Penguin Books. 2007 p. 160]

In summarizing Cheney's deeds and character, there can be no better source than G.H.W. Bush, the man who obviously got him to help out his son, George W., in his son's new role as President. Cheney had even served as G.H.W. Bush's Secretary of War. Bush Sr. kept his silence until November 2015 with the publication of his biography, "*Destiny and Power: The American Odyssey of George Herbert Walker Bush.*" Bush told John Meacham, his biographer, that Dick "had his own empire" in the White House "and marched to his own drummer." (Wright, D & LoBianco, T., 2015) [Wright, D. and LoBianco, T., "Bush 41 hits 43's aides in new biography." CNN Politics, 11/6/2015.]

"I don't know, he just became very hard line and very different from the Dick Cheney I knew and worked with. The reaction to (the 9/11 terrorists attacks) what to do about the Middle East. Just iron-ass. His seeming under to the real hard-charging guys who want to fight about everything, use force to get our way in the Middle East.....You know, I've concluded that Lynne Cheney is a lot of the *eminence grise* here—iron ass, tough as nails, driving." (Wright, D. et al., supra)

If you couldn't believe all of the things that Dick did during his term as VP, you might at least take it from Bush 41, the horse's mouth, that Dick was not a nice guy. His own drummer, his own empire, his hard-ass approach, tells us that he was a Machiavellian, part of the Dark Triad. He is our chosen avatar of the Anomic Personality's drive for power.

Rumsfeld gets an E from Bush 41, compared with Cheney's D minus. Here is the man with the idée fixe. "I didn't like what he did, and I think it hurt the President, having his iron-ass idea of everything. There's a lack of humility, a lack of seeing what the other guy thinks. He's more kick-ass and take names, take numbers. I think he paid a price for that." (Wright, D. et al., supra.) "Kick-ass" could be the trait that captures the quintessence of the Mach!

CHAPTER SEVEN

SOCIAL CHARACTER
RELATIVE DEPRIVATION AND INEQUALITIES
ANOMIC PERSONALITY: AN ADAPTATION TO CAPITALISM AND INEQUALITY
OBAMA, HILLARY AND BERNIE SANDERS
A RANK ORDERING OF CATASTROPHE
A RAY OF SUNSHINE? TWO "RECENT" SUPREME COURT DECISIONS
THE ROOTS OF ANOMIC PERSONALITY: ECONOMIC, HEREDITARY, RELIGIOUS, ETHNIC AND CHILD REARING

This book is about the excessive deregulation of the economy (a state of anomie) and its association with the deregulation of the individual, resulting in a sharp increase in an anomic deregulated personality type. This personality type is so widespread in the United States that it has become a culturally patterned defect. It is no longer just a type of individual pathology. Instead it has become a dominant feature of the *social character* of Americans, particularly of many American men.

Before we look at the origins of the anomic personality type, it would be best to review once more the characteristics of this type, and their relation to the clinical concepts of aggressive narcissism and psychopathy.

Factor 1: Aggressive Narcissism

Glibness, superficial charm
Grandiose sense of self-worth
Pathological lying
Cunning/manipulative
Lack of remorse or guilt
Emotionally shallow
Callous/lack of empathy
Failure to accept responsibility for own action

These traits were based on a factor analysis of responses to the Hare Psychopathy Checklist (see Chapter 2).

The traits of the anomic personality, (shown below) as I have defined it, are strikingly similar to the characteristics of the psychopath (Factor 1, aggressive narcissism) Indeed, Robert Hare, perhaps the leading expert on psychopathy, has said: "In my book, *Without Conscience*, I argued that we live in a "camouflage society," a society in which some psychopathic traits-egocentricity, lack of concern for others, superficiality, style over substance, being "cool," manipulativeness, and so forth–increasingly are tolerated and even valued." (Hare, R.D., 1996) [Hare. R.D., "Psychopathy and Antisocial Personality: A Case of Diagnostic Confusion" *Psychiatric Times*: February 1996, Vol. XIII, Issue 2]

In addition to the psychopathic traits, I have placed special emphasis on the possession of limitless goals. This limitlessness, or deregulation, is the essence of Durkheim's concept of anomie as he found it in the financial marketplace (with its high suicide rates), in the higher suicide rates of deregulated unmarried males compared with married males (sexual anomie), and in the higher suicide rates of the relatively deregulated Protestants, compared with Catholics in the same countries. The relentless striving for unlimited (deregulated) goals is virtually a definition of grandiosity.

The Anomic Personality (A Recap) Since this concept has been introduced by me for the first time in this book, I feel it is helpful to repeat it at different points.

1.They pursue their goals relentlessly.

3.Their goals are limitless. They are grandiose.They treat other people as objects.

4. They are cunning and use language to justify their acquisitive or aggressive behavior.

5. They are often pathological liars, and deny their offenses and predations when these are discovered.

6. They are usually charismatic, and use their charm and interpersonal skills to gain power and possession. Many politicians (as well as con artists) are smooth talkers.

7. Sexual addiction, combined with charisma and *a strong drive to attain power*, is often found in political leaders and some very successful or wealthy individuals or "stars." (Sexual addiction is the only trait they share with the criminal element in Hare's Factor 2.)

Based on the congruence of the anomic personality and psychopathy, we can summarize by saying that the anomic personality is a culturally patterned defect which would be classified as a range of psychopathology (mental/emotional disorder) from mild to severe (narcissist, Machiavellian, and psychopath) were it not for its prevalence and general acceptance in our culture.

Social Character

It is my contention that the anomic personality has recently become the dominant social character of our nation, though some of its traits have been observed as early as 1835 (de Tocqueville).

We have been talking about social character from the very first chapters of this book. In this chapter it will be necessary to backtrack a bit, and ask what the terms "social character" (and its cousin "national character,") really mean. As Einstein noted, if you look at a bouncing ball from 90 degrees to its path, it shows a zigzag pattern. But if it is coming towards you, it just seems to be bouncing up and down. The observer's position; her social class or his native country, may well influence or even determine the types of social character he or she find in their observations and studies of nations and cultures.

We looked at the descriptions of American character by de Tocqueville, who emphasized "striving and the restless passion for more," while Margaret Mead saw practicality as dominant. Karen Horney, in The Neurotic Personality of Our Time, saw Americans as engaged in a struggle for prestige, power and possession. Not only does national character change over time, but different observers have seen or emphasized different aspects of those national and social characters.

"Social character is a difficult concept that crosses academic boundaries of psychology, sociology, anthropology and economics."(Maccoby, M. 2000) [Maccoby, M. "Social Character in a Mexican Village," M. Maccoby, 2000-1.pdf.] Depending on the historical period and the culture under consideration, social scientists have used a variety of terms to describe national and social character. As discussed by Maccoby (supra) Freud's types were "libidinal, erotic, obsessive and narcissist." Fromm's types, based on Freud's, were "receptive, hoarding, exploitative and marketing." Maccoby came up with social character types linked to historical change. He divided them into productive and unproductive types. He saw changes in the U.S. social character. The period of "narcissistic productive entrepreneurs" (Henry Ford, Rockefeller) was followed by the "productive obsessive *bureaucratic*" character in the mid twentieth century. This was followed by a shift to a service society. In the 90's, information technology changed the social character to "*interactive*." This focused on "innovation, interactive networks, teamwork and flexibility." {Maccoby, *supra*.)

Clearly, the means of production have been a very strong influence on the growth of and changes in the U.S. social character. (We will review other influences later in this chapter.) The shift from a manufacturing/exporting economy to a service economy, and subsequently the rapid growth of globalization, have created extreme inequality in the U.S. (Stiglitz, Berman, and Picketty among others have documented this.) Later in this chapter I will discuss their view on inequality and the future of our democracy. For now, I feel it necessary to say that Picketty and Stiglitz have narrower definitions of inequality than mine, because they are economists. Inequalities in mathematics are represented by < and > signs. (Picketty, T., 2014) [Picketty, T. Capital in the Twenty-First Century,

Cambridge, Mass: Harvard University Press (Belknap), 2014.] Picketty focuses on the inequality caused by the disparity between wealth and earned income. The opposing figures are the rentier who lives on inherited wealth, and the worker who receives wages. Wealth and earned income are objective measures of inequality. Picketty admits that inequality has a large subjective dimension. "Hence there will always be a fundamentally subjective and psychological dimension to inequality, which inevitably gives rise to political conflict that no purportedly scientific analysis can alleviate." (Picketty, T., 2014, p. 2).

Relative Deprivation and Inequalities

A good example of this psychological or *subjective* dimension is the study by Stauffer et al.in *The American Soldier* (*supra*), where Stauffer was the first to develop the concept of "relative deprivation." The dissatisfaction of American soldiers overseas depended on their "reference group."

"If we take the questions that refer to 'personal esprit' and 'personal commitment' alone, we discover that the less educated, the older men, and the married men come out with more negative attitudes than the better educated, the younger men, and the unmarried men. An explanation for this is offered by the concept of relative deprivation, which suggests that one feels better or worse on the basis of whether one has been treated better or worse than other people who are around. The older men compare themselves with the younger, feel it is unfair they should have to give up careers, jobs, etc., and have less personal esprit and commitment. The married men compare themselves with the unmarried, and go through the same line of reasoning." (Young, J. 1999) [Young J. *The Exclusive Society,* Sage, 1999, quoted by Amy Jackson, "The Wide World of Cybercrime," found under "Relative Deprivation Theory-Angelfire"] Young is describing but actually attacking the concept of relative deprivation!

So it is not just objective deprivation, but *feelings of deprivation relative to your reference group* that can make you disaffected or angry. *Incredibly, many of our poorest citizens have millionaires as their reference group.* As noted before, Michael Moore, the maker of movies critical of our lack of democracy, said that the reason many of the poor vote for Republicans, against their own interests, is that they feel sure that one day *they too* will be millionaires! The CEOs are their reference group, but clearly not their membership group.

For fear of writing a tome comparable in length to a "history of the British Navy" (a quote from the hilarious "Soaked in Seaweed, or Upset in the Ocean, An Old-Fashioned Sea Story," by Stephen Leacock), I must *briefly* mention some of the many inequalities that exist in our society. This list focuses on inequalities that are primarily objective. They are not due to the imagination of their victims. They really exist. They may be *exacerbated* by subjective comparisons with other groups or individuals, but the inequality and deprivation is not imaginary. Women's salaries, for example, fall in the objective measures of wealth and income inequality that are comparatively "hard data", and are dear to economists.

The Gender Gap: Women's salaries are consistently lower than those of men with the same skills. Men are more likely to be promoted over women with the same skills. Remember, it is only about 100 years ago that women have even been able to vote (August 1920). Control over women's sexuality is much harsher than that of men; the fight against abortion and "choice" continues. Prostitutes are arrested, but "Johns" go free.

Height Inequality: Short people are less likely to get jobs and promotions. They are more likely to be bullied.

Physical Inequality: Beautiful women and handsome men get better jobs, more promotions, and higher salaries. A few pretty girls do most of the dating, leaving a large percentage of teens as comparative wallflowers. (Subjective physical inequality is widespread. For example, many American girls are convinced that they are overweight by comparing themselves to Twiggy-like models and stars. This often leads to anorexia and severe illness.)

Race Inequality: African-Americans still come closest to an American caste. Hispanics and Native Americans, similar to African Americans, have lower income, less education, and are more subject to arrest than Whites for the exact same behavior. Minorities are underrepresented in the professions and highly skilled jobs. African Americans are more likely to be arrested, jailed, found guilty, given longer sentences, for the same offenses than other racial groups. It is harder for them to get jobs, regardless of their level of skill or education.

Regional Inequality: Appalachian poor whites and those in "small towns in the Midwest" essentially bypassed by the government were described by Obama to a wealthy fund-raising audience. "And it's not surprising they get bitter. They cling to their guns or religion or antipathy toward people who are not like them…" *Of those in poverty* in 2011, 41.4% were White non-Hispanic, 28.6% were Hispanic, (any race), 25.4% were African-American, alone or in combination, and 4.3% were Asian. (Inequality.org. 2012) [Inequality.org. 2012, "Poverty more than a matter of Black and White."] In contrast, *the proportion of each ethnic group in poverty* was White 10%, Black 27%, and Hispanic 24%. In proportion to their numbers in the population, half as many Whites were in poverty as Blacks and Hispanics in 2013. (The Henry Kaiser Family Foundation, "Poverty Rate by Race/Ethnicity, U.S. 2013)

Religious inequality: The U.S. has been a predominantly Protestant country. The "mainline" Protestant churches include the Methodist, Lutheran, Presbyterian, Episcopal, Congregationalist, Baptist, and Quakers, and others. Even within this group there is an implicit hierarchy. I once read a short biography of a Southern author returning to his roots to "dry out." He said that his home town was such a backwater that "*even* the Episcopalians were snake-handlers." That brings us to the lower ranking evangelical and fundamentalist sects that conjure up images of the Holy Rollers and "speaking in tongues." Catholicism has grown in the U.S, due in part to the growth of the Hispanic population, now comprising one third of the nation. Catholics and Jews, once despised and persecuted groups, have now become generally accepted, but are still stereotyped. Lowest on the U.S. religious totem-pole may be the Muslims, largely due to the conflict in the Middle East. There is intolerance and physical violence directed at them. The history of the Mormons is one of vicious massacres, though Mormons are generally accepted today. The U.S. forbade their original polygamy in 1890. There is currently prejudice against atheists and native-American religious cults.

"Even when localities recognized the drug (peyote) as legal 'Indians have… [suffered] criminal justice harassments, arrests, prosecutions, convictions, and jail time." In 1997 "The Supreme Court struck down the Religious Freedom Act of 1993, which would have allowed Native Americans to use such substances as peyote if they were a traditional and legitimate part of their ceremonies. The Court ruled 6-3 that the act was an infringement of states' rights. (Rasmussen, K and Smith, C.R., 1998) [Rasmussen, K and Smith, C.R. Native Americans and Religious Freedom: The Case for a "Re-Vision" of the First Amendment. The Center for First Amendment Studies, CFAS, White Papers.pub. in 1997 Free Speech Yearbook, (SCA: Washington, D.C., 1998)]

Sexual inequality: LGBT (Lesbian, gay, bisexual and transgender) discrimination is still rife in the U.S. The inequality ranges from the workplace (exclusion from jobs, harassment on the job) to the occasional violent attack or murder, based on anger at and fear of LGBTs. Much of the past persecution of gays, for example, was done by politicians in the McCarthy era who were in fact homosexuals themselves.

In 2014, the Supreme Court found for the Hobby Lobby Corporation, a chain of craft stores, and opened up a can of worms by ruling that the "person" with religious beliefs referred to in the federal Religious Freedom Restoration Act (RFRA) could be a closely held for-profit corporation. These companies (and their religious owners) could not be forced to pay for insurance for contraception needed by their female employees. That would be considered a breach of the religious freedom of the owners! It was, in effect, another attack on Obamacare (Affordable Care Act). Then on March 26th, 2015, Governor Mike Pence of Indiana signed the Indiana Religious Freedom Restoration Act. This would have expanded the Hobby Lobby description of "closely-held for-profit corporations" to include "a partnership, a limited liability company, a corporation, a company, a firm, a society, a joint-stock company, an unincorporated association, or another entity." "An RFRA of some kind is not, *in the abstract*, a terrible idea (my emphasis)….. The inspiration for RFRAs was the prosecution of Native Americans for rituals involving peyote." (Davidson, A., 2015) [Davidson, A. "Why a G.O.P. Gambit Backfired in Indiana." The New Yorker, March 31, 2015.] As of April 2nd, Indiana's legislative leaders "fixed" the wording in Pence's Act, under the guidance of business leaders. Some of the speakers were "Allison Melangton, who headed planning for the 2012 Superbowl in Indianapolis, Jim Morris, vice chairman of the Pacers, and Salesforce Marketing Cloud CEO Scott McCorkle." (Indy Star, 2015) [Tony Cook and Tom LoBianco, Indiana business leaders embrace RFRA fix, Indy Star, April 2, 2015]. If concern for LGBT individuals is weak, perhaps the self-interests of the business community will jump in to protect against the most outrageous discrimination. Note that the Citizens United decision of the Supreme Court was the first to find that corporations are individuals (persons) with the right of free speech. From this decision, it is not a giant leap to find that these corporate "individuals" suffer religious discrimination because they don't want to be forced to provide contraception to bisexuals, don't want to be forced to bake a wedding cake for a gay wedding, or provide flowers for a transgendered funeral!. The deceptive language skills of the anomic lawyers and politicians are part and parcel of the dark triad's traits of cunning and manipulation. The morphing of the corporation into a "person" is a Machiavellian move by skilled wordsmiths who long ago gave us such oxymorons as "benign neglect" and "compassionate conservatism." A revised "religious freedom" bill was signed in Arkansas, inspired by the uproar over the Indiana bill. Bills in Georgia and North Carolina that allow discrimination against LGBTs are being held up, due to the nationally discussed controversy.

Inequality of justice: "African Americans are incarcerated at nearly six times the rate of whites. Together, African Americans and Hispanics comprised 58% of all prisoners in 2008, even though African Americans and Hispanics make up approximately one quarter of the U.S. population." (NAACP Criminal Justice Fact Sheet) Upon return to the community, prisoners are subject to further inequality. It is hard to get a job if you have a record of arrest, even for a minor offense.

Veterans' inequality: The suicide rates of veterans have gone through the roof. Between 2005 and 2011, 49,000 veterans took their own lives. "The annual suicide rate among veterans is 30 for every 100,000 of the population, compared to a civilian rate of 14 per 100,000. (Hargarten, J. 2014) [Hargarten, J. et al. "Suicide rate for Veterans far exceeds that of civilian population" Center for Public Integrity 5/19/2014]. Although the Veteran's Affairs mental health staff has grown by nearly 40% since 2009, much more funding for prevention, treatment, and research is needed.

Mental Health inequality: For a discussion of the effect of education on mental health, *vide infra*.

We could go on and list the inequality of the many specific minorities, ethnic groups, and religious groups. Several volumes would be needed. By looking at socioeconomic status in relation to the growth of the anomic personality type, I hope to have covered most of the minorities in our country who suffer from inequality and discrimination. (For example, Native Americans.) Almost all of these inequalities are grist for the fear, anger and hatred of the prejudiced. In 2006, Virginia Republican Senator George Allen called a 20-year-old Democratic volunteer of East Indian descent a "macaca," a term based on the macaque monkeys. This "animalization" is commonly applied to enemies, to make them subhuman, and thus acceptable as targets. There is no guilt when you attack a policeman who is a "pig." The Germans have combined two despised animals in the term "*schweinhund*," or pig-dog. Sometimes epithets partake of two or more inequalities. A man murdered by a distant cousin of mine told his wife "You have two strikes against you. You are not only a Jew, but also a midget." A man who is "effeminate" or a women who is "too assertive," (i.e. masculine) are targets for disapproval.

I think much of the angry disapproval of Hillary Clinton springs from her assertiveness. It takes a lot of what used to be called "moxie" or "backbone" to run for president.

The list of racial, ethnic and regional slurs (see Wikipedia, List of ethnic slurs by ethnicity) is a long one. Here are a few examples: African-American; nigger, spade, coon, Sambo; Asian; Jap, Chink, gook, Oriental; Hispanic; spic, wetback, beaner; White; cracker, gringo, honkey, red-neck, hick. When Berman (*infra*) rails against the torn social fabric of America, he is talking about the above listed inequalities and the hatreds exemplified by the endless list of slurs.

Anomic Personality: An Adaptation to Capitalism and Inequality

I would add that this recent dramatic spurt of inequality (at the very least a spurt of objective inequality of wealth and income) has made the striving, competition, and the other traits of the anomic personality even more accentuated. These traits are found in the general population, but are called out or exacerbated as adaptations to capitalism and its inequalities.

Grandiosity: (Goals and self-image out of line with reality) may become endemic if millions are striving for high-level jobs where only thousands of jobs actually exist. There are about ten million prime-age men who are not working, but there are only 4.8 million job openings for men and women of all ages, according to the most recent federal data." (Applebaum, B. 2014) ["The Vanishing Male Worker," Binyamin Applebaum, The NY Times, 12/11/2014.]

Lack of empathy is advantageous if you are going to outstrip your neighbor or minority members in wealth and possessions without guilt. *Cunning and manipulative verbal skills* are needed in the race for money and power, especially when money and power are more concentrated in the "1%."

Treating others as objects is a means of gaining an edge over others without spoiling your positive self-image (anon.) Elsewhere I have compared the Community (Gemeinschaft) with the Society (Gesellschaft) after the manner of Ferdinand Toennies. (Toennies, F. 1963) [Toennies, F. *Gemeinschaft and Gesellschaft, Edited and translated by Charles P. Loomis (Original edition 1887, New York: Harper & Rowe, 1957, 1963).*] "In the Community, social relations are 'natural' (intrinsic); people are loved for what they are, not for what they can give you (valued as ends, not as means to an end). In the Society (read present-day U.S.) social relationships are seen as means to an end, as in 'networking' (instrumental)." I have tried to illustrate the fact that these traits, and this personality type, are a good "fit" to the demands of the deregulated anomic culture in which we Americans live. But Kenneth Burke, mentioned before, warned us that the "goodness of fit" of traits and behavior to the demands of a particular culture can be misleading. His characterization of the bureaucratic personality as being "fit in an unfit fitness" tells the story. (He termed his phrase "echolalic" in reference to echolalia, a compulsive repetition of another person's phrases or vocalizations, common in autism.) For example, if you are a good fit to the demands of a totalitarian society, as in Nazi Germany, then you are not really fit (healthy) even though you are surrounded by others just like you and are not "deviant."

Again, this is not to say that the rise of the anomic personality is an adaptation to *only* one factor, the economic factor of the recent rapid growth of inequality. The national history, the myth of the American Dream, child rearing for success and cutthroat competition, and many other factors have laid the groundwork and promoted the growth of the anomics. I previously quoted a review of the movie "The Hunger Games." Its heroine, Katniss Everdeen, the huntress with bow and arrows competing with her teen peers to stay alive in a murderous kleptocracy, is the epitome of the high-school anomic. If she survives, maybe she will grow up to be a CEO, or at least a professional. High grades, athletic prowess, trendy clothes, hooking up, and having the latest electronic device are the signs of adolescent success and a "state of grace" in the modern teen. Martin Luther would be horrified. But your conspicuous consumption (and maybe your hard work) still tells God (and your peers) that you or your parents have worked hard.

Maccoby (*supra*) stresses the lifelong influence (not just economic determinism) on social character, presumably to avoid the once popular and almost exclusive emphasis on early childhood factors. "Social character is formed in childhood and continuously by work, schooling and play." This statement would have upset the "pisspot determinists" writing in the days of my college and graduate training. (anon.) They seized on breast feeding and weaning, toilet training, and swaddling as keys to national character. During World War II there were numerous books diagnosing "culture at a distance." Since we could not interview the enemy, we relied heavily on guesswork to describe him. *The Chrysanthemum and the Sword*, by Ruth Benedict on Japanese social character, and *"Is Germany Incurable,"* by Richard Brickner, are two examples. In *The People of Great Russia*, Geoffrey Gorer and John Rickman claimed that traditional Russians of our World War II ally swaddled their children tightly. This practice "irreversibly rendered the mass of Soviet citizens inclined toward passivity and submission, even as they suffered intense bouts of longing for personal freedom." (Turner, F. "Margaret Mead's Countercultures,") [Turner, Fred. http://www.publicbooks.org/nonfiction/margaret-meads-countercultures, in a review of *Return from the Natives*, by Peter Mandler] Despite the naiveté of some of the "culture and personality" studies (Gorer and Brickner, in particular), "through their books, Mead and Benedict offered Americans an opportunity to embrace an extraordinary range of sexual, racial, and cultural differences." (Turner, op. cit.)

Tiger, Bernie, Dick and Donald are the outliers and avatars that I have used to illustrate in detail the behavior (and the emotions when data are available in biographies) that are prevalent in the anomics of our time. But anomics lie on a continuum. Those exhibiting the most unbridled ambition, extreme lack of empathy, and manipulation of others are part of the Dark Triad (Goleman, D. 2007, pp. 117-132). Yet the large majority of the population exhibits only a few of the traits of the psychopath, the Machiavellian, or the Aggressive Narcissist. Who are they, and what makes them anomic? They are garden-variety narcissists, and they are us.

They are the people who cheat on their income taxes. They are the butcher who puts his thumb on the scale. How many times have we read of candidates for political office who have failed to qualify for office because they hired an illegal immigrant as a baby sitter or housekeeper? They bear some resemblance to the mother who encouraged her daughter to bully her classmate on the internet until the victim committed suicide.

Morris Berman (Berman, M. 2006) [Berman, M. *Dark Ages America: The Final Days of Empire.* New York, NY, W.W. Norton & Co., 2006 paperback, p. 37] describes an incident where a man lay shot at a gas station and was bleeding. No one paid any attention to him. One man looked at the injured body, pumped some gas into his own car, and left without a word. The injured man lay in the street for hours before anyone called the police. The case of Kitty Genovese in 1964 is still a shocker, even in the days of television violence and Isis beheadings. She cried out for help, while being stabbed during three episodes over the course of one half hour. A total of 38 people heard her cry for help, and some of them actually saw her being killed, but not one of them called the police. They didn't want to get involved. Kew Gardens, Queens was a staid middle-class area. This suggests a gaping hole in the social fabric.

Incidents such as these can be seen as milder examples of the narcissism and self-regard that is widespread. Using the expression, "I'm all right, Jack" (originally "Fuck you, Jack, I'm all right!") doesn't necessarily put you in the dark triad/tetrad but it signals a regrettable change in our national moral fiber. Its origin is believed to stem from the rejecting and selfish attitude of civilians toward British sailors (jacks) returning home from war.

There is no doubt that ours is a narcissistic nation. Decades ago, in his book, *The Culture of Narcissism*, (Lasch, C., 1979) [Lasch, Christopher The Culture of Narcissism, New York, Norton, 1979] Christopher Lasch found that the everyday behavior of the nation coincided with the traits and symptoms of pathological narcissism found in psychiatric patients. Of course, there have been jeremiads decrying the seven deadly sins of the human race ever since time began, and were probably written on the walls of the caves in Altamira, Spain during the Cro-Magnon period in symbols we don't understand. One trait mentioned by Lasch, (op. cit.) the narcissist's excessive concern with fear of dying, gets little attention from other authors. Yet for me, the fact that Republicans have shown a greater fear of dying than Democrats in "terror management" studies, has great political significance. This is felt to have made them more prone to vote for George W. Bush, who rode in on a wave of fear after 9/11 prompted by GOP lies about Saddam Hussein's WMD's (Weapons of Mass Destruction). (anon.) 2009, supra) The GOP's greater bellicosity and stand against gun control may stem in part from this same propensity to thanatophobia, though gun manufacturer's money is clearly the main motivation.

The proliferation of the selfie photograph, made simple and popular by the new technology of the cell phone, surely is narcissistic. [Twenge, J.M. and Campbell, W.K... *The Narcissism Epidemic*, New York: Simon & Schuster, atria paperback, 2013.] Twenge and Campbell, 2013, give extensive examples of the part of narcissism that is called vanity. The face book, and the gathering of hundreds of "friends" is a relatively harmless phenomenon, but the desire for publicity, fame and fortune is behind the anomic outliers (as well as these less harmful garden-variety types) whose unlimited striving for success has cost us so much in crime, wars and in damage to the economy through inequality.

One of the main traits of the narcissist is the need for attention and recognition. Several serial killers have sought recognition by contacting news reporters. This is a recurrent theme in television murder mysteries. The Zodiac Killer in California, who shot young couples, sent taunting encrypted letters to the press. He killed at least ten people, and perhaps many more. He was never caught.

Dennis Rader tortured animals as a child (behavior known to be prognostic of clinical psychopathy). As an adult, he earned a B.A. in administration of justice *(sic!)*. He was married, with two children, and held a series of jobs. He seemed an exemplary citizen, having been elected president of the church council of Christ Lutheran Church. He was also a Cub Scout leader. He killed ten people, mostly by strangulation, before being caught,. His modus operandi was encoded in his signature, "BTK", standing for "Bind, Torture, Kill," which appeared on numerous letters he sent to the police and the newspapers. His quest for fame was his undoing. He sent a floppy disk to KSAS-TV in Wichita, with his usual writings. In a deleted MS Word document on the disk, unknown to him, were the words "Christ Lutheran Church" and "last modified by Dennis." The obvious lesson is, "Buy your own floppy disks!" (Dennis Rader, Wikipedia)

While BTK and the Zodiac Killer were psychopaths by definition, and might be expected to show an extreme need for attention, the desire for publicity, fame, and recognition is widespread. Celebrities were found to be generally more narcissistic than the average person in a study using the Narcissistic Personality Inventory. (Surprised?) "Narcissists are masters at staying in the spotlight; they love attention and will do almost anything to get it." (Twenge, supra). In this era there are many people who are "famous for being famous." These include Paris Hilton, Lindsay Lohan, and Britney Spears. Kim Kardashian West is now the front runner. (Why are these famous/famous leaders all women? There are plenty of male zeros out there.) It has been a given that the recruitment for show business; acting, dancing, singing and musical performance, catches narcissists. They are people who want to be "on stage."

But in our anomic society, a much larger proportion of the population than those in show business and serial killers wants to be in the spotlight. "In 2006, 51% of 18-to-25-year-olds said that "becoming famous" was an important goal..... In 2005, 31% of American high school students said they expected to become famous some day." (Twenge, supra). The American Dream, though rapidly becoming a myth, lives on.

We looked at the way social character has been studied and described, and covered some of the pitfalls of these studies. The prevalence of narcissism in our culture was described. The "fit" of the anomic personality to the demands of a competitive, winner-take-all, zero-sum society (capitalism?) was noted. The traits of the anomic personality, with its narcissism, were shown to be an adaptation to the shortage of jobs when compared with the number of job seekers. But the economy is only one of the roots of the social character, "anomic personality."

Now we should take time to review the factors that may possibly have produced social character in general, and the social character called the anomic personality in particular. Social character has to be the product of many factors.

The **historical roots** of the anomic personality were reviewed in earlier chapters. These were the Reformation and the Protestant ethic. Work, as proof of grace, led to "secular asceticism." (The austerity and self-denial of the monk's life was transferred to everyday life, marked by hard work, possessions and production as proof of a state of grace.) With the advent of the industrial revolution and the mass production of consumer goods, came conspicuous consumption. The American Dream was the product of the social character of the New Englanders described so well by de Tocqueville. Combined with the Westward Expansion and unlimited opportunity, it led to the belief that everyone could be president, or at least successful. With time, of course, land became scarcer, housing more expensive, and opportunity much more limited. Waves of immigrants eventually found that the streets of the New World were not paved with gold. Inequality was mitigated briefly after World War II, but according to Piketty (Piketty, T. *Capital in the Twenty-First Century, supra) it was on a sharp upward trajectory from the 1970s on.* Inequality (in income, diet, education, housing, medical care, access to information, and other areas) is a major factor in producing changes in social character.

Obama, Hillary and Bernie Sanders

President Obama, in his 2015 State of the Union address, set an ambitious domestic agenda. These were making community college free for most students, enhancing tax credits for education and child care, and imposing new taxes and fees on high income earners and large financial institutions. He wanted to lift the trade embargo on Cuba, and requested legislation authorizing the fight against ISIS, the Islamic State. I have covered all the major domestic incentives, and much more. The sad truth is that not much could be done in the final year of a "lame duck" president. The GOP vowed to block his every move toward building a better safety net "for the middle class." I felt, along with perhaps half the nation that our best hope lay in a resurgence of the Democrats.

I thought that Hillary Clinton would turn out to be more liberal because of Bernie Sanders pulling her to the left. She presented herself as a populist. I thought she would become our first woman president, with the help of women voters. She did get help from our leading misogynist,

Donald Trump, criticizing Carly Fiorina's looks on the televised GOP debates in 2015, and calling Alicia Machado, a former Miss Universe from Venezuela, "Miss Piggy" and "Miss Housekeeping" (because she is Hispanic). But Hillary didn't win over many Republican women

Donald Trump not only survived the many debates with his numerous fellow GOP presidential candidates, but prevailed over them. At this point I hesitate to relate in *full* detail his character, his ideations, and his behavior directly to the subject matter of this book, the Anomic Personality. I hesitate to do this, because I have found that he has been involved in some 3500 lawsuits, and many others have already made extensive opinions and judgements based on his behavior and ideation. But the Anomic Personality is a widespread American phenomenon, and he is one of us. I too, have been driven; worked seven years for a doctorate, and struggled to get professorial appointments from universities and fellowships from (anon.) many foundations. Like Trump, I have been "tantalized" at each level of success to go further. That is the only place where we are similar. We are members of an excessively striving society that will only become more so with explosive inequality during Trump's presidency. To be clear, in political ideology (and I hope in most other aspects of personality) we are at opposite ends of the universe.

"An exclusive USA TODAY analysis of legal filings across the United States finds that the presumptive Republican presidential nominee and his businesses have been involved in at least 3,500 legal actions in federal and state courts during the past three decades. They range from skirmishes with casino patrons to million-dollar real estate suits to personal defamation lawsuits."(Penzenstadler, N & Page, S., 2016) [Nick Penzenstadler and Susan Page, "Exclusive: Trump's 3,500 lawsuits unprecedented for a presidential nominee USA Today. 6/2/2016]

Trump's litigiousness (and primarily his constant striving for more power, more money and more adulation) shows his good fit to the Anomic Personality type. The description of the Anomic, and particularly the Machiavellian, seem to fit him like a glove. I choose to let others who have written about his symptomatology in detail speak for themselves. Let's just quote one of these experts, who seems to agree at least on his narcissism. This expert, psychiatrist Justin Frank, goes even further:

(Frank, J. 11/4/2016) [Frank J. "Crazy in Love or Crazy in Fear?" Justin Frank Official Website, 11/4/2016, p. 6.]

"So, here are some clues about psychotic elements that are present in and expressed openly by Donald Trump: He presents a preponderance of destructive impulses so great that even the impulses to love are suffused by them and turned to sadism. We see this in his attacks on women, immigrants, the handicapped, Muslims (even the Gold Star Khan family), and – of course on his opponent he still calls "Crooked Hillary."

"He also shows a hatred of external reality, which, as Freud pointed out, is extended to all aspects of the psyche that make for awareness of it. He makes up stories to fit his fantasies, and never checks them for veracity. He simply says he will deport 11 million immigrants or build a giant wall without thinking twice about reality. He denies the reality of his destructiveness—a complete denial of reality and responsibility that is also psychotic.

He also hates internal reality and all that makes for awareness of it. He has said repeatedly that he never looks at himself in the mirror, and one can see that when looking into his vacant eyes during a speech. He refuses any and all introspection, ultimately blinding himself to his inner world. This hatred of his own psychic truths makes it impossible for him to feel empathy for others, or to take responsibility for his actions."

"In the consulting room, one characteristic of psychotic functioning is when a patient immediately develops an intense set of feelings about the therapist – an intense attachment whose thinness (the patient barely knows the therapist) is of marked contrast to the tenacity with which it is maintained. This intense *attachment* (my emphasis) stems from a need for comfort and safety, protecting against deep inarticulate fears of annihilation." (Frank, J. op.cit.)

Because of his character, Trump has great appeal to a large portion of the nation's voters. His displays of anger, his "tough" persona, his misogyny, his possible modeling on Hitler, and his fear of the "other" (Muslims, blacks, Hispanics and immigrants) are part of the belief system of a startling number of our citizens. Later on, I will try to connect Trump's appeal to his base (what Hilary unfortunately called his "basket of deplorables") to a series of facts and hypotheses:1) the short life span of the Cro-Magnons 2) the need for strong child-parent attachment during prehistoric times, due to predators 3) modern carry-over of DNA for strong attachment need, predators now mostly human 4) emotional attachment to a leader which overrides any personal political issues, and 5) substitution of the leader's issues and platform for any personal issues or independent political philosophy. This emotional attachment (4) is similar to the "thin attachment" or immediate transference to the therapist, mentioned by Frank, (*supra*) and starkly different from gradual attachment based on mutual familiarity and interaction between patient and therapist.

Returning to events prior to the election, Hillary had a huge boost around mid-2016, when Trump accused Obama of founding ISIS and attacked the parents of an American Muslin U.S. Army Specialist, Kareem Rashad Sultan Khan, who was killed in Iraq. Trump's propensity to improvise and ad lib, rather than follow the teleprompter, might have lost him some of his White Collar male voters, and some of the financial support of the establishment GOP. Hillary was then ahead by ten points in the polls.

Bernie Sanders, the Vermont Senator (Independent) and Hillary's only real primary rival, drew huge crowds to hear his populist stump speech. I think that his label of "democratic socialist" weighed heavily against him. A major weakness, from the liberal viewpoint, was on gun control, and he talked little of foreign policy at a time of crisis in the Middle East and confrontation with Russia and China. His Jeremiads against inequality and the greed of the 1% are rarely heard from other politicians. Gradually Hillary moved from presenting herself as a moderate to calling herself a progressive. Bernie emphasized that he was a progressive, and did not use his label as democratic socialist in the later debates with Hillary.

I admire Bernie's honesty, and indeed, his idées fixes, (mass movement, single payer health care, break up the big banks, reinstate Glass-Steagall) for to me they are good ones. He outlined a program that included most of the major policy points I have suggested. (Regulate, Redistribute and Rebuild.) Paul Krugman, whom I greatly admire, unfortunately came out with an Op Ed labeling Sanders as "naïve' and believing that change can come about by "transformational rhetoric." He depicted Hillary as exhibiting "hardheaded realism." Sanders actually made clear that a "political revolution" is needed, and for this to happen, there has to be a mass movement. People of good will have to get out and vote and participate actively in politics. "History shows that Sanders' (actual) view of how change happens, through mass movements, is far more accurate than Krugman's view that change happens through enlightened elites willing to compromise with their adversaries." (Hetland, G., 2016) [Hetland, G., "Paul Krugman is Wrong About Bernie Sanders-and About How Social Change Works." Web Only/Views, 1/25/2016.] (See also Palermo, J.P., 2016) [Palermo, J.P., "Paul Krugman on the 'Happy Dreams' of Bernie Sanders," *Huffpost Politics,* 1/24/2016.]

A Ray of Sunshine? Two Recent Supreme Court Decisions

Just when you're thinking that things couldn't get worse, there is often a ray of sunshine. (No, Barbara Ehrenreich, this isn't the product of "bright-sided" unrealistic "positive thinking.") On June 25th, 2015 the Supreme Court ruled 6 to 3 that the federal subsidies (tax credits) that help people pay their premiums for Obamacare are legal under the Affordable Care Act. This avoids a potential leap in premium prices in 34 states, and avoids the potential loss of coverage for 8 million people. It was a major victory for Obama, since conservatives have consistently tried to destroy his health program. On the following day, the Supreme Court ruled 5 to 4 that the Constitution gives same-sex couples the right to marry. States cannot ban same-sex marriages under the Constitutional guarantees of due process and equal protection under the law. Gay marriage is now legal in all fifty states. Obama was the first sitting president to speak out in favor of gay marriage. In addition to "getting more people to have good lives." as Thomas Edsall says, it gives a victory to Obama and will greatly enhance his historical record of accomplishments. It also gave the Democrats a potential lift in votes before the 2016 presidential election. Obama's February 2015 veto of the XL Pipeline was a brave move politically, for it defied the power of the energy corporations. It could have given impetus to the fight against global warming, in which the U.S. may appeared to have been the world leader in facing up to coal and oil corporate power. That hope died once Trump became president

Bernie Sanders certainly helped to move the Democrats a little to the left from dead center. That was of great service to the country. What was of great concern was that the Middle East and the attacks by ISIS then reached the level of a crisis.(By 2018, ISIS had become comparatively weak.) (The GOP blamed Hillary, focusing on the embassy slaying in Benghazi, Libya, the massacres in France, upheaval in Turkey, and the battle for Syria. Numerous conflagrations and confrontations were busting out all over (like June in the Rodgers and Hammerstein song from *Oklahoma*). Hillary, while more conservative than her former rival candidate, had the necessary skills and contacts with foreign leaders needed to help in this emergency. As former Secretary of State, she had years of experience during similarly troubled times. Trump has none, and still gives no evidence of having any detailed knowledge of foreign policy.

The GOP campaign against Hillary focused on the word "liar." They wished to smear Hillary over her supposed failure to protect our ambassador to Libya, by supplying enough funds to afford full complements of soldiers and equipment at all our embassies. As Secretary of State, she had asked for more funds, but Congress cut those funds by millions of dollars. The GOP lied in its efforts to defame her. The weeping mother of a soldier killed at the Embassy (on television, July 18th, the first night of the Republican National Convention) said her son was killed by Hillary's underfunding. Not true. It was conservative members of Congress, both Democrats and Republicans, who typically fund less for security than requested. They ignored Hillary's warning, in 2011, that the embassies were underfunded for personnel and protection.

The level of discourse, the lying, and the calumny exhibited at the Republican National Convention should have acted as a warning on a small scale of what might happen if Trump should win, and unexpectedly he did.

It has become obvious that much of the speech of Trump's wife, Melania, at the GOP Convention, was plagiarized from a speech of Michelle Obama. It confirms the impression that Trump is not the manager he claims to be. He or his staff cannot even pick a reliable speechwriter for his wife's speech on the opening night of his Convention! How could he manage the daily international upheavals we are seeing? In the same way he has managed several businesses into bankruptcy? Vice President Joseph Biden recently asked how we could trust this man with the code for the "nuclear football" which could set off a worldwide nuclear Armageddon.

A Revised Rank Ordering Of Catastrophe and Threats

At the beginning of this book I tried to rank order the various threats to our nation and the world. That list was written some time ago, and the election of Donald Trump changed or increased those threats. This section is an attempt to bring those threats up to date and to add further explanation of their relative importance.

Depending on our personality, our social class and income, our age and perhaps our gender, we are bound to have differing views on what threatens us the most. My ranking of threats has been heavily affected by what I read, what I hear from family and friends, and my advanced age. Contrary to the politician's short-term view, I think in terms of my wife, my (anon.) children, my (anon.) grandchildren and the future generations. While the nuclear threat is still with us, what seemed like a crisis between the US. and North Korea has simmered down. But global warming seems like a time-bomb, ready to go off if we do not take drastic steps to stop or mitigate it. Other short and long-term threats, national or international, are also of concern:

1. Global Warming
2. Nuclear War: arming and attack by rogue states (Isis), or North Korea, or less likely by Russia or China.
3. Middle East Wars possibly escalating to World War III: Sunnis versus Shiites vs Kurds, Israelis vs Palestinians. Opposing armed groups are fighting in Libya, Syria and Yemen.
4. Over-population, Massive Migration, Food Shortages. These are all possible even without Global Warming or Nuclear War. They are happening right now.
5. With the election of Trump, *two* conservative appointments (Gorsuch and Kavanaugh) to the Supreme Court, leading to perhaps 30 years of conservative decisions. Kavanaugh's appointment was confirmed despite his record of numerous very conservative decisions and testimony in his confirmation hearings suggesting his sexual abuse of a minor during his teens.The fact that he wrote an opinion that a sitting president cannot be indicted makes the reason for Trump's choosing him as a candidate crystal clear.

6. A continuing Republican majority in theSenate. The Democrats won a mid-term majority in the House of Representatives. This means that action against global warming and the investigation of Trump may be slowed down but not stopped in its tracks. The House Democrats can initiate their own investigation of the Russian Affair, even if Trump stops Mueller's investigaton through a biased Attrney General.

The meeting between the U.S. and China might have set an example for other nations to follow, but Trump's withdrawal from the Paris Agreement in June, 2017, was a severe blow. How will future historians look upon decisions made by a single hypomanic narcissist about the future of the world's weather?

7. Given that nearly half the U.S. voting population has shown itself partial to a regressive platform of: racial, religious and ethnic discrimination and misogyny, elimination of the current or Democrat-proposed social safety net (including Social Security and Obama Care, public school support, free college education for families under $125,000, minimum wage of $15, and LGBT recognition,) a resurgence of anger and violence may follow the pssible impeachmernt or indictment of Trump. The threat is that a large portion of the disaffected, especially high-school and lower-educated White males, who have voted against their best interests, will see the loss of their leader, to whom they have developed a *blind attachment*, as a direct attack on themselves. They are already blinded by anger and by the twisting of truth by skilled G.O.P. wordsmiths. As discussed previously, their sudden leap in suicide, alcoholism and addiction rates, in contrast to those of other demographic subgroups, is cause for alarm. "Anger in" as shown in these rates can suddenly turn to "anger out," in the growth of U.S homegrown militias and racist organizations. A recent comment struck me dumbfounded; that the Trump campaign and his current tweets are still full of the famous "dogwhistle" statements and slogans. Remember that actual dogwhistles are beyond the range of the human ear, but German Shepherds can hear them. Similarly, statements like "Make America Great Again." a major Trump slogan, actually fall on his followers' ears as "Make

America White again." "Lock her up," a chant at some Trump campaign gatherings, is *still* part of his attack on Hillary, claiming that she is a criminal because she disregarded State Department cybersecurity guidelines by using a private email account and server. How clever of the campaign managers to take part of the well-known children's song, "London Bridge Is Falling Down," and apply it to Hillary; "Take a key and **lock her up**, my fair lady." This cry is still being repeated at pep rallies in preparation fot the 2020 elections!

8. Inequality. I have devoted many pages to a discussion of how a recent worldwide leap of inequality of all kinds, but especially inequality of income and wealth, may lead to the destruction of our capitalism as we now know it—a system only partially leavened by the creation of a safety network of social supports. The anomic personality thrives in a societal condition of excessive decontrol, (anomie) and makes for extreme striving for sex, money and power at the expense of others.

9. Child-rearing. In survey after survey the large proportion of parents who are punitive, cold, or labile in relation to their children threatens to continue to produce children who are depressed, anxious, or antisocial. Some of these children become leaders who are narcissists. Machiavellians, or even psychopaths. Many fail to care for other human beings due to their early treatment by their parents. The anger engendered especially by antisocial and narcissistic parents prepares young men and women for war, where they can *legally* "act out" their anger, instead of going into depression or crime. Education of parents and teachers in child rearing is of some hope in avoiding wars that we as a nation initiate.

Hillary versus Donald T., Views On The Greatest Threats

Global Warming: Hillary believes in the scientific findings on global warming. She would probably have followed in the footsteps of Obama, who held talks with China about global warming. Donald, on the other hand, doesn't believe in global warming!

On the dark side, the replacement of Justice Scalia and Justice Kennedy with two very conservative justices will give us years of a 6-4 conservative majority under Trump and his successors. SCOTUS appointments last a lifetime. Congress blocked Obama's candidate for Chief Justice, thus handing the appointment to Trump. This was a major blow to our movement toward greater equality under Obama. (Trump nominated Neil Gorsuch and Brett Kavanaugh, both extremely conservative judges. They were approved, and now the SCOTUS is 6 to 4, in favor of conservatives.)

The Roots of the Anomic Personality

Heredity: First we must consider the fact that information on heredity and political persuasion is very hard to come by, and until much more data are gathered, must remain largely in the realm of conjecture. In one study, 54 pairs of identical twins (monozgotic) and 46 pairs of fraternal twins, all separated at birth, were adopted and reared by parents of differing backgrounds. "A conservatism scale showed a difference between the identical and the fraternal twins equivalent to a correlation of 0.56, showing a large genetic influence. This would suggest that genetics, or the difference between one egg and two egg twins, accounts for about 30% of the variance in conservatism (as measured by scores on the conservatism scale). For example, identical twins are much more likely to *both* be conservative or *both* be liberal than fraternal twins or siblings." (anon.) (Bouchard, T.J. Jr. et al. 2003) [Bouchard, T.J. Jr. et al. "Evidence for the Construct Validity and Heritability of the Wilson-Patterson *Conservatism* Scale." *Personality and Individual Differences, 34:959-969, 2003*] The *identical* twins seem to have maintained much of their genetic *individual character* structure despite the influence of later parenting by the assumed differences in adoptive parents, subsequent schooling, peer groups, later work settings and other life experiences. The timing of the adoption may be of critical importance.

Another possible inherited trait may be due to brain structure; the presence or absence of mirror and spindle cells. One of the salient characteristics of anomics and the dark triad of narcissists is their lack of empathy. Mirror and spindle cells are necessary for being able to understand what another person is feeling. That is empathy. (It is not sympathy, often confused with empathy.) The higher apes have mirror cells, but the other primates (except for man) do not have them. (Parr, L.A. et al. 2008) [Parr, L.A. et al. "Emotional Communication in Primates: *Implications for Neurobiology*" *Current Opinion in Neurobiology, 15:716-720, 2008.*] It is possible that people with little regard for others lack or have a low number of mirror or spindle cells, but to my knowledge no brain scans of empathic and non-empathic people have been done focusing specifically on these cells.

A study which comes very close to being a test of mirror cells and empathy was recently done at the University of Chicago. "…Researchers conducted functional brain imaging on 80 prisoners ages 18 to 50, all of whom had tests done to measure their levels of psychopathy" (which includes lack of empathy). Then they posed some scenarios of someone being hurt purposely, as well as had them watch videos of pained facial expressions. Researchers found that those who scored higher on the psychopathy test experienced less activation in the amygdala, ventromedial prefrontal cortex, lateral orbitofrontal cortex, and periaqueductal gray brain regions, compared with those who scored lower on the test. Those who scored higher on the psychopathy test had more activation of the striatum and insula brain regions – the insula brain region is known to play a role in emotion, researchers noted." (Huffpost, 2014 "Psychopaths' Brains Aren't Wired to Show Empathy, Study Finds." Hufffpost, December 18, 2014.) Since most people in prison might be expected to score higher than average on a psychopathy test, the fact that there was a significant difference in brain region activity associated with psychopathy (as a measure of empathy) *within* a population with a constricted range of (high) psychopathy, adds strength to these findings.

Religion. I mentioned the Puritan character of the early English-Scotch New England settlers. We derive our adjective "puritanical," meaning "of a rigid morality," for good reason. Their religion seems unforgiving, with a punitive god, and infant damnation. Their tough, stubborn, dogged, rather dour persona may have been in part the result of being "hard-bitten" by those terrible early winters and the high death rate. But Calvinism, according to Barbara Ehrenreich, (Ehrenreich, B., 2010) [Ehrenreich, B. *Bright-Sided. New York, NY,* Henry Holt & Co. Picador 2010] "could be described as a system of socially prescribed depression." "Through predestination, only those chosen by God *before birth* would get into heaven, and Hell and Purgatory awaited the rest. The task for the living was to constantly examine 'the loathsome abominations that lie in his bosom,' seeking to uproot the sinful thoughts that are a sure sign of damnation." (Ehrenreich, pp. 74-5.) Labor on the farm or in business was the only alternative to this self-examination.

The parallel between Calvinism's emphasis on work *as an outlet* and the "secular asceticism" that followed Martin Luther's Reformation is noteworthy, since hard work and the possessions that followed gave you a chance at a state of grace. Max Weber was clear that new technology (the printing press, the steam engine, and the making of steel) also had a great influence on the rise of capitalism, as well as the Protestant Ethic. These made colonialism and the great Armadas possible. The search for spices to cover up the odor of rotting teeth in Europe also gave impetus to worldwide exploration, to changes in the economies, and thence to changes in social character. Then capitalism followed, and finally globalism, with its striving, relatively unproductive, anomic personalities.

Ethnic Background: This "factor" obviously includes an ethnic group's history, religion, economy, parental practices, religion, and so forth, but ethnicity is helpful shorthand. Let's look at the Scots-Irish, for their contrast with the New England Puritans. Jim Webb has been a senator from Virginia, a combat Marine in Vietnam, an assistant secretary of defense, Secretary of the Navy, and author. In November 2014 he announced a run for U.S. President in 2016, as a Democrat. In his book, *Born Fighting,* he gives a detailed description of the social character of his own people, the Scots-Irish. (Webb, J. 2004) [Webb, J. *Born Fighting.* New York: Broadway. 2004.] They emigrated from the Scottish border country (between England and Scotland) to Ireland and then to Appalachia in the U.S. due to British persecution. Quotations from reviews of Webb's book give some idea of the Scots-Irish social character.

"The Scots-Irish culture of isolation, bad luck, stubbornness, and mistrust of the nation's elite formed and still dominates blue-collar America, the military service, the Bible Belt, and country music" (http://www.jameswebb.com/books/born-fighting)

"The…..ethnic group that has created the core beliefs of democracy American style: our rights come from God, not the government; all of us are born equal, and born aristocrats don't exist…" (Tom Wolfe).

"Pugnacious, bibulous, pious, the Scots-Irish….." (Booklist:" Kirkus Reviews.)

"…..fierce individualism, persistent egalitarianism, and a strong sense of personal honor." "…..ongoing Scots-Irish legacy…..fundamentalist Christianity (a potent combination of Scottish Calvinism and headstrong populism}…..and country music." (Booklist.)

A less complimentary view, previously quoted, was given by Bageant (Bageant, 2007, infra.) "The Scots-Irish working class culture…often comes down to this: Drink, pray, fight and fuck." Bageant revisited his Scots-Irish roots in Appalachia, so his assessment is somewhat harsher than that of Scots-Irish politicians like James Webb, who must run for office. Bageant's assessment of right-wing *and* liberal Americans is no less harsh. He blames conservatives for ignoring the poor, not just in Appalachia. He blames liberals for overlooking the Appalachians, while focusing on a safety net for non-white minorities. (Bageant, J., 2007) [Bageant, J. *Deer Hunting with Jesus,* New York: Crown, 2007.]

The Puritans of New England and the Scots-Irish of Appalachia (Virginia in particular).were both originally Presbyterians. By 1800 the Scots-Irish in Virginia had become predominantly Baptist and Methodist. While New Englanders maintained their character to a great extent (for example, Robert Frost's crusty isolationist "Good fences make good neighbors.") the Bible Belt of the South became famous for its drift away from the puritanical to open expression of religious fervor. I read a review of a book by a former alcoholic (name forgotten) who returned to his Southern roots to "dry out." He said that the town he came from was "such a backwater that even the Episcopalians were snake-handlers." (This remark is also attributed to Dan Rather.) The lesson of the divergence of these two subgroups of Protestant immigrants is that you need to know their history of religious persecution (the Puritans) or the Borders' (Ulster Scots) migration to the Plantation of Ulster, a colonization planned and enforced by the British and Scottish kings.

*Child Rearing_*Especially after the days of Dr. Benjamin Spock, considered by some as spoiling the children of the "me" generation, child rearing practices may have been a crucial factor in the U.S. leading to the growth of the anomic personality and its marked narcissism. But consider that there are narcissists in many countries with much stricter child rearing practices. Narcissism has been believed to be in part due to a "narcissistic injury" First posited by Freud, "Loss of love and failure leave behind them a permanent injury to self-regard in the form of a narcissistic scar." (Freud, S. 1984) [Freud, S. On Metapsychology, Penguin Freud Library 11, Pelican, paperback, International edition. 1984. p. 291.] Freud's later emphasis on loss of the breast and the infant's own treasured feces, the castration fear in men and penis envy in women led to the "pisspot determinism" of the 1930s described before. But his early emphasis on loss of love and failure offers us a much broader set of culprits in the formation of narcissism.

Psychoanalysts after Freud continued to contribute to the theory and treatment of narcissism, which included work by Karl Abraham, Otto Fenichel, Edmund Bergler, and Heinz Kohut. (See Wikipedia, "Narcissistic rage and narcissistic injury.") Much attention was paid to the loss of the "primary narcissism" of infancy, a grandiose natural self-centeredness which must eventually yield to the reality of our relative state of impotence as the child grows into adolescence and adulthood. But this loss must be the experience of *every* child, because we all grow up to realize the limits of the bloated self-esteem of our coddled infancy. So why doesn't every human infant eventually become a narcissist?

Let's return to Freud's broader first formulation, that loss of love and failure are the drivers of narcissism (and thus of the anomic personality whose aggressive narcissism is his main characteristic). Loss of love may occur at any stage of life, but it is most damaging in infancy and childhood. It is connected to fear of dying, because of the inevitable periods of separation between parent and infant, when the child fears abandonment and death. (See anon.) where I discuss Bowlby's attachment theory and its link to death fear, which is a stronger trait in narcissists than in most other personality types.) Bowlby reminds us that any prolonged separation actually means death to an infant. Separation anxiety is then reinforced when a *narcissistic parent* is so self-absorbed that he or she cannot give love, affection, or even attention to the infant or child. Not all parents are narcissists, and this answers our question, "Why doesn't every infant become a narcissist due to loss of the grandiose self-esteem of infancy."

Concern with the effect of narcissistic parents on infants and children has a long history. Sandor Ferenczi, Heinz Kohut, Karen Horney, Donald Winnicott, Alice Miller, and Arno Gruen have all made major contributions to the subject of the genesis of narcissism through parent-child interaction.(See "Narcissistic abuse," Wikipedia, and Winnicott's concept of the "true self" and the "false self" (Winnicott, D.W., 1960) [Winnicott, D.W. 1960. *Ego Distortion in Terms of True and False Self,*" in The Maturational Process and the Facilitating Environment: Studies in the theory of Emotional Development. New York: International UP, 1965, pp. 140=1252.] Winnicott laid the foundation for later elaboration by others, with his concepts of the "true self" and the "false self." I have been especially impressed by the further conceptualization of both Miller and Gruen.

Gruen describes the process whereby the child's *original self* is lost, a *false self* is created, and some of the self is *disowned*. To get love, the child surrenders autonomy by submission to the parents' will. The child sees her submissiveness as a bargain, forcing the parents to take care of her. "First, children accept their parents' evaluation of them without reservation; introjection is therefore a process of collaboration through submission. Second, this means that children begin to hate everything in themselves that could bring them into conflict with parental expectations (a *false self is created*). And third, out of this self-hatred grows a readiness for even more submission." (Italics my comment) (Gruen, 1992, p. 4.) [Gruen, A. *The Insanity of Normality: Realism as Sickness: Toward Understanding Human Destructiveness.* Translated by Hildegarde & Hunter Hannum. New York: Grove Weidenfeld, 1992.]

Gruen and Miller feel that giving up so much of their autonomy and true self to win or maintain their parents' (conditional) love creates in children a lasting rage. Other therapists have commented on narcissistic rage. This rage is directed at the self, resulting in depression. It is also directed outward, toward others they blame for their losses (but typically not their parents). Minorities, other ethnic groups, and foreigners become culturally legitimate targets of this rage.

Another target of narcissistic rage is one's spouse, as in spousal murder (though it is, of course, not culturally approved). Half of American marriages now end in divorce but only a small number end with the killing of a former spouse. The loss of love through divorce, separation or breakup taken together does result in enough murders to suspect that the more narcissistic partners will kill. If you read the papers or go on the internet, you will be deluged by reports of spousal killings. These partings must represent a tremendous loss of self-esteem to provide the rage that ends in killing. The FBI figures for 1995 show "men murdered by girlfriends/wives as 3% of 15,848, (total men murdered) or 475. In contrast, "women murdered by boyfriends/husbands" comprised 30% of 2,711 (total women murdered) or 813. So 63% of "spousal" ("couples"?) murders were by men and only 37% were by women. The traits of the aggressive narcissist (and the psychopath) seem to fit American men better than women, and these murder rates seem to support that impression.

The rage created in children of narcissistic parents is the key to so many of the traits we discussed. The grandiose goals are a compensation for the poor self-esteem created by the loss of the true autonomous self. These goals are abetted by the American Dream myth and by parents' wishing to "live through" their children, or to attain prestige through their child's accomplishments. Do better at sports, excel at school, look prettier, and be more popular than others, and so on. The lack of empathy, remorse or guilt enables the narcissistic anomic personality to walk over all others on the way to fame and fortune. Hurting others is easier when you have been hurt. Does some of this remind you of Gruen's view that the "disowned self" (as labeled by Harville Hendrix) is created by the child as he struggles to blame himself for his parents' rejection and abandonment of him. In effect, it is an attempt to preserve the illusion of parental love. It results, however, in a negative self-image, "self-hatred and self-contempt, a state of perceived weakness that can be overcome only by striving for power." (anon., 2002, op. cit., p. 202.)

Then it is not so much the "spoiling" of children with too much attention and power, (as Twenge and Johnson would have it, *supra*) but the lack of love and affection given to children by narcissistic parents that is operating in the production of narcissists. In my study of mental disorder in a random sample of children (anon.et al.) [anon.et al.) parental practices factors (cold parents, punitive parents, and "labile" parents {parental mood swings} leading to alternating displays of love and rejection of the child) were the best predictors of psychopathology in the children 5 years later, out of a total of 25 predictors. While parenting has probably changed somewhat toward the less authoritarian in the years since the study was done,

(Anon.) this was still a time of Dr. Spock's strong influence. If parents were so strongly affected by Spock's *supposed* influence toward permissive child-rearing, these parents would have reported very mild practices. On the contrary, there were positive responses to questions indicating traditional, authoritarian, and often destructive parental practices. (Incidentally, Spock never recommended permissiveness; only kindness, love, and respect for the child's individuality.) In the late 60s, Norman Vincent Peale blamed Spock's "permissiveness" for the Vietnam War protesters, and this attack was followed by Vice President Spiro Agnew and other conservatives who were strong supporters of the war. (Wikipedia, Benjamin Spock.)

Questions answered by mothers in the two hour interviews were factor analyzed, and certain items "loaded" high on these factors. For example, the highest loading items on the factor "Parents Cold" were "Parents rarely hug and kiss the child" and "Parents do not show affection easily to child." Highest loading items on the "Parents Punitive" factor were "Parents spank child with strap or stick," and "Parents often use deprivation of privileges." The highest loading items on the factor "Mother Excitable-Rejecting" were "Mother often screams at child," "Mother is very changeable in handling him (her)," and "Mother has problems which keep her from getting pleasure from him (her)." (anon.) Spanking with a strap or stick and screaming are not socially approved parental behaviors, yet some parents within all social classes reported such behavior. My guess is that the extremely "permissive" parents described by Twenge and Johnson come from the wealthiest layer of our society. They can afford to hire "false paparazzi" to follow their children around and create a bogus little celebrity. (Twenge, J.M. et al. supra.)

A lack of empathy is one of the defining characteristics of the psychopath, and of the anomic personality in his excessive striving for success, which inevitably involves the failure of others in a zero-sum society. The following prediction of adult empathy from parental behavior over a quarter century is an amazing feat.

"Eleven parenting dimensions (were) derived from maternal interviews when the subjects were 5 years old. Taken together, the parenting dimensions predicted the level of empathic concern at age 31. Adult levels of empathic concern were most strongly related to paternal involvement in child care, maternal tolerance of dependent behavior, maternal inhibition of child's aggression, and maternal satisfaction with the role of mother." (Koestner, R. et. al. 1990) [Koestner, R. et. al. "The family origins of empathic concern: A 28 year longitudinal study." *Journal of Personality and Social Psychology,* Vol. 548 (4), Apr. 1990, 709-717.]

If only we could change parenting in a more loving direction, then the dyed-in-the-wool Democrat in me would predict a Republican Party left in the dust. But maybe the G.O.P. can continue to win elections, even though the country will soon be over 33% Latino, and African-Americans will remain at 12%. The conservative mantra, "When the going gets tough, the tough get going," or other forms of "tough love" and "benign neglect" may yet enable them to convince (deceive) the poor and minorities that they will do better under a Republican administration. I discussed the Trump phenomenon in Chapter 1. How did a presumed billionaire persuade so many poor and middle-class people that he was on their side?

There are many fascinating studies that throw light on the origins of psychopathy and the traits of the anomic personality. Callous and unemotional children are probably on their way to various levels of psychopathy in adulthood. A study of children with oppositional defiant disorder, "assessed for callous-unemotional traits," and matched controls, looked at the mother-child eye contact for each dyad. The authors hypothesized that "psychopathic disorder begins as a failure to attend to the eyes of attachment figures." "Those (children) with high levels of callous-unemotional traits showed low levels of eye contact toward their mothers." (Surprisingly) "Low eye contact was not correlated with maternal coercive parenting or feelings toward the child, but was correlated with psychopathic fearlessness in their fathers." (Dadds, MR., 2011) [Dadds, Mark R., Allen, Jennifer L. et al, "Love, eye contact and the developmental origins of empathy v. psychopathy." British Journal of Psychiatry, published online ahead of print August 18, 2011.] It would be of great interest to know the sex ratio of the experimental subjects, since the fathers' character might provide greater reinforcement for the sons' tendency toward psychopathy as the sons mature. Again, a study tells us the great importance of early attachment, especially to mother, for healthy child development, as John Bowlby has told us in several volumes.

Nicholas Kristof, in "How do we increase empathy?" (*The New York Times*, 1/29/2015) [Kristof, N. "How do we increase empathy?" *The New York Times*, 1/29/2015] briefly reviews several studies and facts which shed light on the relationship between political conservatism and lack of empathy. "One study by psychologists at the University of California at Berkeley finds that the drivers of luxury cars are more likely to cut off other motorists and ignore pedestrians at a crosswalk. Likewise, heart rates of wealthier research subjects are less affected when they watch a video of children with cancer." Kristof says such studies suggest that "wealth may impede empathy." I would prefer to say that *too much empathy impedes the accumulation of wealth,* and impedes the anomic personality in his (or her) "relentless pursuit of limitless goals," the hallmark of this social character. And the most typical limitless goal is money, and more money; the Almighty Dollar. Sex and power are of course obtainable without money, but money makes sex and power much easier to obtain. Tiger had ready access to extramarital sex once he achieved wealth and fame as a champion golfer. Dick became a wealthy CEO before he became the most powerful vice president in U.S. history. Bernie had an extramarital relationship with Sheryl Weinstein, the chief financial officer of Hadassah. She led Hadassah to invest $40 million, and also invested her own family's money, with Madoff. Oy veh! Money makes sex and power more available. You might call it The Golden Triad.

Kristof goes on to say that "Among Democratic politicians, personal wealth is a predictor of supporting legislation that would increase inequality, according to a journal article last year by Michael W. Kraus and Bennett Callaghan." Moreover, the "wealthiest 20% of Americans give significantly less to charity as a fraction of income (1.4%) than do the poorest 20% (3.5%)." In addition, "Wealthy people who live in economically diverse areas are more generous than those who live in exclusively wealthy areas." Those who live in gated communities are acting in accord with the principle of "differential association," whereby you act in accordance with the behavior of the people with whom you are in contact, and learn by them through imitation, modeling or group pressure. You are more likely to move to a gated community if you have a lot of money (it costs) and your attitudes are similar to those within the gates. That is preselection. Changes in dressing, language, or eating habits may be seen as "anticipatory socialization" among the nouveau riche who wish to move up in the system.

It would be only fair to mention a conflicting view of the origins of empathy. Three psychologists take the position that empathy is a matter of choice. (Cameron, D. et al.) [Cameron, D. et al. "Empathy is Actually a Choice." *The New York Times*, July 10, 2015, Op-Ed.] "While we concede that the exercise of empathy is, in practice, often far too limited in scope, we dispute the idea that this shortcoming is inherent, a permanent flaw in the emotion itself.….we believe that empathy is a *choice* that we make whether to extend ourselves to others.….People with a higher sense of power exhibit less empathy because they have less incentive to interact with others."

The longitudinal and experimental studies I have previously cited seem to refute the hypothesis that empathy is merely a choice. These studies are among many others suggesting the early origins of empathy. A longitudinal study predicted adult empathy levels based upon parental behavior 26 years previously. This shows that empathic ability starts to form early, since the initial measures of parental behavior were taken at the child's age of 5. In another study, children with high "callous-unemotional" traits showed lower levels of eye contact with their mothers than a control group. This is in line with the famous work of Bowlby, who emphasized the importance of early attachment of child to mother, including physical contact. Brain structures (mirror cells) seem related to the ability to experience empathy. In experiments with prisoners exposed to pictures of people in pain, those scoring low on empathy showed lower activity in the amygdala (an emotional center) and prefrontal cortex (cognitive ability) and other brain activity changes. The evidence seems overwhelming; empathy is not simply a choice.

It cannot be emphasized enough that in addition to any other factors, such as heredity, child rearing, ethnic background, and religion (the Protestant Ethic), the current form of capitalism in the U.S., with its inequality of wealth, income, job opportunity, education, health, and so forth, makes for an excessive striving for the success (or even survival) crumbs left on the table. The traits found in psychopathy and the anomic personality are specifically fitted for the survival and success of those in a winner-take-all society. Glibness and lying help you in business and social climbing. Lack of guilt or remorse protects you from the emotional suffering caused by guilt feelings and a negative self-image because of the damage you have done to others in your climb up the ladder. Callousness again is a protection against the pain of a negative self-image. Charisma, glibness, and manipulative language skills aid in the climb to success. Your parents may have pushed you to succeed, and laid the groundwork for the development of an anomic personality. But when you're an adult, your anomic personality traits shield you against any guilt feelings that a capitalist society, with its rampant inequality, might engender. Grandiosity helps you to ignore your moral shortcomings; after all, you are bigger, better and smarter than the average Joe. You deserve to be top dog in this fight, despite your lack of empathy. Those who are without means have not worked hard enough, are lazy, or think they are entitled to take from those who have means.

Isn't this a contradiction? How can psychopathology be adaptive? How can psychopathy, even in its mildest forms, be helpful to the individual? Many examples can be found. The hysterical paralyses that occurred so frequently in the time of Janet, Charcot and Freud were considered a compromise, a defense against the surfacing of a repressed sexual wish. The paralysis is certainly dysfunctional, but it is in the service of reducing anxiety over the sexual wish. The alcoholic may be suffering from depression, let's say from a job loss or from unrequited love. The drinking temporarily lifts the depression, but the alcohol in the long run acts to depress general functioning, and eventually can cause nerve and brain damage, as in Korsakoff's psychosis. Again, heavy drinking may be adaptive in the short run (similar to the hysterical paralysis of an arm or leg), but maladaptive in the long run.

Abram Kardiner, a well-known psychiatrist and psychoanalyst, (anon.) told of a "hit man" who came to him with a paralyzed trigger-finger. He said "If you don't cure me, Doc, I'll go to another shrink, get cured, and come back and shoot you." What was Dr. Kardiner to do? He decided to save his own life. We never found out if the trigger-finger paralysis was due to the conflict between the hit man's values and his deadly profession, or some deep Freudian conflict concerning repressed sexuality.

In discussing lack of empathy, lack of remorse or guilt, glibness and lying, grandiosity, and other anomic personality traits as adaptive mechanisms in a capitalist society with rapidly growing inequality, we were inevitably forced to discuss the impact of economic factors on the development of the phenomenon of the anomic personality. There is more to be said on this subject in the following chapter.

For the moment, let's return to the role of parenting in producing the anomic personality. Parents in the U.S. tend more than parents in most other countries to push their children to succeed and excel, but perhaps not to the extent of the Japanese and Chinese, for example. We hear of 3-year-old Japanese children learning to play the violin, using the Suzuki method. A Chinese-American mother, Amy Chua, said in her book, *Battle Hymn of the Tiger Mother* (Chua, A. 2011) [Chua, A. *Battle Hymn of the Tiger Mother*. New York: Penguin Group. 2011] that she pushed her daughters hard to become successful. She faults *most* American mothers for being too soft and undemanding. She, in contrast, is the epitome of "tough love," which has been so dear to some pundits and politicians on the right wing. "Here are some things my daughters, Sophia and Louisa, were never allowed to do: attend a sleepover, have a play date, be in a school play, watch TV or play computer games, get any grade less than an A, not play the piano or violin," (and so on). Instrument practice is a minimum of 3 hours a day. Other studies indicate that compared to Western parents, Chinese parents spend approximately 10 times as long every day drilling academic activities with their children." (Chua, A., 2011) [Chua, A. "Why Chinese Mothers Are Superior." *The Wall Street Journal*, January 8, 2011.]

There are Tiger parents (not to be confused with Tiger Woods) at every socioeconomic level, but they tend to be more numerous in high income communities. Palo Alto and Gunn high schools have had a total of eight suicides since 2009. This set the community to asking why. This is Silicon Valley, so you might figure that the parents are already overachievers. "Madeline Levine, a Bay Area psychologist who treats depressed, anxious and suicidal tech-industry executives, workers and their children, (says) "They all say, 'All I care about is that you're happy,' and then the kid walks in the door and the first question is, 'How did you do on the math test?'" (Richtel, M., 2015) [Richtel, Matt. "Push, don't crush the students." *The New York Times*, Sunday Review, 4/24/2015.] This parental doublespeak is on a par with the language in George Orwell's novel, *Animal Farm; "All animals are equal, but some animals are more equal than others."* The anomic parents partake of the doublespeak of the political wordsmiths, but they have no need to coin oxymorons such as "benign neglect" and "death taxes." The message, "Strive!" gets through by contradictory scripts, by tone of voice, and body language.

A good example of anomic parenting if found in the case of Kathryn DeWitt. (Scelfo, J.,2015) [Scelfo, J. "Suicide on Campus and the Pressure of Perfection." *The New York Times, July 27, 2015*. Education Life.] "Kathryn DeWitt conquered high school like a gold-medal decathlete. She ran track, represented her school at a statewide girls' leadership program and took eight Advanced Placement tests. Expectations were high. Every day at 5 p.m. test scores and updated grades were posted online. Her mother would be the first to comment should her grades go down. "I would come home from track and she would say 'I see your grade dropped." I would say 'Mom, I think it's a mistake." (And it *was* a typing error. Kathryn got straight A's.) At the University of Pennsylvania "she was surrounded by people with seemingly greater drive and ability" (Shades of Dick Cheney at Yale. See *supra*.) "Friends lives, as told through selfies, showed them having more fun, making more friends and going to better parties." (Relative deprivation.) Despite her cheery countenance and assiduous completion of assignments, Ms. DeWitt had already bought razor blades and written a stack of goodbye letters to loved ones"… "Several times in high school she had found herself attracted to other girls, but believing her parents and church did not fully accept homosexuality, she had pushed aside those feelings." (Adoption of a false self.) In college, 'noticing a cute girl in her dorm, she had a terrifying realization: 'I couldn't deny it anymore."

"Then came a crushing blow:" (narcissistic injury) "a score in the low 60s on her calculus midterm." (She thought she would fail, but in reality the course was graded on a curve.) This grade, she thought, was "dooming her plan to major in math and to teach……She began cutting herself to prepare for the pain" of suicide. Her roommate told a resident advisor of Kathryn's suicide plans, the Dean was contacted, and Kathryn was hospitalized. After counseling, a leave of absence, and a non-profit internship, Kathryn returned to college. "When Ms. DeWitt's mother came to visit her in the hospital, one of the first things she brought up was the readmittance process." (Let us hope that she at least said hello and kissed her first before getting back on the Tiger-mom track.)

Were Tiger Woods' parents "Tiger Parents" too? Well, his father spent years training him in golf and other athletics, and this clearly paid off. Sports are one of the few ways for minority males to rise high in the system. Bernie's parents were in the competitive business of investment, and his mother's early brush with the S.E.C. (Securities and Exchange Commission) gives us reason to suspect that there was some modeling on a crooked model. But no evidence of a Tiger Mom or Dad. Bernie's first job was as a life-saver, though this athletic skill was not his passport to fame and fortune. Dick excelled in sports and in his studies through high school, and only met with failure at Yale. It is tempting to guess that Dick's rage and Darth Vader persona is due to the narcissistic injury of *failure* he suffered when he flunked out twice at Yale and didn't make the freshman athletic teams either. His quest for power as CEO and VP surely sprang from the injured self-esteem of his college days. No mention of a Tiger Mom or Dad in Dick's childhood. Is it possible, since Obama achieved the presidency, that there will be more African-American Tiger parents pushing their children to succeed?

There may be many more factors making for the rise of the anomics in our society. We've mentioned history, (immigration, unlimited land in the West, the shift to a service economy), genetics and heredity (mirror cells and other brain characteristics), religion, ethnic background and child rearing. Perhaps diet and environmental factors also enter the picture. While all of these probably make a contribution to the overwhelming growth of the anomic social character, the major factor discussed throughout this book is the economic factor. It would be wonderful to be able to put all these factors into a multiple regression equation, and then see how much of a contribution each factor made to the dependent variable, anomic personality (as measured by traits in a given population.) Alas, even if we could accurately measure such variables as religion, or religiosity or churchgoing, or the various means of production, or the genomes of the population, the job would take years, and the largest computer ever built.

CHAPTER EIGHT

ECONOMIC FACTORS
INEQUALITIES OF WEALTH, INCOME AND "RENT"
A PLATFORM: REGULATE, REDISTRIBUTE, AND REBUILD
INEQUALITIES OF EDUCATION AND MENTAL HEALTH
A DOUBTFUL REMEDY
THE ELECTION

Economic Factors

Economic factors have been discussed intermittently throughout this book. That is because they are similar to other potential causal factors, and are intertwined with all the other "usual suspects." The industrial revolution made the middle class possible, and in time these were the people who envied the trappings of royalty and aspired to own more of what royalty already possessed. Economics (poverty) was the cause of much of the historical immigration to the U.S. Lincoln's Homestead Act of 1862 gave 160 acres of free land to those who would farm it for five years, resulting in a vast Westward Movement. With mass production and new technology, new products became accessible, and these were followed by newer products. Conspicuous consumption followed.

The changes in the economy and the financial world were a major factor in the rise of the anomic personality. In particular, the recent rise of inequality, the shift to a service economy and away from manufacturing, the growth of globalization with its concomitant outsourcing and the consequent U.S. unskilled and semi-skilled job loss, have caused greater competition for the remaining shrunken opportunities. An increase in population, especially at low and middle income levels, combined with a shrinkage of appropriate jobs, has helped to make the believers in the American Dream mythology more ruthless in pursuit of their goals, more grandiose in their ambitions, more callous, and more lacking in empathy, remorse or guilt for what they have done to others while on the road to success.

Mark Twain famously said "Everybody talks about the weather, but nobody does anything about it." "The Warmists want to not only talk about the weather (hurricanes, tornadoes, floods, droughts, etc.) but they also want to do something about it by regulating, taxing, and signing treaties to change the weather!" (This quote comes surprisingly from a global-warming *denier* web site, "Climate Depot.") Yes, it is true, we can do something about the weather, and we *can* do something about inequality. But there are those who deny inequality, or deny that we can do anything about it. I review what they say briefly, below.

Just how are we to escape the rapid growth of U.S. inequality and its destruction of our moral fiber and our social fabric? At first a change in parenting comes to mind. Why not create parents who don't push their children so hard to excel and trample others? The main reason training parents won't work *in the short run* is that despite the influence of experts like Spock and Ferber, parental practices are slow to change. The findings of one of my studies, with response data elicited from over 2000 mothers during the wave of "permissiveness," suggest that parents had maintained the "tough love" and cold or punitive practices they learned from their own parents. Changing parenting is a big job. *I think changing the pressures on parents to protect their children and help them succeed in a system with great inequality of income and opportunity will have more immediate effect than trying to change parenting practices directly.* True equality of opportunity, free and better education, access to a single payer health system for all, similar to Medicare, and most of all, enough jobs at different skill levels to provide work and self-esteem for all who need it, is the way to win back the social solidarity we once had during and shortly after World War II. *Reducing the prevalence of ruthlessly striving anomics who care not for their fellow-men can possibly be best achieved by diminishing inequality in all its forms.*

Just because changing parenting is a long process requiring effort over at least several generations doesn't mean it should not be employed to reduce *inequality over time as social character changes away from the anomic personality.* Training for parenthood can take place at different life stages. 1) In childhood, by modeling on good parents or older siblings. 2) In school, by teens taking responsibility for children in younger grades, or modeling on teachers. 3) In high-school, by taking a course in parenting and child care, combining lectures with small discussion groups. 4) Instruction for primagravidae and their husbands or boyfriends, during the middle months of pregnancy, and the year following birth, with instruction by various doctors, pediatricians, nurses, and members of various professions, such as child and adolescent psychiatry, psychology, and social work.

Inequalities of Wealth, Income and Rent

Let's see what several history and economics experts (among many) think about the threat of rapidly rising inequality that is so damaging to our democracy, and plays a major role in creating a social character I call the anomic personality, ranging from narcissists to psychopaths. Do they say "you can't do anything about the weather (inequality) or do they look on the bright side, and suggest ways to improve or save our democracy? (I have tried to avoid delving into the mathematical mysteries of economics, which I cannot fully understand, and which would bore most of my readers. Instead I have tried to simplify the positions taken by three economists, without the math and technical language. I have chosen three who differ widely in their Weltanschauung, from dark to positive.) First a brief summary of each position is needed.

Berman, in his book *Dark Ages America*, (*supra*) sees no hope for our democracy. For him, our inequality is so great, and our democracy so deteriorated and weakened by our imperialist adventures, that we will revert to the social level of the Dark Ages. In his view, the social fabric is so torn that no intervention can save it.

Picketty, in his book *Capital in the Twenty-First Century (supra)*, while feeling that global inequality can destroy democracies, including our own, holds out hope for a global wealth tax of 5% to 10% on billionaires. This tax on all assets could slow the current progress toward extreme inequality. He also proposes a progressive tax on the wealth (all assets) of the top 10% wealthiest. He is more hopeful about the future of democracy than Berman. His emphasis on taxing *unearned* income (wealth) as opposed to earned income, would diminish the inequality between the top 1% who live off capital, and the rest of us.

Stiglitz, the 2001 Nobel Laureate in Economics, in *The Price of Inequality*, (Stiglitz, J., 2012) [Stiglitz, J. *The Price of Inequality.* New York: W.W. Norton & Co., 2012.] *feels that we can reverse inequality. He doesn't see democracy's downhill slide* as irreversible. He thinks that better wages, support of education, and stricter regulation of corporations along with increasing capital gains taxes (taxes on unearned income) will help to equalize income inequality. More on Berman, Picketty and Stiglitz follows.

Berman (Berman, M., op.cit.) attributes the recent leap in inequality to the repeal of the Bretton Woods Treaty in 1971 during the Nixon administration. The Bretton Woods agreement put limits on the ability of international exchange rates to fluctuate. The repeal of Bretton Woods allowed traders in money to take advantage of even small changes in exchange rates to make billions in profits. This put developing nations at great disadvantage, and often made their currencies weak or worthless. The deregulation of Bretton Woods set the stage for the creation of new investment vehicles and cycles of boom and bust. (I discussed the process of securitization and the creation of derivatives in Chapter Four.)

The recent crash (2007-2008) and depression due to insider trading and securitization of sub-prime mortgages by the banks is still with us, in the form of a very slow recovery. Mortgages based primarily on "underwater" properties were sold in "tranches" to unaware investors. Those worthless mortgages were a principal cause of the housing crash.

"Its (Bretton Woods') repeal in 1971 set the stage for a 'predatory' economy, both at home and abroad. The floating exchange rates that resulted stimulated the growth of finance (i.e., speculative and investment) capitalism, which in turn led to a huge gap between rich and poor, as well as to a "Wall Street-Treasury Department" complex that had a powerful (and baleful) impact on American domestic and foreign policy. These policies, which have eroded democracy and led to a much more aggressive foreign policy, have destabilized the American empire at home and abroad. The repeal of Bretton Woods, in short, is a major factor in our decline." (Berman, M., op. cit., p. 50.)

Well, Berman may be right in blaming Bretton Woods' repeal and its consequences for our current dilemma, but there has always been inequality in the U.S. This was true in the early colonies, where the class differences of the English settlers were maintained. The era of large plantations, such as belonged to Washington and Jefferson, and the slave economy that supported these demesnes, exemplified extreme stratification and inequality. The rum and slave trade made fortunes for the ship-owning families of New England, while many laborers in both North and South were slaves or indentured servants.

The fifties through the seventies, the thirty years after World War II, were times of relative equality. The G.I. Bill enabled many poor servicemen to gain a higher education. How times have changed! The 2016 Democratic platform called for free public colleges. (anon.)

Recently (2015) the richest people, (those in the 39.6% tax bracket) who have most of their taxable income from capital investments, are subject to a capital gains tax of only 20 %. The rest of the country pays a much higher percentage of their income in taxes, because it is earned income, not based on capital gains. No wonder the Republican mantra has been "no more taxes." George H.W. Bush famously said it in 1988 as he accepted the Republican presidential nomination; "Read my lips: no new taxes."

To get an update on income and wealth disparity, I decided to get it "straight from the (conservative) horse's mouth," Forbes Magazine. "The average income of the top 1 percent is $717, 000, compared with the rest of the population, which is around $51,000. The real disparity between the classes isn't in income, however, but in net value: The 1 percent are worth about $8.4 million, or 70 times the worth of the lower classes......
Altogether, the top 1 percent control 43 percent of the wealth in the nation;

the next 4 percent control an additional 29 percent." (Dunn, A., 2012) [Alan Dunn, "Average American vs the One Percent," Forbes, 3/21/2012] *So the top 5% control 72 percent of the wealth; almost three quarters of it! Objective inequality of everything else; education medical care, housing, employment, leisure time, etc., follows.*

While inequality in wealth is exorbitant, the inequality in *earned* income is also shocking "CEOs were paid an average of $15.2 million in 2013–296 times more than the typical worker." This means the typical worker earned $51,351 per year, a figure which is suspiciously high.) The ratio of executive to workers pay was 20 to 1 in 1965. "CEO pay increased 937 percent since 1978. Compensation for the typical worker grew 10.2 percent in that time." (Economic Policy Institute, 2014) [Economic Policy Institute press release, "CEOs Made 296 Times Typical Workers in 2013." 6/12/2014.] While productivity is "skyrocketing," workers are making less, and CEOs are obviously skimming off whatever increased productivity yields. These figures on the disparity in earned income between Chief Executive Officers of corporations and typical workers in those corporations suggest that we are living in a kleptocracy, not a democracy.

The newest big factor in inequality (which will exacerbate the competitive struggle of the anomics and create a great increase in inequality) is the Supreme Court decision called "Citizens United." This decision considers corporations to be individuals, with a right to free speech. That "speech" includes the contribution to political campaigns, individuals, or lobbyists without the identification of the donor. With corporations able to put politicians "in their pockets," the struggle for power, prestige and possession will become like the battle of Armageddon. Already, as detailed before, the members of the dark triad/tetrad and their lesser brothers have made the financial system into a battlefield. New investment vehicles are being churned out. This "securitization" usually has as its hidden purpose the bilking of even the smartest of investors.

The Citizens United decision (January 2010) makes us question the primacy of economics (globalization and automation) in causing the downhill course of democracy. Once corporations are considered "individuals" with the right of free speech, there is no limit to their political contributions. As Stiglitz and others see it, *the political power of the wealthy over legislative and regulatory processes is the primary cause of national disintegration. Politics shapes the market, not the reverse.* Conservative money, now part of "free speech," buys the politicians who make or break the laws governing the market and the financial world. This conservative (free speech) money comes largely from corporations whose primary purpose is to make money for its CEO's and stockholders. They do create jobs, but we know that much of their work is now outsourced to foreign countries with cheap labor. A list of the "corporate hall of shame" distributed by Corporate Accountability International shows how much damage these companies do here and abroad. Without political protection, they could not continue this depredation. To summarize, TransCanada (Keystone XL oil pipeline, mass environmental damage), GM (10 years to recall defective ignition switches, 13 deaths), Chevron (dumped 18.5 billion gallons of toxic chemicals into Ecuadorean Amazon, no clean up), Monsanto (toxic chemicals, genetically engineered seeds exacerbate food scarcity globally), Veolia (privatizing drinking water. Originally a French corporation), Bayer (pesticides "linked to alarming die-off of bees), Philip Morris international (addicting thousands of new smokers a day, with lung cancer as proven consequence), Credit Suisse, (loans to Fannie Mae and Freddie Mac to help precipitate the 2007 financial crisis.) "Free speech" money can "*pay* politicians *to* let corporations *play*" and vote the way corporations want them to, simply by funding the campaigns of the Senators and Representatives.

Stiglitz focuses on the concept of "rent" and its contribution to the rise of inequality. This is not a new concept. It goes back to the work of Henry George and Wilfredo Pareto. There are many overlapping definitions of "rent," but the one that seems to get at the common core of them all is "an excess (of return) where there is no enterprise or costs of production. ("Of return" is my addition to this summary definition by Wikipedia, "Economic Rent.")

In a review of Stiglitz' writings, James Surowiecki clarifies the concept of "rent" by giving examples. (Stiglitz) "sees the boom in the incomes of the one percent as largely the result of what economists call 'rent-seeking.' …..So the extra profit a monopolist earns because he faces no competition is a rent. The extra profits that big banks earn because they have the implicit backing of the government, which will bail them out if things go wrong, are a rent. And the extra profits that pharmaceutical companies make because their products are protected by patents are rents as well." (Surowiecki, J., 2015) [Surowiecki, James "Why the Rich Are So Much Richer." The New York Review of Books, September 24, 2015.]

Guilds and unions also create a form of rent. For example. The American Medical Association limits the number of doctors who can be trained at medical schools. This in part accounts for the large salaries of physicians, who are always in demand due to shortages. Stiglitz says that rent-seeking leaves the finance and pharmaceutical industries with more than their fair share of rewards. As noted before, CEOs have been taking a progressively larger share of the corporate profits pie, while productivity is rising, and workers are not getting commensurate increases. CEO profit-skimming is another form of rent.

Stiglitz feels that this "predatory rent-seeking" hurts the society and the economy. It erodes America's "sense of identity, in which fair play, equality of opportunity, and a sense of community are so important." It alienates people from the system.(Surowiecki, supra) Where Surowiecki tends to part company with Stiglitz is when Stiglitz claims that inequality does damage to economic growth. Looking across countries, there seems to be little consistent relationship between high inequality and factors that would slow economic growth, such as excessive debt, as people and banks borrow to make up for their stagnant incomes financial instability

Stiglitz, and his critic, Surowiecki, essentially agree on what should be done to alleviate inequality First, raise tax rates on the wealthy, including the capital gains tax. Raise the inheritance tax rates. Pass laws supportive of stronger unions, and raise minimum wages. Increase regulation of banks, and of corporate boards that give a pass to exorbitant CEO salaries and bonuses. Increase investment in schools, infrastructure and basic research. Where Surowiecki is less sanguine (bright sided?) than Stiglitz is not in *what has to be done* to diminish inequality. "Of course, the political challenge in doing any of this (let alone all of it) is immense, in part because inequality makes it harder to fix inequality (*because of the power of wealth, my insert*). And even for progressives, the very familiarity of the tax and transfer agenda may make it seem less appealing." (Surowiecki, *supra.*

As Berman points out, the sharp decline of the unions has furthered U.S. inequality, since the bargaining power of its once lower-middle-class membership has been decimated. This means that many who could have had an above average life with security and pensions, have been thrown into the scramble for money on their own. This will make for more and more anomic strivers in a stratum that was once (relatively) content in a middle-class protected life. The workers' pensions are rarer than ever. The right wing has made concerted and consistent attempts to gut Social Security, Obama Care, education (see discussion of Diane Ravitch below) and housing. All the more reason for everyone to struggle without stint to get to the top; to get security. The media display the wealth and perks of the movie stars, top athletes, and the rich, which adds to the incentive for the limitless striving of the anomic.

Just how much money gap is there? Where it was once the goal to become a millionaire, they are a "dime a dozen" nowadays. "The United States had 492 *billionaires* on the Forbes list. This was the most of any country in the world. China followed with 152, and Russia came in third, with 111. Worldwide there were 1,645 billionaires. Of this group, 67% were self-made, 13% inherited their wealth, and 20% "combined inheritance and business acumen." (Wikipedia, "The World's Billionaires.") There's detailed discussion of billionaires in Chapter 1. The more billionaires, the less wealth for the rest of us. Doesn't it seem as if a cap on wealth were called for? Picketty calls for a cap worldwide, but how is this to be enforced? Unless the Democrats win both the House and Senate majorities in 2020, there is no way that major increases in tax rates will become law. Likewise, do we expect the Saudis to give up their wealth without a fight? Bill Gates gives up millions for good causes, but he is currently worth $81 billion. The Koch brothers have a combined wealth of $82 billion, but they contribute heavily to their own political agenda.

Given the various factors that fed the recent rapid growth of inequality, the resulting struggle for survival has produced a social character that falls heavily into the dark triad of narcissism, Machiavellianism, and psychopathy. (NB: The term "psychopathology" would include the full range of mental and emotional disorders. "Psychopathy" refers specifically to psychopaths.) Child rearing practices have played a large part in producing this change in national character, but the excessive preparation of children for success in a zero-sum culture is an adaptation to the scarcity of opportunity. Parental anxiety over the reality of limited opportunity drives them to be Tiger mothers and fathers. The anomic personality, marked by its excessive striving, is the result of scarcity and inequality. My conclusion is that while changes in parenting and education may help reduce the spread of the anomic personality, the reduction of scarcity and inequality deserves primacy in any program of short term amelioration. *This in turn means more political involvement and action on the part of the political center-left. This does not mean that the improvement of parenting and more generous funding of public education should be put on a back burner.*

A Platform For The Future: Regulate, Redistribute, Rebuild

This section of the book was written before Trump won the 2016 election. Although seemingly "outdated," it is included to show the contrast between the Democratic positions and those of Trump and the G.O.P. "Regulation" and "Redistribution" are anathema to Republicans. "Rebuilding the infrastructure" under the new Republican administration will be done by such means as making toll roads through low cost loans to entrepreneurs. The public will pay tolls indefinitely, filling the pockets of the investors in perpetuity. This is privatization of the highways.

Here are some suggestions for a "platform for the future" to reduce inequality. It might be called the "Three Rs," a sequel; to "Reading, and Writing, and 'Rithmetic." Note that it does not differ in many respects from the platforms of the two Democratic frontrunners in the 2016 presidential elections, but is somewhat closer to those of Vermont Senator Bernie Sanders than to those of Hillary Clinton, former Secretary of State.

Several positions taken by Sanders were incorporated in the Democratic Platform. This may well have been due to pressure on Hillary and the Democratic Party once she became the Democratic nominee, to appeal to the many younger Bernie followers. Some of these are a $15 minimum wage (while Hillary opted for $12 during her campaign), marijuana legalization, reinstating the Glass-Steagall Act (to control the banks' acting as stockbrokers and traders), and a tax on financial transaction.

Regulate

Install a single-payer health care system, modeled on Medicare.

Regulate banks back to the Glass Steagall Act. Crack down on legal scams.

Control stock brokers, mortgages, and lending rates See early chapters for creation and control of new investment types, underwater mortgages etc.

Regulate the environment; air, water, drug production, drug costs.

Promote equal justice, strengthen the S.E.C. (Securities and Exchange Commission); enlarge the Bureau of Consumer Protection. Pass laws supportive of stronger unions.

Regulate corporate boards that give a pass to exorbitant CEO salaries and bonuses.

Raise taxes on corporations that outsource to foreign countries, and give tax breaks to those that limit their outsourcing, in order to create more jobs in the U.S.

Redistribute wealth through taxation, à la Picketty. Reinstate high inheritance taxes. Make the highest tax bracket much higher. A few examples of the highest tax bracket (tax rate percentage of income in the past) are 1924, 73%; 1944, 94%; 1960, 91%; 2004-2008, 34%. Today's tax rates are very low compared with the last 60 years. They dropped precipitously in the1980s. Raise the capital gains tax back to the 35% level from 15-20%. It is part of unearned income. Raise the minimum wage. Lower the federal estate tax exemption. In 2015, $5.43 million could be passed on to the next generation without any federal estate tax. In 2013, those few who paid estate taxes had an average rate of only 16.6% (share of the estate's value).

Rebuild infrastructure; public housing, schools, hospitals, bridges, roads, all in the public domain. Increase investment in pre-school, grade school, college and graduate education. Increase investment in basic research through universities and the National Institutes of Health.

There are several special areas where increased government funding could do much to alleviate inequality (among many, such as a single payer system like Medicare for all ages). I have chosen to discuss only two in any detail.

Education and Inequality: Education *for parenting* has already been discussed in detail. Education for empathy by those *outside* the family can start in pre-school, with books about caring for others. Caring for animals (and younger children) in the classroom may help to breed empathy.

Later in grade and high school, books about empathic and caring people; Lincoln, Mother Teresa, Florence Nightingale, or self-sacrificing heroes can be assigned. Novels by such authors as Don DeLillo and Alice Munro can put you "in the shoes of others," (as explained by Kristof, supra). Classroom discussion and criticism of bullying, online and off, should make for greater empathy and a reduction in teen violence. The tenets of the great religions can be discussed, stressing love for thy neighbor and injunctions against stealing and coveting someone else's wife, husband, girlfriend, or boyfriend. This could aid in bringing home the message of democracy and brotherly love. Self-sacrificing heroes, such as Casey Jones, who saved a trainload of people, can be used in classrooms. His song can be sung. Several people laid down their lives to save total strangers from the Nazis. Many resisted the Nazis, helped rescue some of the Nazi's victims, and were executed, such as Dietrich Bonhoeffer. A class screening and discussion of several movies such as *Schindler's List* could be the basis of essay assignments. The message; the reward of good deeds (compassion, caring, altruism) and empathy is enhanced self-esteem and kudos from one's peers and community.

Education accounts for a much greater portion of the difference in wages between those with and without a college education than the decline of the unions or immigration. "Most estimates of the impact of declining unionization on wage inequality show that about 10 to 20 percent of increased wage inequality for men (and almost none for women) can be explained by the ebbing strength of unions. (Declining unionization) "accounts for just (*only!*) three percentage points out of the total increase in the college wage premium of 23 percentage points.....Most of the slowdown in college attainment has been due to a *slowdown in attendance by the native-born population*," (not by the legal or illegal *immigrant* population. "Only!" is my inserted emphasis). (Goldin, C. and Katz, L.F., 2009) [Goldin, C. and Katz, L.F. "The Future of Inequality," Digital Access to Scholarship at Harvard, p. 5, 2009.]

The quality of our public schools continues to be disgraceful. In 2003 "American 15 year olds ranked 24th of 38 (nations) in mathematics, 19th of 38 in science, 12th of 38 in reading, and 26th of 38 in problem solving." (OECD's Programme, Wikipedia) [OECD's Programme for International Student Assessment, cited in Wikipedia.] "White and Asian students in the

United States are generally among the best performing pupils in the world; black and Hispanic students in the U.S. are among the lowest-achieving pupils." (ibid.) Public schooling funding is based primarily on local taxes (40-50%) and only 10% by the Federal Government. The balance is state funded, but this varies widely from state to state. Wealthy communities can vote to raise property taxes and thus spend more money on their children's schooling. Only a few developed countries in the world pay more for the public education of rich children than of poor children. Public grade school teachers in New York City have been known to buy not only pencils and paper for their students, but also toilet paper. Extreme conservatives have suggested dismantling the U.S. Department of Education. This attitude may keep McDonalds, Burger King and Wendy's supplied with cheap labor, but aside from its inhumanity, it costs the U.S. billions and trillions over time, because of a decrease in GDP (Gross Domestic Product). This hurts the pocketbooks of the wealthy, in the long run. As with so many behaviors, people, rich or poor, often do not act in their own best interests.

According to Goldin and Katz (*supra*), 20 percentage points out of the total increase in the college wage premium of 23 percentalge points are due to a slowdown in college attendance (by the native-born). A 23% difference in income between college and non-college graduates is a big gap. It is clear that the public schools are not preparing a large portion of their students for college, and this in turn exacerbates inequality not only of income, but of coping skills, which I will discuss shortly.

Jonathan Zimmerman, in "He Transformed the Schools, But..." (Zimmerman, J., 2015) [Zimmerman, J. N.Y. Review of Books, March 5, 2015, Vol. LXll, NO. 4, in a review of Klein, Joel. *Lessons of Hope: How to Fix Our Schools. Harper Collins.*] presents the opposing approaches to public education of Joel Klein, former Chancellor 0f New York City Schools, and his adversary, Diane Ravitch, a leading scholar of public education, and former U.S. Assistant Secretary of Education. To sum up the difference, Klein stood for small schools, Charter schools, trimming administration, grading schools, teachers and principals and pegging their salaries based on pupils' performance on standardized tests. Klein also favored "decentralization." He closed the community school boards (which were ripe with corruption) and also closed the New York City Board of Education. But Zimmerman says that Klein replaced the Board of Education "with a panel that was firmly under the Mayor's (Bloomberg) control."

Ravitch once supported "reform by testing and school choice" but changed her mind around 2003 after the "No Child Left Behind" program took effect, and stated why in several books. She and her supporters argue that Klein and his financial backers, Bill Gates and Eli Broad, have set out consciously to destroy the Public School System. Zimmerman doubts this was conscious, but suggests it is having the same effect, be it conscious or unconscious. Ravitch sees the Charter School and the privatization that goes with it as a way of avoiding the full federal government funding of public schools. She shows that Charter Schools are not functioning any better than public schools, and are diverting public school funding. The exclusionary policies of the Charters are in fact cherry-picking the brighter students to boost the Charter schools' average test scores. The more capable teachers and principals have been attracted with salaries up to $125,000 due to private funding, but this level of compensation is unrealistic on any but the small scale of the Charters. She criticizes the control of school textbooks by schoolboards, and the distortion of content, especially in the case of history. Note that in some states references to evolution play down Darwin's contribution, and still devote a lot of their biology textbooks to a discussion of "intelligent design." Ravitch supports the teachers' unions while Klein et al. see teachers' unions as corrupt and blocking innovation. She criticizes "teaching to the test", which limits the creativity of the teacher and severely narrows the content of what is taught. The arts and literature, in particular, are given short shrift. (To shrive meant "to hear the confession of and give absolution to a penitent." Criminals about to be executed were given "short shrift."

It is almost beyond belief that there are people in positions of power who would gladly destroy our public educational system. On March 13th, 2015, Senator Rand Paul "won applause at a speech in Maryland for saying he would eliminate the Departments of Commerce and Education if he could, a move that would eliminate corporate welfare and give power back to the states, respectively." (Kasperowicz, P., 2015) [The Blaze, 3/13/2015 Posted by Pete Kasperowicz.] Paul is an M.D. ophthalmologist. He supports the Tea Party Movement, and generally follows the conservative Libertarian doctrine. He is for states' rights over the federal government on almost any issue. You know that some states, particularly in the South, would be glad to slash their public school budget to the bone. It is the first item to be cut when there is a shortage of state funds. To my mind, as a Republican contender for the 2016 presidency, Paul shone by comparison with his running mates. Shining was made easy by comparison with Paul's other Republican opponents. However, on the February 1st G.O.P. caucus, Paul came in last.

Klein was funded by conservatives. His Leadership Academy trained a new group of principals. "Klein's book is vague about what this academy taught, other than the latest jargon from American business schools; its advisory committee was chaired by (former) General Electric CEO Jack Welch, who hosted the first class of novice principals" (at his Jack Welch Leadership Center) "and instructed them to focus zealously on 'targets' and the proper 'incentives' for meeting them." (Zimmerman, J., 2002. op. cit.).Welch is worth $720 million. He is a chemical engineer and the son of a railroad conductor.

Welch looks like a good candidate for the anomic personality award. He is "the toughest boss in America" and "manager of the 20th Century" according to Fortune Magazine. (Trigaux, R., 2002) [Trigaux, R. "Welch divorce will deflate superhero myth" St. Petersburg Times, March 24, 2002.] He has married three times, and has paid a king's ransom in alimony. He is another high achiever with no limitations or little regulation in his intimate personal life, clearly strong self-regulation as CEO in his business life, but who no doubt wanted deregulation of G.E. by the government in his role as CEO.

Earlier, (Chapter One) when discussing Trump's post-victory choices for his cabinet, I cited his appointment of Betsy DeVos, a billionairess, to the position of Secretary of Education. She has devoted herself to the creation of Charter Schools, and by so doing is laying the groundwork for the eventual destruction (and privatization) of public school education. This is one of many examples of the fox guarding the henhouse.

Education and Mental Health Inequality

It may seem strange to say that education is linked to *mental* health and mental disorder. It is easy to see why those of low socioeconomic status (SES, as measured by years of education, income and occupational level, for example) get worse medical care, less nutritious food or less food, are more exposed to the elements and environmental toxins through poor housing and inadequate clothing, and are thus less *physically* healthy than those of higher SES.

But why do those of low SES have worse *mental* health? Study after study has shown that the low SES group has higher rates of psychosis and character disorders,(low levels of social conscientiousness) while personality disorders; [*paranoid, schizoid, dissocial, emotionally histrionic, obsessive-compulsive, anxious (avoidant), and dependent/unstable* (borderline type and impulsive type),] are more common at middle and high SES levels (associated with anxiety and depression and what used to be called neuroses). Is it simply a "slam dunk" to answer this question? Mental and physical health go hand in hand, a correlation. And high SES individuals have better health because of diet, medical care, etc. Ergo, low SES individuals have worse mental **and** physical health? This correlation (going hand in hand) doesn't necessarily explain causation.

Do low SES people have tougher lives? Yes. But if we try to hold "life stresses" constant, as I did in a major study (and look at the "slope" of the relationship between the number of life stresses and a seven-point mental health "impairment rating" made by psychiatrists from home interviews (anon.) a striking relationship appears. The slopes of the graphs show that *for any given number of "life stresses,"* such as loss of a child, death of a spouse, divorce, many major operations, a large number of hospitalizations, major accidents, etc., *the impairment level of the low SES (socioeconomic) group is much greater than the middle or high SES group.* The low SES has a steep slope, while the middle and high SES have gradual slopes, with the high SES the most gradual.

What does this indicate? It shows that holding stress constant (as best we can using interview data), the low SES group shows *less resistance and less resilience.* It is not difficult to attribute some of this difference to a lack of coping skills of particular kinds that assure survival and even success in our society. Where are these skills learned? Verbal skills are learned at home first, and then in school. Very low SES families have vocabularies of only a few hundred words! This includes vocabularies in their native languages, as well as English vocabularies. Poor public schools do little to improve this deficit. Parents and schools at high SES levels offer a variety of coping mechanisms that are lacking at low SES levels. Reading, playing musical instruments, the arts in general are what rich people often fall back on in times of stress. Language skill, especially the use of "jaw-jaw" instead of "war-war," as Winston Churchill put it, allows high SES people to talk it out, rather than having to "act out" their anger, and thus avoid jail terms.

A Doubtful Remedy: Moving Children Out of High Poverty Neighborhoods

There have been many intervention programs, such as "No Child Left Behind," under G.W. Bush, and "Race to the Top" under Barack Obama, but Ravitch has shown their faults. Klein's success (see above) was based on privatization of public education. This is "helping" the public in the fashion of the Veolia Corporation, which privatizes (public) drinking water. Literally thousands of studies have looked at school curricula, teacher training, child rearing, parental behavior, and so on. I have discussed a few of them. Very few have a direct impact on improving lives in the U.S. But here comes Thomas B. Edsall, reviewing several interventions that really *did* improve the lives and life chances of children from the low socioeconomic group. The solution; *move children out of high poverty neighborhoods.* (Edsall, T.B., 2015) [Edsall, Thomas B, "How Do We Get More People to Have Good Lives?" *The New York Times,* June 3, 2015, contributing op-ed writer.] After briefly reviewing some of the same factors that make for low upward mobility that I have discussed previously (low job availability, lack of cognitive and non-cognitive [coping and "character"] skills, and poor public schools) Edsall cites several intervention studies; 1) The Moving to Opportunity Experiment ("a five-city program running since 1994 in which randomly selected poor families were given vouchers to move out of high poverty neighborhoods ......generated significant improvements among children under age 13 at the time of the move." 2) The Effects of Exposure to Better Neighborhoods on Children, Chetty Raj et al., *The New York Times,* May 4, 2015, "Moving to a lower-poverty neighborhood significantly improves college attendance rates and earnings for children who were young when their families moved. (They are) less likely to become single parents.....have an annual income that is $3477 or 31% higher on average relative to a mean (average) of $11,270 in the control group in their mid-twenties." 3) James Heckman and colleagues analyzed longitudinal results of the Perry Program conducted 1962-1967 in Ypsilanti, Michigan. The sample consisted of "123 low-income low-IQ children ages 3-4 considered to be at high risk of school failure. Fifty-eight were assigned to an intensive (2.5 hour sessions five days a week) preschool training project, while the remaining 65 were not, in order to serve as a control group. The Perry Program "did not increase long-term IQ, but it did raise scores on tests measuring achievement, as opposed to cognitive ability. He and his colleagues argue that 'increased personality skills promote learning, which in turn, boosts achievement test scores.'" "The participants in the Perry program had higher incomes at age 27 than the control group, better high school graduation rates, lower arrest records, higher levels of employment at age 40, and more home and car ownership, Heckman reported." 4) "Similar, but not identical, benefits were enjoyed by participants in the Carolina Abecedarian Project, which followed 101 low income children from infancy in 1972 to age 35." This again was a preschool intervention program from 4 months to 5-year-old kindergarten, "focusing on social, emotional and cognitive areas."

Edsall's final comments bear repeating. "If these three experimental programs are further validated over time and can be successfully replicated, there is reason to be cautiously optimistic about well-designed, adequately funded, carefully assessed intervention in early childhood. The modest but genuine success of the most fully conceived programs of this nature suggests that a disadvantaged class marked by test scores at the bottom of the ability distribution is not inevitable. *Instead, the question of what to do becomes a political issue about the distribution of resources —both private and public— and, above all, about the will of the electorate.*" (Italics are my emphasis). In an earlier part of his op-ed piece, Edsall says "Without substantial policy intervention, however, these trends (relegation of less-skilled workers to the bottom) are likely, if not certain, to continue, and the current balance of power in Congress suggests that few such interventions will be undertaken."

Though I have been a researcher in epidemiological studies of mental disorder in children, adults and the elderly, these were not interventional studies. They were meant to add knowledge for those who do intervene, and to point up the critical shortages of mental health services. In addition, *random community samples yield a very different picture of the etiology (causal factors) of mental disorder than preselected samples of patients.* My response to Edsall's successful intervention examples is 1) The better studies took 35 and 40 years to get full results on adult functioning. Remarkably well done, but at what a cost in time; one or two generations! 2) Even Edsall, who seems somewhat "bright-sided" (to use Barbara Ehrenreich's term for unrealistic "positive thinking") doubts that there is the political and public will to really intervene on a large scale, pre-school, in school, and afterward. 3) Moving people out of the slums seems like a great idea, but where do you stop? Have you created suburban slums when you move half of the low income residents there? How will the suburbs accept a large influx of poor people? They already exclude them through high taxes and discrimination against applicants of color. 4) By this time we know that cognitive and non-cognitive skills must be developed early. Study after study has shown this to be true. It is time to use the knowledge at hand to intervene on a large scale. That means improving the schools should be our first priority. Why not improve the rotten schools right where they are? Fix them up, hire enough teachers and pay them decent salaries. Build new schools employing the manual skills of slum parents who desperately need jobs at this level. Schools are part of the "infrastructure" we have been promised. 5) Parents in the slums need jobs, many of which have been out-sourced to third-world countries. Until the parents can get jobs at their own skill level, we should tax outsourcing heavily, or at least give tax breaks to corporations that don't outsource beyond the U.S. 6) At a certain point the gathering of additional knowledge should be secondary to direct large-scale intervention. Forming a committee or commission to "study" a problem has historically been a way to put off doing much about it. Sometimes studies can perform the same delaying function. There is no reason why studies can't continue at the same time that massive overhauling is going on, based on what we already know has to be done.

The 2016 Election

A brief look back at the some of the events leading up to Trump's victory may shed a bit of light on why Hillary won over Bernie Sanders, and why Trump bested Hillary.

"Appearing on Fox News on Friday, a spokesperson for Republican frontrunner Donald Trump threatened that the business mogul would be willing to use nuclear weapons if he were elected to serve as commander in chief. 'What good does it do to have a good nuclear triad if you're afraid to use it?' campaign spokesperson Katrina Pierson asked on Fox's *The O'Reilly Factor*."

"Pierson went on to suggest that while other Republican candidates may threaten war, Trump would actually be willing to use the nuclear triad to fix problems around the world. 'That's where we are today,' she said. 'We need to be discussing how we fix their problems, not just complaining and name-calling about who started this and who started that.'" (Trump Spokesperson, 2015.) [Trump Spokesperson: Why Have Nuclear Weapons 'If You're Afraid To Use' Them? Think Progress. 12/19/2015.]

Hillary spent much of her stint as Secretary of State under Obama trying to stop nuclear proliferation and nuclear threats. Progress on reducing the nuclear arsenals of Russia and the U.S. was being made. In a June 2013 speech in Berlin, President Obama suggested that the two powers negotiate an additional one-third reduction of deployed nuclear weapons. But a recent reversal has taken place, and a new arms race is on.

"Part of the reason, as explained by James Carroll, is that [in] order to get the votes of Senate Republicans to ratify the START treaty, Obama made what turned out to be a devil's bargain. He agreed to lay the groundwork for a vast 'modernization' of the US nuclear arsenal, which, in the name of updating an aged system, is already morphing into a full-blown reinvention of the arms cache at an estimated future cost of more than a trillion dollars. In the process, the Navy wants ... twelve new strategic submarines; the Air Force wants... a new long-range strike bomber force. Bombers and submarines would ... both be outfitted with next-generation missiles.' Modernization, under the guise of "life extension" for existing weapons, also involves creation of upgraded warheads, contrary to intentions stated in the 2010 Nuclear Posture Review.'" (Elliott, J., 2016) [Judy Elliott. "Asking Hillary About Nuclear Weapons." Governing Under the Influence, Bird Dog Reports. 9/18/2016.]

Hillary did not come out with a clear statement about where she stood on this expensive nuclear modernization program. However, in contrast to Trump and his spokeswoman, she has *never* advocated "nuking" another country or entity such as ISIS.

Because of the possibility of Trump's actually using the "nuclear triad," (strategic bombers, intercontinental ballistic missiles [ICBMs], and submarine-launched ballistic missiles [SLBMs]), and his denial of global warming, we in the U.S. and the rest of the world are in great danger.

We can be sure that Donald T. is consistently on the wrong side of the major threats, since his decisions are based on what is good for business, especially *his* business. Negotiations for hotels with the Trump brand have gone on with Taiwan, Pakistan and other countries.

On November 29th, 2018, Trump's former personal lawyer and "fixit man," Michael Cohen, testified that he made efforts as early as 2016 to give Putin a $50 million penthouse in exchange for approval of a Trump Tower in Moscow. Trump's presidency could hang on whether he knew of, or even directed, these negotiations. The slow juggernaut of the Mueller investigation has finally arrived at the door of the White House.

Donald's personal phone calls to foreign leaders flout years of diplomatic tradition and caution. What's good for the world, the planet, for women and minorities, for the "others" in this world, is not his concern. Nuking ISIS or even other nations is O.K. Global warming is a hoax. The election of Donald Trump as President of the United States and his continuation in office is clearly a threat to people of all persuasions and eventually all social classes in the U.S. and worldwide.

The United Nations report tells us that we have only twelve more years in which to try to reverse climate change and global warming. After that time it will be ***irreversible***! Can we let one very sick man use up another six years, or one half of our "chance of survival" time?

Index